Afro-Cuban Voices

CONTEMPORARY
CUBA

Contemporary Cuba
Edited by John M. Kirk

A multidisciplinary series focusing on balanced, current, and provocative aspects of Cuban history, culture, society, and politics. Of special interest are works that examine the dramatic changes in Cuba since 1959, such as the role of the military, the nature of economic reforms, and the impact of foreign investments, human rights treaties, and tourism on the island.

Afro-Cuban Voices: On Race and Identity in Contemporary Cuba,
by Pedro Pérez Sarduy and Jean Stubbs (2000)
Cuba, the United States, and the Helms-Burton Doctrine: International Reactions,
by Joaquín Roy (2000)

Afro-Cuban Voices

On Race and Identity in Contemporary Cuba

Edited by Pedro Pérez Sarduy
and Jean Stubbs

University Press of Florida

Gainesville · Tallahassee · Tampa · Boca Raton
Pensacola · Orlando · Miami · Jacksonville

05 04 03 02 01   6 5 4 3 2

Library of Congress Cataloging-in-Publication Data
Pérez Sarduy, Pedro, 1943–
Afro-Cuban voices: on race and identity in contemporary Cuba /
Pedro Pérez Sarduy and Jean Stubbs.
p. cm. — (Contemporary Cuba)
Includes bibliographical references.
ISBN 0-8130-1735-1 (cloth: alk. paper)
1. Blacks—Race identity—Cuba. 2. Blacks in art. 3. Blacks in
literature. 4. Blacks—Cuba—Social conditions. 5. Cuba—Race
relations. I. Stubbs, Jean, 1946– . II. Title. III. Series.
F1789.N3 P47 2000
305.896'07291—dc21   99-053467

The University Press of Florida is the scholarly publishing agency
for the State University System of Florida, comprising Florida
A&M University, Florida Atlantic University, Florida International
University, Florida State University, University of Central Florida,
University of Florida, University of North Florida, University of
South Florida, and University of West Florida.

University Press of Florida
15 Northwest 15th Street
Gainesville, FL 32611-2079
http://www.upf.com

CONTENTS

SERIES EDITOR'S FOREWORD

Cuba is a fascinating study. Witness the continuing debate over whether Washington should normalize relations with Havana, nearly forty years after the United States severed relations with the Castro government, or the changes in the Cuban American community in recent years. U.S. business interest in Cuba has also grown dramatically, with many trade missions visiting the island in preparation for the day when the blockade will be lifted. From Jack Nicholson to the Baltimore Orioles, from former Secretary of State Henry Kissinger to leading U.S. industrialists, it is clear that domestic interest in things Cuban is increasing.

In international matters, too, Cuba—a country of just 11 million—continues to play a role that belies its relatively small size. The importance of the visit of Pope John Paul II in January 1998 has received justifiable attention. But in 1998 alone Cuba was also visited by the leaders of ten countries (from the prime minister of Canada to the president of Colombia) and no less than twenty-five foreign ministers.

Given this growing fascination with Cuba, the University Press of Florida has decided to launch a series of books examining contemporary Cuba (defined loosely, but not exclusively, as Cuba since 1959). The basic concept is of a number of academic studies that examine—from a variety of perspectives, and over a range of disciplines—the nature of Cuba today. (The Press welcomes proposals from all potential contributors.)

This book on the thorny issue of race relations is the first volume in the series. It is important because strengthening racial equality and eradicating racial discrimination have long been major goals of the Cuban revolutionary process. The racism that existed in Batista's Cuba has been well documented—but what of life in Cuba today?

This volume by Pedro Pérez Sarduy and Jean Stubbs, their latest on the question of racial identity, is a courageous attempt to deal head-on with the issue of race in Cuba today. How Cuba has dealt with the "racial question" in a revolutionary socialist society is extremely important because it represents a major challenge to the Cuban government. After all, black Cubans, along with women and peasants, stood to gain the most from the revolutionary process. The social distortions resulting from the demise of the Soviet Union, and from the post-1980s Special Period, as Cuba opened up rapidly to foreign investment and domestic economic reform—what Fidel Castro termed a "pact with the devil"—have only aggravated the situation.

So how has the Cuban government fared in pursuing this policy? No race riots have occurred, such as those seen in major cities of the developed world, and access to social benefits (including free education and health care) is indeed possible. Yet tensions still exist. Pérez Sarduy and Stubbs seek to put a human face on this debate, and do so well. The book will be received with relief by some and with frustration by others. Controversial it will undoubtedly be, since—as with most things Cuban—strong emotions are a given assumption. It will be an admirable beginning for the series and, it is hoped, will spark a much-needed debate in the United States on many aspects of the "Cuban question." It is about time.

John M. Kirk

FOREWORD

Pedro Pérez Sarduy and Jean Stubbs have brought together a powerful collection of critical commentaries and essays that interpret and explain the richness of the Afro-Cuban contemporary experience. Race and culture interact in Cuba in a manner which is distinctive, yet which also illuminates the structures of power. At a time when Cuba is undergoing immense economic and social changes, race becomes a kind of cultural litmus test for the national identity. *Afro-Cuban Voices* presents the insights of black Cubans who have a deep belief in the Cuban Revolution but who at the same time identify with the integrity and beauty of black Cuban people. These artists and writers seek a path for constructing a national identity that ultimately transcends the contradictions of both racial stereotyping and cultural assimilation. This anthology illustrates fully that it is possible to be both revolutionary and black in Cuba.

Manning Marable
Director, Institute for Research in African-American Studies
Columbia University

In privileging the Afro-Cuban voice, Pedro Pérez Sarduy and Jean Stubbs provide platform and soundscape for higher visibility and broader amplification of varied, yet racially problematic sociocultural, political, and economic realities of Afro-Cubans in today's socialist Cuba. Through interviews the reader is engaged by the internal perspectives of nationally and internationally recognized Afro-Cubans in scholarship, arts, media, medicine, and other professions who call for foregrounding race in public dialogue in ways that will constructively counter the officially privileged discourse about a prototypical national identity that both obscures and facilitates racial and national stereotypes and material inequality. This book is as much about nation-building as about racial identity, racial discrimination, and racial democracy. Through experiential voice, interviewees explore complexities and contradictions of racial identity and discrimination, comment on national achievements, identify challenges, and recommend actions before the still-unfolding Cuban nationhood. The privileged Afro-Cuban voices convey a positive and hopeful message that Cuba can be renewed by careful and frank acknowledgment of the historic and contemporary contributions of Afro-Cubans in the construction of national life and national identity. The authors of *Afro-Cuban Voices,* also key actors in the new, unfolding dialogue about race in Cuba, make a seminal contribution through a forthright critique of "racial blind spots" in official history and present-day racial discrimination, and through their review of and suggestions about the strengths and weaknesses of old and new methods of racial analysis. From this reader's perspective, *Afro-Cuban Voices* will be instructional for those concerned with building a strong, organic national unity and identity that can maximize public-spiritedness in internal development and patriotism in the face of external threats, as well as demonstrate leadership in a hemisphere and world where issues of race, racism, and racial identity are central elements in global and statecraft.

James Early
Director, Cultural Studies and Communication
Smithsonian Institution

PREFACE

Privileging the Afro-Cuban Voice

"Why, explain to me why, after three decades [of revolution], do I have to think again in race terms?" The question was put to us almost ten years ago at our home in London by a black Cuban colleague who was on a short visit to Britain. Yet the memory of it remains as clear as if it had been asked yesterday. This was the first of many encounters, on and off the island, each of which confirmed to us the need for a book such as the current volume. Black Cuban colleagues and friends, some of whom had never seen race as a key issue in their everyday or professional lives, wanted to talk as they grappled in their own minds with the experience of a resurgent island racism. Many felt discomfort at having to think more in racial terms; however, there was also an affirmation and pride in being black.

Controversially perhaps, in a Cuban, Caribbean, or Latin American context the term "black" is often used, both in the interviews and by us, in its broadest sense: that is, more or less synonymous with the term "Afro-Cuban," inclusive of both "negro" (black) and "mulato" (mulatto or brown), in juxtaposition to "Euro-" or "Hispano-Cuban." It should be stressed that this is done neither to essentialize nor to simplify blackness or the African diaspora. Reflecting current usage in Cuba, the term "black" is used to encapsulate a broader problematic to which attention is being drawn. This in itself points to a key issue underlying the book: the historical and contemporary validity of theoretical and conceptual models that have been constructed to aid in the understanding of race in Cuba.

Cuba's African-descended identities and cultures are jostled between asserting a sense of difference and recognizing transculturation. In Cuba more than anywhere else, it might be argued, blacks have demonstrated great individual and collective achievement, awareness, and organization in challenging oppression, eliciting official concern and recognition, gaining power, becoming accepted within the culture, and establishing their national self-identity.

In the nineteenth century, Afro-Cubans fought a dual struggle for abolition of slavery and independence from Spain. In the twentieth century they fought along race, class, and nationalist lines, the latter two assuming primacy after the 1912 Race War and during the 1933 and 1959 revolutions. Within a broad agenda of economic redistribution, social justice, and cultural regeneration, the 1959 revolution accorded primacy to class over race in forging a new national unity, greatly benefiting many poorer Cubans of all skin colors. The revolution has managed to survive under threat amidst the post-1989 crisis, but not without renewed contradictory trends where race is concerned.

Economic crisis, rather than government policy, is largely held accountable for this. Increasingly, however, ambivalence and reticence over articulating a race agenda are seen as contributing to the current resurfacing of denigration and stigmatization of darker skin color. Polarization of 1990s thinking on the race question has been quite marked. On the one hand, there is a denial of racism, often embedded in the current of thinking that there is no such thing as race, and a decrying even of the use of the term "Afro-Cuban," on the grounds that it is divisive and that everyone is simply Cuban. To paraphrase the words of José Martí, the founder of the nation, Cuba is more than white, black, or mulatto. On the other, there is a tendency to home in on race, especially in attributing causality to present-day negative phenomena.

Our intention in writing and editing this book has been to reflect all of this thinking and to outline various approaches to the question. We certainly do not wish to reduce and thereby simplify the complexities of race, not only as phenotype or genotype but also in far-reaching politico-economic and sociocultural terms. Indeed, taken as a whole, the book draws attention to all the nuances associated with race in Cuba. It does, however, make the case that the issue of race, no matter how hard to define, cannot be ignored.

We do not view this discussion as intended policy. The revolutionary government moved swiftly in its early years to pass legislation designed to end racial discrimination. Nonetheless, neither racial discrimination nor racial prejudice were ever entirely erased, and policies instituted to ride out the 1990s crisis have had racial implications. Therefore, the book includes policy-related issues, raised by the frank discussion of race, pertaining to both the 1959–89 and the post-1989 periods.

The book has taken shape over several years and in several places and might be read as a sequel to our earlier edited volume, *Afro-Cuba: An Anthology of Cuban Writing on Race, Politics and Culture* (Pérez Sarduy and Stubbs 1993). Our primary objective in launching that first volume was to provide for the non-Spanish-reading public outside Cuba an English-language compilation of work published by Cuban scholars on the island, thereby dispelling the myth that race was a "non-topic" in Cuba. The scholars included in that collection crossed the color spectrum in being phenotypically white, brown, and black.

By the time we were putting the finishing touches to that manuscript, our concerns were shifting. As we wrote the introduction, our fear was that racism would be heightened in Cuba's current crisis; our hope was that, in some small way, the anthology might contribute to a renewed debate on race and nation—in the knowledge that there was concern among the Afro-Cuban population as to their increasing marginalization and exclusion, and that debate was needed to help inform policy and social values.

We saw our fear and hope materialize, as reports of racial discrimination and prejudice increased, and the book became a focal point of discussion inside Cuba and abroad. Since that time, new publications on race in the Americas and Cuba have documented issues raised in the interviews; we discuss these publications in the introduction to this volume. Given that much of what has been written about Cuba has been published abroad and/or by white authors, and that the race issue has become increasingly complex in the 1990s, providing an Afro-Cuban island perspective seemed all the more timely. Trying to understand Cuba without such a perspective, in the words of one of our black West Indian colleagues in London, would be like reading *Hamlet* with no prince.

The book makes no claim to historical truth or contemporary representativeness through the interviews. Nor do we, as editors, necessarily endorse all the views expressed. Indeed, contradictory views come through. Rather, we wished to give voice to a cross section of Afro-Cubans who, for the first time in one volume, urgently call for an end to what they see as the silences and distortions of history and more contemporary times. These, they argue, have a direct bearing not only on the continuance and resurgence of racial discrimination and prejudice, but also on the very conceptualization of what it is to be Cuban and how Cuban nationalism is defined, in present-day Cuba. They all remain committed to the aims and ideals of the Cuban Revolution, while critical of aspects of policy and practice.

The interviews were conducted during the period 1995–97 by Pedro Pérez Sarduy in Cuba, except for one, conducted in 1996 by Jean Stubbs in the United States. All those interviewed were known to one or both of us, and we felt they had valuable voices to contribute. The interviews were recorded, transcribed, and edited. They were designed to be open-ended, allowing interviewees to speak of their own personal experiences and perceptions of the crisis in the broader context of race, revolution, and nation, with the intent of helping to inform wider debate.

All those interviewed are Afro-Cuban professionals, some of them leading figures in their fields, in industry, medicine, media and the arts, ethnology, and cultural studies. All reside on the island and range in age from late twenties to seventies. Some were born and grew up during the revolution; others have first-hand knowledge and experience of both pre- and post-revolutionary Cuba. Some acquired their skills and professions during the revolution, others come from a long line of professional families.

Their experiences of the different parts of the island from which they come find expression in their ideas. Of the major cities, the national capital of Havana in the west has been whiter, the eastern capital of Santiago de Cuba blacker, though both have had relatively fluid societies; Matanzas (east of Havana) has declined from being *the* nineteenth-century city after Havana, having served Cuba's prime hinterland of sugar and slavery; central Santa Clara and central-eastern Camagüey were twentieth-century sugar heartlands of pre-revolutionary racist segregation.

Sarduy was in Cuba for the Second Nation and Migration Conference, convened by the Cuban government in November 1995. The conference brought to Havana some 400 Cubans resident in 35 countries abroad, to discuss issues related to Cuba and to their situations in those countries. Approximately forty of the participants were Afro-Cubans, men and women living in countries as far removed from each other as Australia, Brazil, Finland, the Congo, and Jamaica, as well as Spain and the United States, where the majority of Cubans living abroad are found. Interestingly, the Afro-Cuban representation was generally proportional to its presence abroad, that is, some 10 percent of the total emigré population. One of the panels was on race and cultural identity. However, discussions were not limited to the conference rooms but spilled over into informal gatherings on the island.

A considerable number of the interviews date back to that period and reflect the mood and events around that time. Cubans were then (and still are) locked into the daily grind for survival, trapped in the island crisis occasioned by the breakdown of Cuba's integration into the Eastern European socialist bloc after the 1989 fall of the Berlin Wall. The then thirty-year-old U.S. embargo on the island had been tightened as a result of the 1992 Torricelli-Graham Act, whose extraterritorial sanctions targeted third-party companies and countries doing business with Cuba. The 1990s Special Period of austerity, replacing the late 1980s period of Rectification, was the Cuban government's response to an economic crisis that reached its depths in 1993. National economic indicators improved between 1994 and 1996 but have dropped back since. They continue, moreover, to be tied primarily to the export sector, especially to a growing—and highly visible— tourist enclave based on foreign currency. There has been little spillover into the domestic economy and people have had to fall back on all kinds of informal mechanisms of subsistence, ranging from the licit to the illicit. These include a highly visible resurgence of tourism hustling and prostitution, aptly dubbed *jineterismo* (which literally translates as jockeying— prostitutes being jockeys, or riders, of people and the crisis).

The capital city of Havana, which shouldered particular stresses and strains, was reeling after the events of summer 1994. August brought the first inner-city disturbances since the 1959 revolution, followed in the same month by the exodus of some 30,000 Cubans taking to sea on makeshift rafts, especially from the Havana coastal region. The latter event was seen as a replay of 1980, when an estimated 125,000 left through what became known as the Mariel Boatlift. It did not go unnoticed that there were more black Cubans involved in the tourist hustling and *jineterismo;* that the disturbances took place in a run-down, densely populated, predominantly black, Havana neighborhood; and that, while their numbers were small, more blacks were among the rafters.

Between the initial interviews in November and December 1995 and subsequent interviews conducted when Sarduy was again in Cuba for the May 1996 and May 1997 Annual Tourism Conventions, two key developments had occurred. The first was the shooting down, by Cuban combat planes, of two planes of the Florida-based, Cuban American exile organization Brothers to the Rescue, which were flying off the Cuban coast on 24 February 1996 (the anniversary of the outbreak of the Second War of Independence against Spain, 1895-1898). After the Cuban and U.S. governments signed new immigration accords whereby rafters were no longer to be picked up and welcomed into Florida, the Brothers persisted—despite Cuban warnings—in other activities, which included leafleting Havana from the air. In the wake of the plane-shooting incident, the Clinton administration signed the Helms-Burton Act, extending the extraterritorial sanctions of the previous Torricelli-Graham Act. Opposed in its extraterritoriality by major U.S. allies, the bill nonetheless had a negative impact on foreign investment and further jeopardized incipient island economic recovery. Coincidentally, February 1996 also saw the return of Havana Carnival from July to its former date, after not having been held at all for five years; but there was little to celebrate as the crisis continued at every level, with race ramifications that are explored here.

"No es fácil" (It's not easy) was the popular island comment for the very personal problems affecting the nation, including the racism, in times that were so hard and so easy to distort. On each visit, Sarduy talked with all those interviewed, and they continued to stand by what they said. They were very aware they were expressing views that needed to be handled sensitively, both nationally and internationally. All felt too, however, that circumstances demanded they air private thoughts, often shared among themselves, that they now recognized needed to inform a wider agenda. It was important to them all to feel comfortable with the interviewer and the intentions behind the interviews, and they deposited their trust in us to transcribe and edit (Sarduy), translate (Stubbs), and contextualize the whole (Sarduy and Stubbs). Our off-island commitment was to convey their voices in the struggle for identity. In the academic and literary circles of Europe, the United States, and the Caribbean, this implied navigating, as honestly and knowledgeably as possible, some highly politicized and polemic waters. Our own perceptions and analysis have been enriched conceptually and comparatively in the process.

Pedro Pérez Sarduy has given presentations on the themes underlying this volume, with audiovisual accompaniment, to audiences as interested as they were dissimilar. Two initial presentations, in March 1996, were given at the Conference on Caribbean Culture in honor of Rex Nettleford at the University of the West Indies, Mona, Jamaica, and at the First International

Symposium on Contemporary Literature of the African Diaspora at the University of Salamanca, Spain. A year later, Sarduy was invited back to Salamanca to teach a week-long seminar on Afro-Cuban culture and literature to Spanish students who knew little about slavery and its legacy in what was once a colony of their country. He also published the article "¿Y qué tienen los negros en Cuba?" (And what do blacks have in Cuba?)—a rhetorical play on words based on the famous 1960s poem "Tengo" (I have) by Cuba's national poet, the late Nicolás Guillén—in *Encuentro de la Cultura Cubana* (Cuban cultural encounter), the new journal of Cuban literary dialogue edited in Madrid (1996).

In July and August 1997 Sarduy was in the United States as an invited participant in a multicultural workshop for Danzante, a Latino arts and cultural organization in Harrisburg, Pennsylvania, and in the biennial National Black Theater Festival in Winston-Salem, North Carolina. At the 1995 festival he had given a presentation on *María Antonia* by Afro-Cuban playwright Eugenio Hernández. Telling the tragic story of a young black woman in a marginal world, the play was unprecedented in 1960s Cuba, both in its conception and in how it was perceived, dealing as it did with ordinary black people and their universal problems of love and sadness, jealousy and envy. For many, it profaned the concept of fine art, though it contained all the ingredients of Greek tragedy. Some practitioners of the Santería religion felt they had been betrayed by having their secrets revealed on stage. In the 1980s, *María Antonia* had made a highly successful stage and film comeback. In 1997, Sarduy's topic was Teatro Negro (Black Theater), the first Cuban company of its kind and the first to bear that name, and its inaugural play, *¿Dónde está Dios?* (Where is God?), by Afro-Cuban actress and playwright Flor Amalia Lugo. The play is a consciousness-raising musical satire about a young black man in search of truth who accuses and questions the Lord, who, in turn, submits him to rigorous trials that strengthen his awareness and spur him on to struggle for the unity of black people.

When Sarduy was the 1997 fall semester's Rockefeller Scholar in the Caribbean 2000 Program at the University of Puerto Rico—on an island so similar to Cuba in many ways yet one that has had such a different destiny—he found himself catapulted into a national race debate that displayed many familiar features, not least the denial of racism and the myth of racial democracy, and also the same passion. During that time and since, at events in

Cuba and on successive lecture tours of universities in the United States and Spain, he found the spirit and intentions of this volume further vindicated. His article "And Where Did the Blacks Go?," written for the New York-based Center for Cuban Studies publication *Cuba UpDate* (1998) and describing Santería and the reactions of the Afro-Cuban population to Pope John Paul II's January 1998 visit to Cuba, reflected this.

Late 1998 brought Spain and Africa together for Sarduy. In November he gave a slide-tape presentation at the First International Congress on Postcolonial Studies at the University of Vigo, as well as at the University of Santiago de Compostela, Lugo, and the University of Oviedo, Spain. In December he traveled to Africa for the first time, as a guest speaker at the Second International Symposium on Afro-Ibero-American Studies, sponsored by UNESCO, the University of Alcalá de Henares, Spain, and the host University of Cocody in Abidjan, Ivory Coast.

Jean Stubbs first systematized the ideas contained in the introduction in an invited paper she presented at the Tulane-Cambridge Atlantic Studies Group Inaugural Conference, "The Atlantic World: From Slavery to Emancipation," in November 1996. That paper was the product of reflection, after her translation of the interviews, in the context of historical and contemporary studies of race in Cuba and the Americas. Since then, she has presented versions of the paper in several fora in the United States, Britain, and the Caribbean, to audiences that have been both receptive and critical. Spending the 1996 fall semester as a visiting scholar in the Center for Latin American Studies at the University of Florida in Gainesville, she had access to excellent library holdings as well as opportunities for stimulating discussions with colleagues, especially those in the Diaspora Group, who were also working on race in Cuba, the Caribbean, Latin America, and the United States.

The University of North London, where she is part of a challenging collective of faculty and students in the Caribbean and Latin American studies programs, granted her sabbatical and research leave during the period 1996–98. The university also provided funding for her to participate in major regional conferences of the Association of Caribbean Historians (Martinique 1997 and Suriname 1998), the Caribbean Studies Association (Colombia 1997 and Antigua 1998), and the Latin American Studies Association (United States 1998). The University of London Institute of Latin American Studies, of which she is an associate fellow, provided funding for her participation in LASA (Mexico 1997).

The Latin American and Caribbean Center and the Department of History, at Florida International University in Miami, jointly enabled her to spend the 1997 summer semester as a visiting scholar, and the University of Miami North-South Center also provided her with associate status. Living and working in the "other" Cuba was to prove fascinating, not least when she was joined by Sarduy and contacts were made with the "invisible" Miami Afro-Cuban community. During a brief fellowship in the Caribbean Department at the Royal Institute of Linguistics and Anthropology in Leiden, she was able to consult further holdings and discuss perspectives with scholars from the Netherlands and the Dutch Caribbean. At the University of Puerto Rico, as 1998 spring semester Rockefeller Scholar in the Caribbean 2000 Program, she too became drawn into the Puerto Rican race debate. Similarly, her exposure to the "other Cuba" debate was augmented by her return to Miami as 1998 summer semester Rockefeller Scholar in the Cuban Research Institute at Florida International University.

During this period we were commissioned to contribute to two volumes. The first was *No Longer Invisible: Afro-Latin Americans Today*, for which we wrote the introduction (Perez Sarduy and Stubbs 1995). Among other things, this book highlighted the need to bridge the gap between the wealth of studies and comparative knowledge on race in Latin America, often (though not exclusively) the work of white scholars, and the more localized knowledge base, vision, and self-perception of Afro-Latin Americans themselves. The chapters on various countries were written predominantly by nationals of each country, many of them black. The chapters on Brazil and Cuba were remarkable for the frustration and anger expressed by their authors over the disempowerment that accompanied each nation's myths of "racial democracy" and for the cry from these black authors for a race-conscious movement to address this issue. These chapters suggested the need for new points of departure in our understanding of race variants and black self-liberation in the Americas, especially where Brazil and Cuba were concerned.

Our second undertaking was to bring together some of those ideas in the form of the Latin America and Cuba sections of *Africana: The Encyclopedia of the African and African American Experience* (Appiah et al. 1999), an encyclopedia on peoples of the African-descended diaspora. The reader unfamiliar with the history of race in pre- and post-revolutionary Cuba would do well to refer to these two publications, in addition to our earlier *Afro-Cuba*. In this present volume, we have deliberately chosen not to retrace all our steps on an already trodden path but rather to highlight those aspects more directly relevant to the contemporary debate.

The confluence of experiences and sharpening of ideas has no doubt strengthened our conviction that the Americas approach the twenty-first century with changing race realities with which the paradigms have not kept pace, and that Cuba is no exception. As the debates rage over whether the terms "black" and "Afro-Cuban" should even be used, so also they continue over concepts such as diaspora and the internal rationale and validity of the race issue as opposed to what is seen as the exportation of a U.S. race model.

It would be out of place, in a book of interviews of this nature, to attempt to do justice to the debates in all their theoretical complexity. The book itself falls between disciplines. It is neither social science nor historical narrative nor literary text. Its strengths lie in first-hand personal accounts and in our attempt, in the introduction, to ground those accounts, historically, conceptually and comparatively, in the context of recently published work. We have also included a glossary of Afro-Cuban terms and a comprehensive bibliography for the more specialized reader. However, we stand by our underlying premise: that meaningful debate cannot be sustained without viewpoints from Afro-Cuban protagonists, hence our *Afro-Cuban Voices*.

As we were finalizing the preface and introduction to this volume, the Spanish-language edition of *AfroCuba: Una antología de escritos cubanos sobre raza, política y cultura* (Pérez Sarduy and Stubbs 1993 [1998]), was going to print. In fact, a trilogy was in the making, as interviews were being conducted and transcribed for a planned third volume on Afro-Cubans abroad.

As always, we are indebted to many institutions, colleagues, and friends who helped us along the way. For this volume, we would like to convey our special thanks to all the institutions mentioned here, and in particular to Barry Chevannes and Rex Nettleford (Jamaica); Olga Barrios, María Belén Martín, Luis Beltrán, Ana María Bringas, Isabel Carrera, Pío Serrano, and Jesús Zapata (Spain); Anthony Badger, Victor Bulmer-Thomas, Rita Christian, Maxine Molyneux, Clem Seecharan, and Betty Wood (United Kingdom); Anthony Bryan, David Cook, Alejandro de la Fuente, Camille Erice, Sylvia Frey, Eduardo Gamarra, David Geggus, Lynne Guitar, Sherry Johnson, Douglas Kincaid, Chester King, Anthony Maingot, Irma McClaurin, Karen Morrison, Jeffrey Needell, Olasope Oyelaran, Lisandro Pérez, Helen

Safa, Alex and Carol Stepick, and Charles Wood (United States); Jaime Arocha and Fernando Urrea (Colombia); Juan José Baldrich, Lowell Fiet, Humberto García, Antonio Gaztambide, Jorge Giovannetti, Juan Giusti, Sybil Lewis, Rocío López, Angel Quintero, Emilio Pantojas, and Aaron Ramos (Puerto Rico); and Michiel Baud, Rosemarijn Hoefte, and Ingrid and Gert Oostindie (the Netherlands). We can only hope that this volume repays in part their intellectual and social generosity.

Most of all, we wish to recognize our Cuban contributors, without whom there would be no book.

Pedro Pérez Sarduy and Jean Stubbs

This book is dedicated to
Reynaldo Peñalver Moral

Introduction
Race and the Politics of Memory in
Contemporary Black Cuban Consciousness

"The blood of Africa runs deep in our veins."

The Cuban Revolution triumphed forty years ago, in 1959, as Third World national liberation movements and decolonization processes were gaining strength. It was also the height of the Cold War and the U.S. Civil Rights movement. In 1960, Fidel Castro, the young, phenotypically white leader of the Cuban Revolution, was in New York for the United Nations General Assembly. Made less than welcome at the midtown Shelbourne Hotel, he moved his delegation to the more modest Hotel Theresa, in the heart of black Harlem. There he was received by cheering crowds and met with world-famous black figures: Malcolm X, Langston Hughes, and President Kwame Nkrumah of Ghana (who, at the United Nations, had condemned U.S. intervention in the Congo).

In 1996, Cuban President Fidel Castro returned to the United Nations. Although rebuffed by Mayor Rudolph Giuliani of New York, he received many other invitations, including one to meet with African American religious leaders at Harlem's Abyssinian Baptist Church. There he spoke before 1,500 people about Cuba and its role in Angola and the overthrow of apartheid in South Africa. Before Castro spoke, Reverend Calvin Butts said, "People ask me, 'Why are you inviting Castro to your church?' and I say to them, 'Because it is in our tradition to invite visionaries who fight for the freedom of all peoples.'"

Many black Cubans were proud of that vision and commitment to struggle. They supported the revolutionary government's involvement in Africa, especially its response to Angolan President Agostinho Neto's 1975 call for help against invading South African forces. It was then that Castro declared: "The blood of Africa runs deep in our veins" and defined Cubans as a Latin American and Latin African people. The sentiment was strengthened when, in 1979, Cuba became chair of the Movement of Non-Aligned Countries and developed its own bilateral programs with African countries.

Cuba's military involvement in the war in Angola was to last a long and costly thirteen years, but it was instrumental in driving back the South Africans and driving a nail in the coffin of apartheid. Therefore it was hardly surprising that Castro should be given a hero's welcome on a visit to South Africa in 1998. In September of that year, he attended the inaugural session of the Twelfth Summit of the Movement of Non-Aligned Countries, as South African President Nelson Mandela began his mandate as chair of the movement. It was an occasion for Mandela to confer on him South Africa's Order of Good Hope. Castro had made an earlier visit to South Africa in 1994, to attend Mandela's investiture as the country's first black leader. For the two elder statesmen, both visits had been emotionally charged.

Conversely, during the 1990s the political and racial division between Cubans on the island (mainly black and brown) and Cubans in Miami (overwhelmingly white) was made apparent in the receptions each group gave South African leader Mandela: in Cuba he was welcomed as a hero, but not so in Miami. In June 1990, shortly before a planned visit to Florida as part of his U.S. tour, four Cuban American mayors of Miami signed a letter declaring Nelson Mandela persona non grata. Any sign of support for Cuba was to be denounced. (Mandela had often expressed appreciation for Cuba's solidarity in ending apartheid.) The African American community declared a boycott of Miami, which was ineffective, and demanded an apology from the Cuban Americans, which was never offered. The conflict also signaled divisions among Cuban Americans, as Afro-Cubans distanced themselves from Cubans of Hispanic descent.

In August 1998, before his trip to South Africa, Castro was closer to home, visiting Jamaica, Barbados, and Grenada. He was given an equally warm welcome in each country. He spoke of the links embracing those countries and Cuba: their shared history of European colonialism, sugar-plantation economy, and African slavery.

Diplomatic relations between the revolutionary government of Cuba and the independent Anglophone Caribbean countries of Trinidad and Tobago, Barbados, Guyana, and Jamaica date back to 1972. Castro was in Jamaica in October 1977 at the invitation of then Prime Minister Michael

Manley; twenty years later, he was there for Manley's funeral; and in May 1998, Jamaican Prime Minister Percival Patterson was in Cuba to sign a joint investment agreement.

In 1993, Cuban construction workers helping to build an international airport in Grenada had faced the forces of the U.S. invasion, in the wake of the imploding Grenadian Revolution of 1979 and the 1983 murder of its leader Maurice Bishop, who had been particularly close to Cuba. Fifteen years later, Grenadian Prime Minister Keith Mitchell thanked the Cuban people and their leader for what they had done for Grenada.

In September 1998, while Castro was in the Dominican Republic for a CARIFORUM meeting of Caribbean heads of state and government, Dominican President Leonel Fernández conferred on him that country's Duarte, Sánchez and Mella Order of Merit. Castro in turn conferred on Fernández the José Martí Order of Cuba. In a moment charged with historic symbolism, Castro visited Baní, birthplace of Dominican General Máximo Gómez, who had fought in Cuba's nineteenth-century wars of independence and was described by Fernández as "a living historical force for justice and the well-being of humanity." Over the last decade, Caribbean nations have welcomed Cuba into their folds and spoken out against the injustice of the U.S. trade embargo on the island. In 1961, the embargo catapulted Cuba into the Soviet camp. It was twice tightened in the 1990s, after the demise of the Soviet bloc, in a pincers-like move to oust Castro and his regime through increasing economic and social hardship. Politically, the regime held sway, but with a widening gulf between vision and reality, one that had internal race implications.

Race in 1990s Cuba

The Fifth Congress of the Cuban Communist Party, held in October 1997, took place in a Cuba that was arguably as beleaguered as in October 1991, when the Fourth Congress was held. The 1997 congress could almost predictably be seen as a battening down of the hatches—both numerically (the Central Committee was actually reduced in number to 150) and ideologically. As in the 1991 congress, noncapitulation was the order of the day. In his closing speech of October 10, symbolically the date commemorating the outbreak of Cuba's first war of independence from Spain (1868–78), Castro declared:

We must erect a mountain of steel that everything will smash against, we must develop a Party of steel and safeguard our Revolution from any deviation and danger, external or internal, today, tomorrow and always. . . . The Cuban Revolution of 1868, as Martí repeatedly said, failed because it was divided; and in the 1895 war there were also problems of leadership. The lesson of history is that there must be leadership and that the leadership must not fail, for there will be no paying the price. This is key and must be guaranteed for a long period to come.

Minister of the Armed Forces Raúl Castro, in turn, contextualizing this in present-day terms, called for keeping the revolution immune from "corrosive viruses from within" because "what happened in the U.S.S.R. and the Eastern European countries will never happen here."

The congress was widely interpreted both inside and outside Cuba as a hard-line tightening of the ranks, militarily and politically, around the rallying calls of anti-imperialism, nationalism, and socialism, with a sidelining of some potentially more reforming elements. One little-mentioned aspect of the congress, however, was its attention to proportional representation within the ranks with regard to youth, blacks, and women. Congress proceedings state:

In the present we must continue the consolidation of the fair policy of promoting blacks and women, especially as cadres, not mechanically but in the same way that the policy has been occurring with youth, a policy that guarantees the moral authority of the party before our people. . . . The Party must insist on the qualities and example set by newly promoted cadres, something that also holds for the state and other institutions in society. The promotion of persons from different generations, men and women, whites, blacks and mestizos, should not be left to spontaneity.

In race terms, this would appear to mark a significant departure. The concept of racial equality was espoused by the revolution from its early days. With overwhelming support, the revolutionary government curtailed class privilege and gave opportunities to the poor on a platform of agrarian reform and nationalization of industry, coupled with extensive educational and health care programs. The early exodus of Cubans, to the United States and Miami in particular, was primarily wealthy and white. On the island, black Cubans regained dignity as the bases for institutionalized racism were dismantled, and the revolution mirrored liberation movements sweeping Asia, Africa, and the Caribbean at the time.

Propelled in no small measure by the United States government's hostile response, ranging from an embargo on trade to espionage, the Cuban government entered the European socialist fold. In 1961, after the failed invasion of U.S.-supported Cuban exiles at the Bay of Pigs, Castro declared the socialist nature of the revolution. The missile crisis of 1962 thrust Cuba into the spotlight of world attention; disaster was averted by the Soviet withdrawal of missiles, in return, among other things, for the U.S. commitment not to invade Cuba. In 1965 the revolutionary forces were regrouped under the new Communist Party of Cuba.

The Cuban government sought to establish a socialist, state-run economy and society. In keeping with the Marxist emphasis on class, the government targeted disparities of class over race, in the belief that addressing the former would correct the latter. After initial declarations on race, it was not until the 1986 party congress that Castro again addressed the question, this time to criticize the persistence of racial stereotypes and prejudice as well as the lack of party representation along race lines. His address came after the major 1980 exodus of 125,000 Cubans through Mariel, which included more of the popular classes and more blacks than before. Aside from certain "quota" policies that were subsequently put in place, there is little evidence that his remarks led to any widespread follow-up action.

The 1989 collapse of Soviet-bloc socialism and the 1990s U.S. embargo, tightened in the form of the 1992 Torricelli-Graham Act and extended in the 1996 Helms-Burton Act, precipitated internal economic collapse, which has disproportionately affected the black population. The economy plummeted by about 50 percent, to its worst depths, in 1993. In summer 1994 there was rioting in Havana, the first of its kind since 1959, and some 30,000 rafters took to the seas in desperation, many of them from poorer and blacker sectors of society. Strategies in joint state and international venture capital created export and tourist industry dollar enclaves in which blacks played a lesser and more menial role: fewer blacks had families abroad to send dollar remittances in an economy in which the dollar had become king. Consequently, more black figures in sports and music turned to professionalism abroad, and more blacks were driven by necessity into the informal underground economy.

At the 1997 party congress, three black provincial first secretaries were promoted to the Politburo. Juan Carlos Robinson Agramonte (Santiago de Cuba), Misael Enamorado Dager (Las Tunas), and Pedro Sáez Montejo (Sancti Spiritus) joined existing black members Juan Almeida Bosque, Esteban Lazo Hernández, and Pedro Ross Leal, making six out of a total of twenty-four Politburo members.

Proportional to the population as a whole, a one-quarter representation might be seen as not far off the mark. However, that depends on whether minimalist estimates of 30 percent or maximalist estimates of 60 to 70 percent of the population are considered, broadly speaking, to be black. There is a growing current of opinion that the latter figure is more accurate (due in part to the greater exodus of whites from the island); that, while welcome, increased party representation among Afro-Cubans is but one change among many needed; and that, however one looks at it, race is an increasingly crucial issue in understanding contemporary Cuba.

The decade of the 1990s has borne witness to paradoxical developments in Cuba. A symbolism of race has been deployed. Most striking is the 1990s noncapitulation to the United States' stepped-up pressure, encapsulated in the concept of the nation as a Baraguá. This is a reference to the 1878 Protest of Baraguá, when General Antonio Maceo, Cuba's nineteenth-century Afro-Cuban independence fighter, refused to capitulate to Spain by signing the Pact of Zanjón, which marked the end of the 1868–78 Ten Years War. More recently, all of Cuba has been likened to a *palenque* (a maroon, or runaway slave, settlement). The current plight of Cuba has been described as a process of "Haitianization," in clear reference to both external reprisals and internal implosion, as well as racialization, of the Haitian conflict, from the time of the 1791–1804 Haitian Revolution to the present.

Other instances are the ways in which black Cuban support for the revolution is invoked (many black Cubans have benefited from the policies of the revolution and today form a significant proportion of professionals in fields such as medicine, biotechnology, and sports) and in which Afro-Cuban culture (music, dance, and religion) is celebrated. The overt increase in Afro-Cuban religions is a considerable change from earlier periods, when all religions, especially the Afro-Cuban religions, were discouraged. The Afro-Cuban religious revival should not be underestimated as a deep and genuine expression of an old African spirituality.

At the same time, racial divides have increased, along with a perceived growing unease about those divides, not least due to the forms of racism generated around them, especially among Afro-Cubans. The divides most discussed relate to the current economic restructuring process, from the primarily Hispano-Cuban tourism and foreign exchange sector, plus dollar remittances from the predominantly white Hispano-Cuban American community, to the blacker second economy that has accompanied the downsizing of the manufacturing and public sectors where many blacks were employed. They are associated with hardening double standards. The reinvigorated Catholicism (of which the pope's 1998 visit was but a part) encompassed a "Catholicizing" of Santería (though the pope himself refused to meet with priests of Santería).

There was also a "demonizing" of other Afro-Cuban religions, as media and popular rumor told of Afro-Cuban *brujos* (witch doctors) sacrificing small white girls and digging up bones from cemetery graveyards for their rituals. This accompanied a general bolstering of Hispano-Cuban historical and cultural hegemony, with Afro-Cubans excluded from meaningful roles in Cuban television and other media while Afro-Cuban folklore was commercialized for the tourist market. As we were writing, it was unclear whether any of this will be turned around by policies and activities. However, there have been encouraging signs. The 1996 Declaration of Havana endorsed UNESCO's "Slave Routes of the Americas" cultural heritage tourism program; and, in November 1998, the race issue was raised at length by the National Union of Writers and Artists of Cuba (UNEAC).

Contemporary developments might be described as having occasioned three broadly parallel trends, all of which find expression in the interviews in this volume. The first is a growing present-day white Cuban manifestation of "blaming-the-victim" syndrome, as more blacks are out of work, on the streets (in petty trading and prostitution), and in the jails. An unintentional outcome of the revolutionary process has been to equate the black with the humble and dispossessed, thereby traveling a slippery slope along which the black goes from being seen as slave (rebel) to member of an underclass (criminal). The second is what might be termed Hispano-Cuban appropriation of Afro-Cuban culture, with white Cubans spearheading art forms, movements, and institutions related to black Cuban culture and claiming legitimacy to do so given the extent of cultural and biological race mixing on the island. The third is the need expressed by Afro-Cubans to articulate a black perspective, which is what this book is about.

What follows aims first and foremost to introduce the book, summarizing key points formulated by those interviewed. A conscious contemporary agenda takes shape in probing the past: what, from the vantage point of the late 1990s, is remembered, why, and to what end? Familiar themes are the experience of slavery and truncated freedom, past and present; concepts of *mestizaje*, "whiteness" and "blackness"; type and stereotype; difference and identity; *africanía, hispanidad, cubanía*. However, there are new departures.

One is to challenge the dominant view of Cuban history, on and off the island, which has all too often played down the long tradition of black Cuban thinking and scholarship. A salient feature emerging from the testimony of those interviewed is a collective affirmation of that tradition. Another is the downplaying, rejection, or rethinking of slavery and its post-emancipation sequel, servitude, as *the* historical markers. Yet another is the call for other markers, such as the deconstruction of Cuban "whiteness" and reconstruction of black achievement, both during and since slavery. Together, they also challenge conventional wisdom that sees Cuba as a racial democracy on the basis of its celebrated *mestizaje* (race mixing). All of this represents a significant shift from ten, twenty, and thirty years ago, when race was seen as much less of an issue and Cuba was perceived as moving more in the direction of a racial democracy.

Given this shift, we endeavor to situate the scenario that emerges from the interviews in a broader, more historical and comparative frame of reference suggested by recent scholarship, especially on the United States, Brazil, and Cuba. The argument endorsed is the need to rethink our conceptual frameworks about nation, to question the binary or bipolar (U.S.) and multiracial (Brazil/Cuba) models, and to understand what appears to be a certain convergence. In this context, we review some of the new historiography and anthropological and sociocultural studies emerging on race and race constructs in Cuba. Finally, we examine recent publications in the social sciences in Cuba, which include recommendations on constructive steps that might be taken in advancing the national race debate.

Race, Representation, and Identity

Part I of the book focuses on race as a lived experience during the periods before and since the 1959 revolution. In chapter 1, retired journalist Reynaldo Peñalver describes his grit and determination to leave the life of the slums behind him and become a journalist in pre-revolutionary Cuba. He worked as a bricklayer's mate at the age of twelve, studied under a street-lamp well into the early morning hours, and rode on the back of the street-car without paying to get to and from journalism school. An early highlight in his career as a journalist was covering Fidel Castro's stay in Harlem in 1960, when he helped arrange a meeting between Castro and Malcolm X and subsequently interviewed Malcolm X himself.

Chapter 2 recounts the life stories of two generations of the Molina-Pérez family, a black Havana family which, thanks to openings provided by the revolution, was in occupational terms upwardly mobile. In the stories of Elpidio de la Trinidad Molina (father), Jorge Molina (son), and Egipcia Pérez (mother), generational and gender differences emerge quite clearly. The father, who holds the high title of National Hero of Labor for his knowledge and innovations in the highly specialized field of emery stone production, sees his advance as testimony to the end of racial discrimination in Cuba. His son sees his own educational and occupational mobility as a product of revolutionary change (after this interview was conducted, in January 1998, he was proudly elected deputy to the National Assembly of People's Power). Here, however, he reflects that he was in many ways buffered by growing up in a black, middle-class professional home and feels the contemporary situation is far more racially divisive. Egipcia, as wife and mother, candidly recounts anecdotes from her life, both before and since the revolution, revealing how she has been the target of racial discrimination and prejudice—first as a bright little black girl at school, then as a maid who was too educated for her own good, and finally as a health worker who would always speak her mind.

The two women doctors in chapter 3 come from different class backgrounds. Lliliam Cordiés Jackson is older and of an established Santiago de Cuba professional family from before the revolution. She specializes in hypertension and is knowledgeable about studies being conducted in the Caribbean and the United States on its more lethal incidence among blacks. Nuria Pérez Sesma is younger and studied hard to become a doctor during the revolution. This was what she most wanted in life, and she achieved her goal, only to find the profession devalued in today's Cuba. In this context, both women reflect on race as it affected their own lives and their patients', and also on their knowledge and experience as black women in the medical profession in Cuba. "Right now, I feel very frustrated," Pérez Sesma declares. "I wanted to be a doctor and I became one, because I like medicine. But this whole situation, in every sense, the economic and social problems, including the racial discrimination that exists . . . thousands of problems we have make me generally depressed." She ends on a poignant note: "There are times, when I'm alone, and I wonder what the future will be like . . . is it so uncertain or is there hope? There are times when I feel tired and think I can't go on. Then I give myself a bit of psychotherapy and go on making an effort, because all that can be very soul-destroying."

Part II explores and critiques racial representation in the conscious and subconscious life of Cuba, linking historical fiction and the contemporary media with present-day attitudes and events. Marta Rojas is a print journalist and Eliseo Altunaga, a scriptwriter. Both have recently turned to historical fiction and make very explicit links between past and present when speaking about their 1999 work. In her interview, Rojas is undecided as to which of two provisional titles to give her latest novel: *Papeles de blanco* (which is wonderfully apt and ambiguous in the Spanish since it translates as both White Papers and White Roles) or *Santa lujuria* (Holy Lust, the title eventually chosen). In chapter 4 she explains, "I wanted to do a trilogy about *mestizaje* in the Americas set in three epochs: one around the eighteenth and nineteenth centuries, that might have something contemporary; one at the start of the twentieth century; and another more contemporary." Altunaga, in chapter 5, describes his new novel titled *A medianoche llegan los muertos* (The Dead Come at Midnight), which he declares is "a postmodernist novel on two narrative planes: that of today, and that of the nineteenth century, 1912 and 1930."

For Santiago de Cuba-born Rojas, there is a logical centrality of *mestizaje,* and she gently mocks notions of whiteness, from that surrounding the colonial painter Vicente Escobar, described in art books as one who was "born black and died white" (because his whiteness was bought for him legally, so that he might paint the Havana nobility), to that of present-day Cuba, where you can get an I.D. and declare yourself white on paper. "Now you don't have to buy it," she jokes, "it's down to consumer taste." Camagüey-born Altunaga, on the other hand, challenges conventional interpretations of blackness. He debunks conventional depictions of Antonio Maceo as a warrior, because he was also an entrepreneur, a man of ideas, a political man. The novel goes on to trace "an atmosphere that has remained hidden, that functions beneath Cuban discourse. The Cuban says one thing, but does another. The black speaks but behind the rhetoric there's a world of frustrations, violence, and discrimination, but that's not said, or seen." Altunaga decries the marginalization and negation of "what is black in Cuban culture," which, he says, "weakens that culture terribly." He concludes, "If they want to perpetuate the nation, the members of that nation must recognize themselves as black as much as white. . . . The idea of a mestizo society is the only one that can save the nation. I think the Cuban has a white aesthetic and a black ethic. That is where the struggle lies. That is the world my novels are about."

After a long career, mainly in radio broadcasting, actress Elvira Cervera, retired and in her seventies, describes in chapter 6 how in 1992 she came to propose Todo en Sepia (All in Sepia), an all-black theater project "to break the apartheid that prevents the black actor from taking on roles of world theater" and "to document, analyze, denounce, and reject the evident limitations on the dark-skinned actor professionally on the Cuban stage." In chapter 7, Camagüey-born and Guantánamo-raised Alden Knight, now in his 60s, argues along the same lines: "Elvira Cervera proposes something I wouldn't have agreed with a few years back, because I had always fought for an integrated theater, like our society, but you realize you have fewer possibilities and you need a place where you do have the possibilities, as she puts it, 'where the magnificent, the mediocre, and the bad can work' because 'the *caras pálidas* [pale-faced] magnificent, mediocre, and bad' can always find work and develop."

Both ask themselves whether racial discrimination has been eliminated and argue it has not, because this is something that can't be legislated but has to be overcome through awareness, and first it has to be recognized that there is discrimination. They rail against stereoptyping of blacks in the media as slaves, servants, and criminals, when in fact blacks can be found in all walks of society, and against the new social structure of the 1990s, in which there is much more discrimination against blacks. And so, as Knight concludes, "Yes, blacks are the backbone of the revolution, but they also protest. . . . You clamor for that for which you shed your blood and died. . . . If what's seen is that if you're black, you're no more than a slave, well, the slave who didn't want to be a slave became a maroon. Today's maroon is protesting oppression by turning criminal. Is the maroon to blame?"

Georgina Herrera, whose writing is now her life, narrates in chapter 8 how she barely read at all, as a child growing up in the predominantly black town of Jovellanos, in Matanzas province, but then started writing poetry. She relates moments important for her as a black woman, such as writing for radio, writing an anthology of poetry on the great African warrior queen N'gola Kiluanji, and forming part of an exciting media women's group called MAGIN (from the word "imagination"). She describes the graphically different focus on the *jineteras* (women prostitutes) of the mainstream Federation of Cuban Women compared with that of MAGIN, while it was still in existence. "The FMC has a completely bourgeois concept of moral values," she declares. "Blacks still face more economic privation, and, in the case of the black woman, who is also exotic and attractive, she has the most difficulties. . . . And so black women were the first to go into *jineterismo*. Needs aside, they know they're attractive. It's a means of survival. . . . MAGIN concludes that for a young, intelligent woman to go out and give her body to bring food home for her family and for herself, she has to have very high self-esteem, she has to be very sure of what her values are and what she's going after. That's the thinking of MAGIN." Since the interview, there has been a crackdown on *jineterismo*, with police swoops rounding up both the prostitutes and pimps, many of whom are black. At the time of this writing, the race dimensions of the crackdown were yet to surface.

Part III opens with filmmaker Gloria Rolando and drummaker Juan Benkomo, who critique dominant concepts of cultural and national identity in contemporary Cuban cinema, music, and religion, with which their own work attempts to break. Forms of representation, and the rethinking of the notions of *africanía, hispanidad,* and *cubanía,* are then linked more broadly with issues of modernity and postmodernity by art critic Guillermina Ramos Cruz and two leading contemporary figures identified with *mestizaje:* ethnographer Rogelio Martínez Furé and poet and literary critic Nancy Morejón.

For Gloria Rolando, the absence of blacks in and on film is a paramount concern that underscores her work. In chapter 9, she describes her motivation and experiences in directing two documentaries: *Oggún* (1993) and *Los hijos de Baraguá* (My Footsteps in Baraguá, 1996). *Oggún* is about the life and work of Lázaro Ross, a longtime key figure in the National Folklore Group, from its founding in the 1960s. Ross is the modern-day griot who tells the legends, the *patakines*. "In that way I was giving voice to him," Rolando says. "I was showing the universality of the values of that culture from Africa, specifically the Yoruba tradition, not only song, dance, and sacrificial ritual, but a whole philosophy and way of life." She was driven by the belief that "we need to show our culture as complex, with many different roots, to help integration, not division."

Her growing fascination with the Caribbean, Caribbean peoples in Cuba, and their contribution to Cuban culture led to the filming of *My Footsteps,* about West Indians who went to work in Cuba in the 1910s and 1920s and who, along with their descendants, still live today in a small sugar town in central Cuba. Like any historian, she faced the challenge of how she was going to tell that story. The threads in the narrative are two old ladies, Miss Jones from Barbados, and Ruby Hunt from Jamaica, along with the Cuban narrator—the daughter of a Jamaican father and Barbadian mother—someone from Baraguá who returns to visit and reflects on the past. Since *My Footsteps,* Rolando has gone on to make *The Eyes of the Rainbow* (1997), a documentary on Assata Shakur, former U.S. Black Panther and Black Liberation Army militant, in exile in Cuba since the 1970s, linking her life with the Afro-Cuban warrior-*orisha* Oyá.

Juan Benkomo is a local Havana craftsman who makes both lay and sacred *batá* drums: the Iyá, Itótele, and Okónkolo. In chapter 10 he shares with us some of the secrets of his drum craft. Berating the cheap commercialism engulfing Santería for the tourist market, he says, "You can't make a drum any day and any hour. When you make a drum for a ceremony, it's not you who's doing the work, it's the dead who are working with you. . . . The drum comes when the dead want to work." The spirits must be in the drum which, like them, needs ritual and food. It is Olofi's punishment for having thrown all those eggs and tomatoes at people leaving in 1980 through Mariel, he mystically declares, that eggs and tomatoes are not plentiful in Cuba today.

Guillermina Ramos Cruz relates in chapter 11 how she started researching *africanía* in greater depth in Cuban painting in 1978, when she joined Grupo Antillano (Antilles Group). "We had left behind the phase of slavery and the slave ship," she says. "Now we were offering a concept from our optic: the flora, the fauna, the strength of African culture and how this translated into the revolutionary context." She recounts how in the 1980s Grupo Volumen Uno (Volume One Group) was founded by young art graduates with a "postmodernist, trans-avant-garde vision," rejecting African roots for a universal modernity beyond cultural identity. They argued that the theme of identity had reached saturation point in Cuba, ever since 1927 when generations of artists had taken it up. In late 1989, postmodernity in Cuban art was successful in Paris, New York, and Madrid, but then, Ramos claims, "The critics began to take an interest in the art with African roots . . . and a subtle and complex story began to unfold, which was an incursion in black culture without the Afro-Cuban artists." She reflects, "When black intellectuals and artists meet and try to organize as a group to reach a common set of ideas, this generates concern. . . . There are certain subtleties, things that are said between the lines, translated by racial prejudice. And there are many omissions. . . ." She concludes, "I think the black continues to be marginalized at the intellectual level. I think this because I live it. My proposition is that we need to unite because we are all dispersed."

In chapter 12, Rogelio Martínez Furé, who trained with Cuban ethnographer Fernando Ortiz, defends Don Fernando's use of the terms "Hispano-Cuban" and "Afro-Cuban" and attacks those who evidently wish to forget that Cuba is the synthesis of the two, referring to Cuban and Afro-Cuban as if Afro-Cuban is something else and Cuban is chemically pure, Hispanic, or white. However, he goes on to declare: "There is, of course, no homogeneous Cuban culture, which is why I also think it is a mistake to speak of a national cultural identity. There is no one national cultural identity. . . . What we must accept is the plural heritage, not homogenizing monomania." The problem for him lies in combating two erroneous camps. "The first, a negative type, is to say 'we are that which makes us different from other people' and the other, mimetic, whereby 'we are like other people. . . .'" He goes on to say, "I think there are elements in common and elements which differentiate us, the product of our historical experience in a specific island called Cuba. But the concept of national identity has changed. . . . Each epoch has its identity."

Nancy Morejón, in chapter 13, sets the issues of race and national identity firmly in the context of the contemporary political world setting in which the ethnic factor is fundamental as the twentieth century, and the millennium, draw to a close. And yet, she declares, in Cuban history, the race question is one "that in us has been extraordinarily linked to the search for a national identity. While I respect the concept of diaspora, the concrete experience and reality of the African diaspora, I believe that diaspora cannot in any way be divorced from the phenomenon of nation." She traces this in the work of black and mulatto women writers of Cuba and argues for a far more profound and rigorously grounded race dialogue: "I think it's a phenomenon of the end of century, of the millennium, for which we must seek an urgent response, because there is evidently a resurgence. I think it's fatal that it feeds on a larger racism that has mushroomed since the demise of the socialist countries. We thought that nations and collectivist societies had resolved their historic ethnic problems. And that wasn't the case." She concludes, "I think there has to be a big antiracist campaign and we have to study racism. We are on the brink of a philosophical rethinking of countries of color, of the emerging cultures, in postmodernist language, of the periphery. That periphery is condemned always to be immigrant and other, the otherness of European."

History and Race Constructs

The graphically changing race dynamic in 1990s Cuba, as expressed in the interviews, has to be understood not only in its national setting, but also in the wider end-of-century, and end-of-millennium, resurgence of racism. What are the historical and contemporary factors that might help explain this? Wherein lie the points of difference and convergence?

In our introduction to *No Longer Invisible: Afro-Latin Americans Today*, we began by writing: "European colonial might did its utmost to strip [Africans] of their freedom, their dignity and their culture, but culture was perhaps the easiest of the three for peoples of African descent to continue to subvert" (Perez Sarduy and Stubbs 1995:1). We noted that the exceptions to racial hostility at the national level were historically thin, testifying to the stigma of a perverse legacy, despite periods of quasi-glorification of notions of *mestizaje* and the "cosmic race."

This, we pointed out, was despite the long-held key variants in race relations in the Americas: the "bipolar" or "two-tiered" black/white division in the United States; the "three-tiered" black/brown/white partitioning in the non-Hispanic Caribbean; and the more fluid "continuum" of race mixing in the Hispanic Caribbean and Iberian Latin America. We outlined the two major lines of reasoning for this in terms of colonial cultures and stages of development.

One side of the argument accounting for the difference is that is it not economic but cultural. Iberians, it is claimed, instituted a more benign form of slavery than did northern Europeans because of the strong Moorish influences on, and the nature of feudalism in, the Iberian Peninsula. The counterargument is that there are powerful underlying economic explanations for racism tied to the growth of plantation economy in the Americas. Thus, it makes little sense to compare Hispanic nineteenth-century Cuba, a booming slave plantation economy, with Hispanic nineteenth-century Puerto Rico, which was an imperial backwater with no significant development of plantation slavery.

Both the "imperial cultures" and the "systadial" (or "stages of development") approaches tend to focus on power structures and official thinking. A third argument highlights the extent to which people have been active agents in shaping their own history, building and abolishing slavery, erecting and transgressing the intricacies of color and class codes. A distinction has been made between public and private, between the rules of behavior regulating contact between racial groups and actual intimate personal relations. According to this view, Iberian differed from non-Iberian America far more in the public sphere than in the private.

No part of the world, it has been claimed, ever witnessed such a gigantic mixing of races as that which took place in the Hispanic Caribbean and Iberian Latin America. At the same time, colonial and postcolonial society partitioned off people, classifying and categorizing skin pigmentation with a bewildering array of legal codes and linguistic terms. In this context, bettering or "whitening" the race denoted upward social mobility, while "blackening" was equated with backwardness, poverty, and underdevelopment. Cuba shares both sides of that history.

After plantation slavery, a renewed hardening of race prejudice occurred, building on nineteenth-century European pseudoscientific eugenics notions. These ideas sat uneasily with currents of thinking that romanticized indigenism and Africanism, celebrated *mestizaje,* or race mixing, as the new symbiosis. As a result, notions of *mestizaje* were also permeated with ideas about the superiority of whitening. Hence the contradiction between the myth of racial democracy and the prevalence of racial discrimination and prejudice. Prevailing currents of history, dominated by a sense of "Europeanness," repeatedly undermined and denied awareness of the African heritage, forcing Afro-Cubans, like their Afro-Latin American brothers and sisters, to rediscover their ancestry and culture and renew the struggle for their rights.

An important lesson of history is that political leadership matters. Race and ethnicity hold strategic, not inherent or absolute value. Ethnic and racial identity take on different meanings in different contexts, depending on who uses them and for what purposes. They are relative, situational categories. Competition and conflict between racial and ethnic groups may occur but need not necessarily do so, and may or may not be institutionalized in the political system at a societal level. Political systems may generate heightened racial or ethnic sentiments, but they can also channel negotiations and cross-cutting alliances, allowing scope for individual and collective action. Any meaningful notion of racial democracy must encompass black self-liberation

Throughout the Americas, the abolition of slavery was followed by post-emancipation societies in which a racist simplism gained currency—one that has been termed "cultural marronage," meaning a flight from all that was black, a denial of the African past—and blacks were pathologized as a obstacle to development. Over subsequent history, blaming the victim has perhaps been the longest-lasting and most damning outcome of the denial of the African past. It is true that, for African Americans, Afro-Latin Americans, and those under analysis here, Afro-Cubans, the dominant experience has been one of oppression, exclusion, and inferiorization. However, during certain periods they have also demonstrated great achievement in challenging their oppression. It is telling how much of that history is silenced and periodically needs to be rediscovered.

The very definitions of race and ethnicity can fluctuate markedly from place to place and over time. Nowhere has this been more graphically evidenced than throughout the Americas, and again Cuba is no exception. Ethnic and racial identities take on different meanings in different contexts, and with different historical markers, depending on who uses them and for what purposes. For the twentieth century alone, it is sufficient to contrast the hegemonic discourse of *café con leche* and mulatta symbolism of Venezuela and Brazil with the demonization of blackness in the Dominican Republic (where blackness was equated with Haitian descent) and the denial of blackness in Puerto Rico (where blackness is now equated with

Dominican descent), or the comparative harmony of racially pluralistic Belize with the intra-race/class divisions of black-majority Haiti and Jamaica, Indo- and Afro-Guyana and Trinidad, Amerindian- and Afro-Dominica, and Amerindian-, Afro-, and Indo-Suriname.[1]

It might be argued that during Cuba's modern history there have been competing variants of race politics and ethnic identity, with varying levels of inclusion and exclusion of race-class groupings. Dominant Hispanic segments of the population may have claimed their identity as the only legitimate one. New power elites from largely the same grouping may have sought legitimacy by promoting a synthetic national culture, tending to discourage racial or ethnic thinking that separated citizens from nation. Or, groups may have shared more equally in the life of the nation in proportion to their share of the population, whereby citizenship encompassed different yet compatible identities, together constituting the life of the nation.

In Cuba's case it might be tempting to attach a lineal time frame to the three variants outlined: the first during the Spanish colonial period, 1492–1898, the second during the twentieth-century pre-revolutionary republican period, and the third during the post-1959 revolutionary period. However, there is a powerful argument for seeing elements of all three throughout and for adopting a more cyclical time frame as to when one or other becomes uppermost. The period 1868–98, which represented thirty years of armed struggle for political independence from Spain and abolition of slavery, and the 1914–45 period of popular struggle to the point of the failed 1933 revolution, populism, and united front, have much in common with the 1959–89 revolutionary period: in all three, the races forged in struggle what might be seen as a "social pact" to usher in a more racially egalitarian and pluralistic third strand.

The years 1898–1914, with two U.S. military occupations and the demobilization of the Liberation Army, along with massive foreign investment and Euro-American immigration, saw the race barriers resurrected to the point of the 1912 Race War and a concomitant strengthening of Hispanicism, as well as North Americanism. A similar, if less racially divided, process can be seen in the years of the late 1940s Cold War, General Fulgencio Batista's 1952 coup, and the ensuing repression. While we do not wish to suggest a modern-day parallel in post-1989 Cuba, there are nonetheless signs of a racial rollback, disturbing enough to have produced an incipient clamor by black Cubans for national debate about increasingly exclusionary rather than inclusionary notions of *cubanidad* along race lines, privileging Hispano- over Afro-Cuban, white over black. Similarly exclusionary patterns are also seen to be operating in tandem with race along class and gender lines, restrengthening middle over working class, and male over female. This book should be read in that context.

Probably it can be safely said that most contemporary scholars of Cuba, as well as most Cubans, of whatever color, know relatively little about the long tradition of black thinking and writing in Cuba.[2] Paradoxically, this appears to have been exacerbated since the revolution. The argument can be made that nineteenth-century *cabildos* and subsequent mutual aid societies (P. Howard 1992; Montejo Arrechea 1933), as well as twentieth-century pre-revolutionary black and mulatto societies, with their emphasis on education and with their own libraries, provided a generational continuity for black history. When they disintegrated under the revolution's 1960s nationalization and revolutionary integration (since they were private, color-segregated institutions), this caused a rupture. As a result, accepted reference for Cuban writing on race undoubtedly privileges white over black authors, with ethnographer Fernando Ortiz taken as *the* point of reference.[3]

The rupture coincided with a revolutionary ideology that strengthened identification of race with class, black struggle with working-class struggle, and working class with nation. The year 1986, which marked the centenary of the final abolition of slavery, occasioned a spate of historical work, written primarily by white historians (Torres Cuevas and Reyes 1986; Barcía 1987; Iznaga 1988; Duharte Jiménez 1986, 1988). Before then, with some very notable exceptions (Moreno Fraginals 1978 [1964], 1983), relatively little of the historiography produced during the revolutionary period had focused on either slavery or abolition. This was clearly a product, intentional or otherwise, of privileging class and nation over race, and gender is only now beginning to make its mark (Castañeda 1995; Stubbs 1995). Key older, often self-taught, black historians whose life work was writing African, Caribbean, and Cuban history, with an emphasis on the black diasporic colonial experience, are now dead (Franco 1959, 1971, 1975a, 1975b, 1977, 1980a, 1980b; Deschamps-Chapeaux 1971, 1974, 1975). Black historians of a new generation have not yet emerged from the mainstream to take their place.

Today's black intellectuals are more often found in the media, literature, and the arts. Older members of these groups, along with some of their contemporaries and forebears, black and white, had in their own work of the 1960s and 1970s chosen to highlight Africa, slavery, and its legacy in both cultural and political terms, emphasizing transculturation as opposed to acculturation (Ortiz 1995 [1940]) and resistance as opposed to accommodation.[4]

The celebration of Cuba's African heritage was legitimized by Cuba's involvement in Africa, especially its thirteen-year military presence in the Angolan conflict starting in 1975. During that period there were signs of a renewed literary look at race in the colonial and postcolonial periods (González 1983a; Bueno 1985; Feijóo 1986), followed by two overview studies of the black in Cuban history, the first of their kind since the revolution of 1959 (Serviat 1986; Fernández Robaina 1990). Since then, some excellent work on race in Cuba has been published by Cuban, Cuban American, and foreign scholars. It is to these, in conjunction with studies undertaken on Brazil and the United States, that we now turn.

Brazil, the United States, and Cuba

In *No Longer Invisible* (see Perez Sarduy and Stubbs 1995), Rosângela Maria Vieira, writing on Brazil, and Gail McGarrity and Osvaldo Cárdenas, writing on Cuba, sought to unravel the pervasive myth of racial democracy. Vieira was impassioned and angry over the stereotyping and denigration of Afro-Brazilians beneath the much-touted racial accord in Brazilian national thinking. Likewise, McGarrity and Cárdenas documented how race as an issue of major historical and contemporary significance had been suppressed and denied in Cuba. Each highlighted how this had come to a head in the 1990s.

Just as 1986 was the centenary year of the abolition of slavery for Cuba, so 1988 was that year for Brazil. Various commemorative events were staged to celebrate emancipation that were shunned by Afro-Brazilian groups repudiating the "farce of abolition." Their actions were described as unprecedented efforts to draw national and international attention to the extensive racial inequality and discrimination that Brazilian blacks—by far the largest concentration of people of African descent in any country in the Western Hemisphere—continue to confront.

The racial conflict and mobilization this occasioned, long almost absent from the Brazilian scene, reopened the debate on Brazilian race dynamics.

Howard Winant, in particular, reexamined Freyre's post-World War II theory of *mestizagem* and the mulatta cult, the 1950s UNESCO studies conflating race and class, Degler's 1960s notions of the "mulatto escape hatch," Do Valle Silva's 1970s race stratification, and the more recent linking of race stratification and ideology by Dzidzienyo and Hasenblag.[5] The 1980s *abertura* (opening), or democratization of Brazil, he argued, had led to a re-emergence of civil society, politicization of racial identities, blacks mobilizing as blacks, and the racial politics of identity as conflictual terrain.

In 1993 Thomas Skidmore[6] took the argument a stage further, to question the continuing validity of the contrast between multiracial Brazil and the bipolar United States. Theories generated on each were located in the historical context of the 1950s, when Brazil was in all respects a less racist society than the United States. Brazil lacked not only the formal segregation but also the negrophobia that had permeated U.S. white society; the Brazilian white elite had elevated the psychosocial phenomenon of the cult of the mulatta to the status of national symbol. Yet data generated since the 1950s graphically demonstrated that Brazil's "racial democracy" did not exist. Conversely, the United States, despite the continuing racism, was no longer the land of lynchings, segregrated facilities, and overt discrimination; there had been the Civil Rights movement, affirmative action, and a rapid growth of the racially mixed Hispanic population; and there were significant (though often neglected and/or dismissed) color and class differentials within the U.S. black community.

Between Brazil and the United States, it was concluded, there were signs of convergence and the assumptions underlying comparative study—the most important of which are multiracial Brazil (whose very essence is an ambiguous, mixed-race, middle category) and the bipolar United States (marked by the "hypodescent" or "one drop of black blood" rule)—had to change. Outlined as requiring further research and debate were the following: analyzing how quantitative evidence is perceived and interpreted and how the two societies' mechanisms evolved for reproducing racial inequality; declaring a moratorium on ahistorical generalizations about race relations in either society; and understanding the causal factors determining the creation and maintenance of systems of race relations and how ideologies behind them interact with the elite's self-image and nationalistic projection.

When considering Cuba, the following questions might be framed: Are there race parallels, both before and after 1959, when Cuba underwent a socialist, not a capitalist, transformation? Did the post-1959 revolutionary process make a difference and, if so, to what extent is that difference eroding today? Historically, where should Cuba lie in the bipolar/multiracial debate? How have more recent studies approached this question for different historical periods?

The 1960s Cuban historiographical vision of slavery and abolition held that, true to the laws of history as understood by Marxism, slavery was rendered obsolete by the advance of technology and its need for wage labor. The most sophisticated rendering of this was to be found in Manuel Moreno Fraginals' seminal 1964 work *El ingenio* (The Sugarmill) and extended in subsequent studies (Moreno Fraginals 1983, 1984, 1987). Fraginals stressed the massive deculturation that accompanied the sugar plantation economy: "African cultural contributions to Latin America and the Caribbean are the result of a cruel class struggle and of a complex transculturation-deculturation process. In such circumstances, the dominant class applies to a maximum its mechanisms of deculturation as hegemonic tools and the dominated class takes refuge in its culture as a means of identity and survival" (Moreno Fraginals 1984).

Jamaican historian Franklin Knight's work on nineteenth-century slave society in Cuba (Knight 1970) and U.S. historian Rebecca Scott's work on slave emancipation in Cuba (Scott 1985) fueled a major revision of Moreno Fraginals. Knight's work centered on a systadial analysis of the very expansion of slavery in the technologically advanced sugar plantations of Cuba. For Scott the focus was on agency rather than structure, that is, the multiple ways in which people's resistance undermined the slave system. A key question posed was why, if technological advance was the cause, the chain of slavery broke precisely in that part of the island where technology and concentrations of slave labor were least in evidence.

Similar questions were raised in the work of U.S. historian Laird Bergad (1989, 1990), on the late-nineteenth-century rise and fall of sugar plantation slavery in Matanzas province and in his collaborative work on Cuban slave markets and slave prices undertaken with Cuban historians Carmen Barcía and Fe Iglesias (1995). Moreover, there were new studies on nineteenth and twentieth-century Cuba by Scott, Knight, and U.S.-based historians Aline Helg (Swiss), Ada Ferrer and Alejandro de La Fuente (Cuban), and Philip Howard and Karen Morrison (African American), as well as by Cuban Raquel Mendieta Costa. The race-class antagonisms and alliances in the intertwined processes of slavery, abolition, and post-emancipation society, on the one hand, and political independence and nation building, on the other, raised questions regarding race constructs and race thinking in Cuba that are pertinent to those outlined for Brazil and the United States.

In this respect, Scott set the stage in the 1990s by conducting comparative historical research on the transition from chattel bondage to legally free labor in the post-emancipation societies of Cuba, Louisiana, and Brazil (Scott 1994, 1996b). The context of emancipation was different in all three: 1860s war and occupation in Louisiana; 1860s and 1870s gradual abolition as a defensive colonial strategy against slave and anticolonial rebels in Cuba; and free workers playing a major role in a declining sugar industry in the Brazilian northeast. Each society witnessed a dramatic post-emancipation history of struggle, but in very different forms of collective action fueled by the desire for racial, economic, and social justice: trade union organizing and political conflict in Reconstruction Louisiana, massive anticolonial insurgency in Cuba, and a large messianic movement in Brazil. These are the contexts in which Scott explores why there were such different responses to patterns of work in post-emancipation sugar: cross-class, interracial movement in Cuba; bitter, racially divided strikes in Louisiana; and a messianic movement but no strikes in Brazil.

Her study of 1895–1912 central Cuba (Scott 1997) began by considering contrasting approaches to the 1912 massacre in eastern Cuba: those of Cathy Duke (1983), who attributed the hardening of racial attitudes to U.S. intervention; Louis A. Pérez (1986), who saw 1912 as essentially a peasant protest for reform and racial equality, which, since it comprised mainly dispossessed Afro-Cubans, was seen, manipulated, and brutally repressed as a race war; and Aline Helg (1995), who emphasized the profound hostility of elite white Cuban nationalists to Afro-Cuban equality.[7] Scott highlighted the work of Ada Ferrer (1991, 1995a, 1995b) on an earlier historical period in what might be seen as a yet another approach, emphasizing Afro-Cuban involvement and leadership in the 1868–98 national liberation struggle with an egalitarian vision of Cuba Libre. Ferrer argued that the transformations in Cuban nationalism, with the rise of slave insurgents and the move from white to multiracial leadership, were not smooth but confrontational, a war between the boundaries of Cuban nationality, in which questions of color and legal status were central.

This formed a prelude to Scott's 1997 study of post-emancipation collective action in the prosperous sugar regions around Cienfuegos, Santa Clara, and Cruces, to suggest ways in which fragile interracial alliances could be either strengthened or weakened. Scott pointed to three characteristics that averted a consolidation of white supremacy similar to that in the U.S. South: planters could not rely solely on black labor; the Hispano-Cuban elite might have displayed tendencies to racism and exclusionism, but there was no political party ready to risk espousing such values as a political platform; a significant group of Afro-Cuban veterans of the war for independence emerged as labor leaders, along with their Hispano-Cuban labor counterparts. Rural Cuba was a long way from the ideals of the independence struggle, but there was a racial heterogeneity to many of the gatherings observed by the occupation forces and the rallying of rural Cubans often operated inclusively rather than exclusively; universal manhood suffrage meant elites had to rely on certain elements of reciprocity and concession, and post-emancipation struggles over working conditions and political rights were also part of a larger struggle over values "sustaining the possibility of cross-racial alliance alongside the potential for racial and ethnic fractioning" (Scott 1997:191).

The work of Helg and De la Fuente helps further contextualize our understanding of specific periods of the race-class dynamic in twentieth-century Cuba. Helg set out to explain the massacre of Afro-Cubans in 1912, led in part by white veterans of the Liberation Army in the province that had earlier been the birthplace of the Cuban nationalist movement. How could this have happened? Focusing on "the historical importance of Afro-Cubans as participants in the building of an independent Cuba and as agents of political and social change during the critical process of transition from a Spanish colony in the 1890s to a nation-state in the 1910s" (Helg 1995:2), she demonstrated the dynamics of race ideology and action among both dominant and subordinate groups, in what she describes as a unique experience deriving from six Cuban particularities. One of them, she argued, was a two-tiered racial system similar to that of the United States, with the significant difference that the line dividing whites from nonwhites was based on visible African ancestry, not on the "one drop of black blood" rule.[8]

Her conclusions for early-twentieth-century Cuba were threefold: race was a fundamental construct articulating the Cuban hierarchy; members of the *raza* or *clase de color* (colored race or class) had a shared experience of white racism that called for a specific agenda, based on their self-perceptions as heroes, not victims; and Afro-Cuban consciousness and autonomous challenge incited the white elite to make more explicit the ideology of white supremacy, diffusing the idea that Cuban slaves had been freed by their masters and that blacks needed to be grateful to whites for their freedom. The formation of a black collective consciousness was undermined by denying the existence of race and of a past discrimination and by resurrecting fears of the Haitian Revolution, African religions and culture, and Afro-Cuban sexuality.

Some but not all of these issues had been drawn out in the two overview studies of black history published in Cuba by Pedro Serviat (1986) and Tomás Fernández Robaina (1990). For Serviat, black separatist politics of any shape or form were anathema. Fernández Robaina differed from Serviat on several counts, which included according greater legitimacy to the separatist stand taken by the Independent Colored Party, but he did not go so far as Helg, who suggested the existence of a coherent ideology of white supremacy and made a comparison with the U.S. two-tiered system.

Mendieta Costa (1989), P. Howard (1992), and Morrison (1997) refocused attention on competing strands of elite and non-elite Afro-Cuban thinking, discourse, and action. For the interwar period of 1878–95, Mendieta Costa highlighted the opposed political thinking and writing of Afro-Cubans Martín Morúa Delgado and Juan Gualberto Gómez, in certain respects uncannily reminiscent of the later scission between Booker T. Washington and W. E. B. DuBois in the United States. Howard's study of nineteenth-century Afro-Cuban *cabildos* situated their growth and development in yet another Afro-Cuban political tradition. Their sequel Afro-Cuban societies and clubs of the twentieth century have yet to be studied in such detail, but Morrison's research on the period 1912–40 suggests the transition of a middle-class Afro-Cuban intellectual discourse from a defensive rebound in the aftermath of 1912 to more assertive definitions of the terms of their inclusion in a national consciousness that was "biracial" and "bicultural." In the context of Euro-Cuban visions remaining profoundly Eurocentric, the period was also witness to 1920s Euro-Cuban *negrismo* (negritude).[9]

According to Morrison, the early-twentieth-century discourse of racial and cultural politics by Afro-Cuban intellectuals revolved around several major areas, and all of these have resonance today: challenging the myth of Cuba's racial democracy, demonstrating through personal example that even their best and brightest were subject to unfair discrimination; constructing and promoting a positive Afro-Cuban history (to be achieved by revealing their proven commitment to the nation in the wars for independence and removing the image of barbarity associated with their African heritage); promotiñg Afro-Cuban self-development (cultural and economic) and unity (social organizations); calling upon Euro-Cubans to seriously address racism and change their attitudes and behaviors for the good of the nation (by strengthening and enforcing antidiscrimination legislation); developing positive images of, and ties with, the African diaspora, especially blacks in the United States; revealing a unique Afro-Cuban aesthetic—especially poetry, folklore, and dance; and questioning traditional Cuban social relations by suggesting changes in class and gender relations.

For Afro-Cuban intellectuals of the time, Morrison argued, these themes signified the terrain through which they could promote their "cultural capital" of blackness and contest Euro-Cuban ideas of race and the nation. Middle class and male almost by definition, they were Afro-Cuban men struggling for cultural and political space in the nation. How Afro-Cuban women constructed their racial and gender identity in the context of competing race patriarchies, a largely white, middle-class feminist movement, and a predominantly black women's involvement in trade unionism is a topic yet to be explored.

De la Fuente's work on race and labor, and on race demographics, politics, and discourse, carried the debate right through twentieth-century pre-and post-revolutionary Cuba.[10] Outlining "two dangers, one solution" for the period 1900–1930 (De la Fuente 1995), he documented the elite's dilemma on publication of the 1899 census: one-third of the population was colored at the same time that there had been an internal population displacement and decline, occasioning the lack of a plentiful and acquiescent labor force. The solution they espoused to solve their "dual dilemma" was to stimulate white immigration, and this only reluctantly gave way to recruiting black Caribbean migrants with the acute demand for seasonal labor in the post-1914 sugar boom.[11] As a result, and not least because of divisionist tactics on the part of the national government, nationality and race divisions permeated society and the labor movement; however, De la Fuente concluded, cross-national differences were often stronger than cross-racial differences, and cross-racial solidarity was often in evidence. This, he argued, accounted for the emergence of class as the most important point of reference in Cuban politics, class consciousness being stronger than race identity among Cuban blacks. In the process, elites had failed to avert "the two dangers": neither was Cuba white, nor had they an acquiescent labor force.

De la Fuente contextualized these developments in terms of race differentials in several key social indicators from 1899 to 1930, which, he concluded, diminished in some (literacy, employment), though in others diminished only for whites and mulattos, not blacks (fertility, mortality). He went on to describe the 1930s as transitional, and the 1940s and 1950s as a period of increasing race differentials, coinciding more or less with growing class differentials, due to the concentration of mulattos and blacks in the lower sectors of society. Between 1959 and 1981, the pattern was reversed, with decreasing race and class differentials (major exceptions were the high correlations between blacks and poor housing and high crime rates). Nonetheless, put simply, in socioeconomic terms, 1899–1930 might be seen as more integrationist and 1930–59 as less, while 1959–81 was the most integrationist of all.

In his work on national discourse (De la Fuente 1997), he used a similar periodization (1899–1930, 1930–59, 1959–89), but told a much more complex story of how national unity was achieved at the expense of racial identities. He characterized the period from 1900 through the 1920s as having a dominant discourse of "racial fraternity, white style," which, to avert division, attempted to silence and deracialize Cubans, against which black Cubans had to fight. The 1930s to 1950s produced an alternative nationalist discourse, spanning Afro-Cubanism, *mestizaje,* and *cubanidad,* and a fused agenda of race and class was articulated by strong worker unions in industry and agriculture. In both periods, however, the black middle class articulated a race agenda, drawing attention to class differentials within race. In the dominant discourse after 1959, race was seen as an economic-class issue that would be resolved through redistributive measures, and the earlier phenomenon of silence and deracialization was reproduced.

Bringing together the two approaches of demographics and discourse (De la Fuente 1998b) led him to also conclude that, during the period 1959–81, key indicators were leveled for whites, blacks, and mulattos, comparing most favorably with countries such as Brazil and the United States, and with resulting minimized racial tension. The same could not be said of the post-1980s Special Period. Though the figures were not available, survey, social science, and more anecdotal studies all pointed to prejudice and discrimination again on the rise.

Policy, Pride, and Prejudice

It should by now be transparent that there have been multiple strands to pre-and post-revolutionary Afro-Cuban political thinking and action. Of particular interest are the implications of the present conjuncture vis-à-vis the pre-revolutionary period and the connections between two key periods of transition, at the turn of both the twentieth and twenty-first centuries.

Knight and Scott have themselves made incursions into linking past and present. Exploring ethnicity and social structure in contemporary Cuba, Knight stated his case:

> Formal institutional barriers to equality . . . were removed by law. . . . But matters of public policy and private action have always been highly contested. . . . Within the private domain, the state is powerless to change the deeply held attitudes of some of its citizens, and these attitudes are especially important for matters of race and ethnicity. The degree to which citizens uphold the law is based on perceptions of self-interest. When conformity brings greater reward than nonconformity, then citizens conform. At the same time, intellectual traditions may not reflect daily conduct at the levels of public and private spheres. . . . Moreover, with the weakening of the administrative and economic structure of the revolution the Cuban government appears increasingly less able to insist on general conformity among the population as it once did. All this has had an incalculable impact on the general attitudes to race and ethnicity, presenting a strange paradox: at the moment when the mutually reinforcing cleavages of race, ethnicity and color appear to be loosening in Cuba, the economic situation threatens to restore the status quo of prerevolutionary days. (Knight 1996)

Like Knight, Scott cautioned against rigidities of race and ethnicity and questioned the concept of race relations as "an ambiguous term which tends to imply a fixity to racial categories themselves and a uniformity of interactions across very different spheres of activity," calling for analysis of the

ways in which issues of race arise—or are subordinated—in specific historical contexts and emphasizing:

> the historical depth of an unusual pattern of simultaneous incorpora-
> tion and exclusion of Cubans of color in the nationalist project. Well
> before 1959, Cuba had established a powerful tradition of cross-ra-
> cial mobilization in pursuit of social goals. Vigorous multiracial alli-
> ances of rural workers, innovative ideologies of anti-racism, and per-
> sistent patterns of racism and discrimination existed side by side . . .
> continuing discrimination did not successfully halt initiatives by Cu-
> bans of color, and black and mulatto Cubans took ever greater roles
> of leadership. Repeatedly, however, elite Cubans attempted to deny
> the complexity of the nation's formative social movements, preferring
> a simpler notion of patriotism and progress. Retrospectively, they
> tended to attribute leadership in key historical developments only to
> whites. . . . (Scott 1995)

This allowed whites to fume against blacks' "ingratitude," which in turn
could reinforce racist imagery of black barbarism and become an element in
brutal repression. Scott concluded by extrapolating to the present and commented on the futility of trying to silence debate through calls for gratitude
and loyalty to the revolutionary project, for they might fall on racially stony
ground.

A linear world turns cyclical and leaves us with a devastating question. Is
a pattern of subordinate human relations emerging that displays similarities
to that of pre-revolutionary Cuba? If so, what is the response of black and
white Cubans?

A 1997 article, provocatively titled "Are Blacks 'Getting out of Control'?
Racial Attitudes, Revolution, and Political Transition in Cuba" (De la Fuente
and Glasco 1997), picked up on the words used by a white Havana resident
in reference to the summer 1994 riot, in which blacks and mulattos were
disproportionately involved. The article analyzed the backdrop in which a
vision tending to racialize the Cuban conflict found fertile ground, especially the history of a black presence in violent antigovernment demonstrations that has traditionally coincided with periods of deep social and political crisis. It also articulated the concern and surprise displayed by Cuban
authorities as understandable: blacks had been considered by many as the

main beneficiaries of the Cuban post-revolutionary social order, with the authorities the "givers" of welfare, in return for which blacks should demonstrate unconditional loyalty and support. In this, the existence of a largely white exile community added a counter racial element to Cuba's current crisis.

The question the article asked was whether blacks could be expected as a group to defend a social order and government from which they had benefited or whether they would participate in cross-racial efforts to oppose the government, as events in 1994 might suggest. The dilemma posed was not only that of weighing the social benefits brought by the revolution against the opportunities of a capitalist restoration, for "in popular imagery and practical terms" the latter would not come alone: it implied some form of restored U.S. and Cuban exile influence.

An exploratory poll of 200 urban respondents (93 in Havana, 97 in Santiago de Cuba, and 10 in Santa Clara; 93 males and 107 females; 72 percent blacks and mulattos) explored opinions on pre-revolutionary racial inequality, the impact of the revolution on race relations, failures of the government to remedy race issues, the impact of the current crisis, and how future political change might affect the black population.

What emerged was a generational rather than a racial divide. Younger Cubans, black and white, were least satisfied in their personal lives. The current crisis had eroded achievements of the revolution to such a degree that young blacks no longer perceived the restoration of capitalism as a major reverse:

> The thin line that separates subjective prejudice from objective discrimination has become more fragile under the crisis and . . . in some highly regarded occupational sectors has been openly broken. . . . These young, more educated, and upwardly mobile blacks were born and raised in racism-free Cuba: the prerevolutionary, discriminatory social order has not affected their lives or shaped their memories the way it has for older respondents. The latter's fears have been transformed by the success of the integrationist program promoted by the revolution into the former's confidence. Cuban authorities' surprise is largely a function of their incapacity to regard these young black citizens not only as beneficiaries of revolution but also as active protagonists of their own well-being and future. (De la Fuente and Glasco 1997:70)

As the attitudinal survey was being conducted, so also was a study on the cultural politics of interracial encounters. U.S. anthropologist Nadine Fernández lived in Central Havana and carried out participant-observation research on race, romance, and revolution. Fernández (1997) explored generational differences of social relations, especially interracial couples, concluding that while the revolution "naturalized" practices of racial integration, it did little to change people's understanding of race. Older generations experienced social mobility and articulated an ideology of equality; youth found themselves in a "taken-for-granted" racial integration but without the same chances for social mobility, not least due to the stagnating and then catastrophically declining economy, but also due to coexisting ideologies of race inequality. Fernández drew on previous generational studies and research on race-endogamous marriage patterns[12] to contextualize her own testimonies of the negative pressures young interracial couples met with from both their peers and their families—paradoxically greater, it would appear, than those experienced by interracial couples in the 1960s and 1970s.

Fernández was part of a growing research interest in Cuba on the race issue. In 1996, *Temas,* a recently established Cuban journal, ran several articles that shifted the terrain from the more social and political to the familial and personal. Anthropologists Juan Antonio Alvarado Ramos and María Magdalena Pérez Alvarez took as their basic premise the eradication of institutionalized racism during the revolutionary period and focused attention on the mechanisms whereby racial prejudice and racist conduct have nonetheless been transmitted in society.

Alvarado singled out the individual, the family, and the social group as key agents of transmission in race relations and racial attitudes, white families in particular stereotyping and denigrating blacks in society. He argued that structural changes in society and living in close proximity have helped break down barriers and prejudice but that interracial couples can occasion serious conflict, often generational, within families and circles of friends. He concluded by highlighting four positives: a general acceptance of the principle that racial prejudice is negative, an understanding of the historical and sociocultural reasons for disadvantaged groups in society, a recognition of biological and cultural race mixing as intrinsic to the Cuban people, and a progressive increase in interracial relations. He also ended, however, with three negatives: the constant reproduction of racial prejudice, especially through the family; the presence of race stereotyping and prejudice in all classes, groups, and generations; and the prevalence of "white cultural values" throughout society.

In her study of racial prejudice in a Havana neighborhood, Pérez emphasized the prevalence of friendship networks, especially couple relationships, within like racial groupings, and related this race endogamy to imagery and socialization patterns linked to the family in particular. She concluded that widespread transculturation had not erased the slave image associated with black and black/white identifications and that pejorative connotations of blackness were common among all racial groupings.

A third article by María del Carmen Cano Secade came closer to a politico-historic and economic analysis and contextualized worsening race relations within the current process of social and political adjustment. She highlighted the relatively brief historical period of the revolution to turn around a phenomenon of historical complexity and stressed the crisis period of the 1990s as a factor for accentuating social, including racial, inequality and racial prejudice. She too accepted widespread transculturation and political consensus on racial equality, but stated:

An emphatic trend in the present crisis is for a greater degree of politicization of the topic, from tendentious interpretations prone to manipulation and overexaggeration of the problem to reactions rejecting the validity of debate on the issue, reducing it to persisting racial prejudice among isolated groups of the population. (Cano Secade 1996:60)

For the revolutionary period as a whole, she emphasized the countervailing weight of social structure to change in terms of race and gender, a process of social integration that failed to significantly alter value systems subordinating black culture, and an overhomogenizing approach to social behavior and identity that had negative repercussions on the black population. This, she argued, had led to sociocultural deformation of patterns of race socialization where blacks are concerned, contributing to their own low social and self-esteem. She concluded by calling for race-affirmative action in the form of sociocultural and political black community projects, backed by the media, that impart a sense of the wealth of black history and culture in Cuba.

A fourth article by Tomás Fernández Robaina, on Afro-Cuban bibliography, refocused the debate on the limitations of the revolution and revolutionary policy. Fernández reached the following conclusions: (1) what has been published since the revolution does not nearly reflect the scope of study conducted the length and breadth of the island; (2) policy on Afro-Cuban studies has been shallow, dogmatic, and superficial; (3) much more attention has been paid to the pre-twentieth-century period than to the twentieth century itself; (4) until the late 1980s, there were no race histories, despite the fact that race was such an important factor in Cuba's history; (5) similarly, few books on Afro-Cuban religion were published before the 1990s; (6) books on race written by Cubans abroad and foreigners outnumber books by Cubans on the island; and (7) the growing interest has given rise to the publication of superficial, stereotypical texts cashing in on the market. Fernández recommended four immediate steps that might be taken: introduce courses beginning in primary school on the African heritage in Cuba, periodically update the Afro-Cuban bibliography, create a special Afro-Cuban collection in the National Library, and organize regular seminars on Afro-Cuban history.

Interestingly, areas such as these are where links with persons and groups outside Cuba can be most valuable. Long-standing links exist between African Americans and Afro-Cubans (Brock and Castañeda 1998) on which to build. The African American community in the United States, in the form of the Congressional Black Caucus, for example, might identify with Afro-Cubans along race rather than political lines, and racial, economic, humanitarian, cultural, and religious bridge building may well prove crucial in this regard. Help could certainly be expected from throughout the Americas and beyond for black studies programs, Africa-centered research and exchange programs, and African diaspora, Afro-Latin American, and Caribbean studies.[13]

The outcome of such efforts might also have valuable policy spinoffs. With the notable exception of the Cuban American National Foundation, which maintains a core Miami base and has proved extremely effective in mounting a powerful lobby not only in Washington but also in Moscow, Madrid, and Brussels, proportionately few Cubans abroad argue for policies of total hostility to Cuba. Similarly, concerns raised by independent observers over such a policy range from fears of an explosion of civil war proportions in Cuba, as people are driven down relentlessly, to fears of another mass exodus, potentially a million strong, comprising Cubans seeking to join family members abroad—the vast majority of whom are concentrated in Florida's Miami and Dade County area.

These same Cubans are in all probability already being provided with crucial support by family abroad. A recent United Nations report contained significant figures: in 1996, Cuban American exiles, individually and through private operations, sent more than US$1,100 million in remittances to the island, US$800 million of which were to family, benefiting almost half the island population, and this did not include the value of food, medication, and other items in kind. The total value of remittances was calculated to exceed Cuban government earnings from either of its major income-generating sectors—tourism (US$1,400 million) and sugar (US $1,000 million)—as well as from all other exports (an overall US$1,000 million). The issue of remittances is one that divides Cubans both on and off the island. Senders are for the most part younger, more recent migrants with considerable island family ties, who are harshly criticized by older, wealthier, first-generation migrant families with fewer ties.[14] Given the race composition of the exile and island populations, senders and recipients are far more likely to be Euro-Cuban. This has to be seen as one of the reasons why Afro-Cubans on the island and abroad (many of whom have their own African American and Caribbean roots) might be adopting a race optic in looking to alternative scenarios that cut across class or national boundaries and ideologies.[15]

A race analysis also helps explain the Caribbean's proactive policy of engagement with Cuba, irrespective of political differences. Caribbean states have embraced Cuba in an attempt to widen and deepen regional integration, within the more recently created Association of Caribbean States (ACS) and the older Caribbean Common Market (CARICOM). Bilaterally and in unison, they have both opposed U.S. policy and resisted the conditionality that has been the increasing stamp of European trade and aid. During 1997, official visits to Cuba were made by Prime Ministers P.J. Patterson (Jamaica), James Mitchell (St. Vincent and the Grenadines), and Keith Mitchell (Grenada). In December three Caribbean-related events took place in Havana: meetings of the CARICOM/Cuba Commission and the UK-based Caribbean Council for Europe, and bilateral Barbados/Cuba talks headed by Foreign Ministers Billie Miller (Barbados) and Roberto Robaina (Cuba). Developments then and during 1998 were such that the Caribbean might be seen as setting an example of constructive engagement that the United States and Europe would do well to follow.

Even one of the regime's more ardent critics on the political and race fronts, Cuban-born Carlos Moore, currently a resident of Trinidad, has moved to advocating an open-door policy to Cuba as the only sane way forward (Moore 1996). Distinguishing between "Model A" and "Model B" societies in what was once the Communist bloc, Moore characterizes Model A societies as relatively homogeneous racially, ethnically, and culturally and ruled by communist institutions, whereas Model B societies were heterogeneous with highly personalized rule. Cuba, he argues, is a Model B society and cannot engage in profound change "without unleashing strong currents of repressed nationalism, ethnicity, racial and cultural demands" (Moore 1996:15).

Moore sees as the monumental issue for the revolution that of accommodating the new ethnodemographic reality created by the revolution: that is, a majority Afro-Cuban share of the population. His argument is that the racial integration of the political structure is not only likely but also crucial to the survival of the Castro regime, and that any political opening might well expose Cuba to the "racially insensitive and undemocratic sectors of the White exile community."(Moore 1996:21) He concludes, "Conscious Afro-Cubans must be opposed to a U.S. policy of hostility, encirclement and harassment of the beleaguered Castro regime . . . and revengeful plans of the Hispanic-Cuban exiles . . . irrespective of their feelings for Fidel Castro and Communism . . . the black Cuban population is highly politicized; highly militarized; highly suspicious of the U.S.; highly opposed to the U.S.-based White exiles" (Moore 1996:23–4).

Counterpoint and Chaos

In the shifting sands of race and ethnicity where Cuba is concerned, there has been a significant Ortiz revival in recent years, both in Cuba and abroad, not least around his concept of transculturation. In 1995, an English-language edition of Ortiz's classic *Cuban Counterpoint: Tobacco and Sugar* was reprinted with a new introduction by Venezuelan anthropologist

Fernando Coronil.[16] Coronil begins by situating the book's initial publication in 1940, at a time when fascism had begun to engulf Western Europe, challenging the fundamentals of Western civilization. In Cuba, strongman Fulgencio Batista was in power. Coronil writes, "*Cuban Counterpoint* has circulated until recent years in a world divided into socialist and capitalist camps and modern and backward nations," all of which were competing "to achieve modernity." Ortiz's book, he states:

> did not quite fit into the terms of this polarized debate. It was unconventional in form and content, did not express explicitly the wisdom of the times or reiterate prevailing currents of thought, and it proposed neither unambiguous solutions nor a blueprint for the future. . . . Half a century later, this edition of *Cuban Counterpoint* addresses a world where cultural differences and political inequalities cannot be mapped out in terms of old polarities. The Second World has drastically contracted and transformed, while the First World is decentering and diversifying. Third World "development" programs of neoliberal design are accelerating the fractures within and among the nations of the "periphery." A number of intimately related processes, in which globalizing forms of capital accumulation and communication are met both with transnationalizing and reconfigured nationalist responses, have unsettled certainties associated with the belief in modernity. (Ortiz 1995:xii)

This is the sense in which *Cuban Counterpoint* has been received as a postmodern text. However, Coronil argues that Ortiz's analysis of what he describes as the complex articulation of stabilizing and disruptive forces throughout Cuban history questions our assumptions about modernity and contributes to our understanding of a world increasingly interrelated and fractured. Ortiz, he says, struggled against Eurocentrism, though within the political and cultural confines of his nation and of reformist nationalist thought. Like Fanon, he used:

> binary oppositions (black and white, West and non-West), in a way that recognizes the experiential value of these terms for people subjected to imperial domination, but that also refuses to imprison an emancipatory politics in them. His allegorical essay recognizes the play of desire in the construction of colonial oppositions, vividly revealing how the colonial encounter forged cognitive categories as well

as structures of sentiment. Ortiz treats binary oppositions not as fixities, but as hybrid and productive, reflecting their transcultural formation and their transitional value in the flow of Cuban history. (Ortiz 1995:xiv)

Coronil's introduction ends with a quote from Ortiz, celebrating the popular imagination and vitality that inspired the work, the "antiphonal prayer of the liturgies of both whites and blacks, the erotic controversy in dance measures of the rumba and . . . the versified counterpoint of the unlettered guajiros and the Afro-Cuban curros" (Ortiz 1995:xlvii).

These are words reminiscent of Antonio Benítez-Rojo, writing on Carnival, at the end of his introduction to *The Repeating Island* (Benítez-Rojo 1992). Inspired by a postmodern perspective of chaos theory, he wrote: "the teasing, the jealousy, the whistles and the faces, the razor that draws blood, death, life, reality in forward and reverse torrents of people who flood the streets, the night lit up like an endless dream, the figure of a centipede *that comes together and then breaks up* [our emphasis], that winds and stretches beneath the ritual's rhythm, always in the rhythm, the beat of the chaos of the islands. . ." (Benítez-Rojo 1992:60).

Interestingly, Benítez-Rojo (1997) himself reflected on what he described as "the binary and cyclically violent tendency" regarding sugar and race in Cuban national discourse. He singled out three moments of black representation in Cuban literary nationalism in terms of power and resistance: 1792–1812/1813–44, the incipient and mature sugar/plantation/slavery complex; 1880–98, after the devastation of the 1868–78 and 1879–80 wars; and the post-1959/post-1989 period of revolution and crisis. He concluded with the concern that, in the context of what is now a majority black and mulatto population, neither the Cuban government nor the Cuban people, nor any one pro- or antidialogue exile Cuban group, appears to be paying sufficient attention to designing a future for Cuba in which blacks can really be equal in political, economic, social, and cultural terms.

This is the precise context in which the present book poses the question, Can there be a just racial order fashioned out of the injustices, chaos, and eclecticism that have shaped Cuba? The contributors firmly believe so. Out of cultural profusion has been born a culture of survival, a significant component part of which is African. In Cuba, as elsewhere in the Americas, a distorted vision of peoples of African descent has been historically refashioned, negating their powers of individual and collective self-determination and expression. Such powers need to be nurtured, for where politics and economics push the races apart, denying, denigrating, or manipulating race difference, people will respond. The Afro-Cubans whose voices fill this book respond by asking for the space and support to find their own paths into the twenty-first century, celebrating the fluidity and "chaos" of their racial pluralism and a *cubanía* that derives from the African as much as any other diaspora.

PART I

The Lived Experience of Race

Cuban blacks have achieved much more freedom and many more rights with the Cuban Revolution. Nobody, no matter how racist, can deny that. My father is a lawyer and my mother a nurse; they achieved more than a lot of others, and they themselves wouldn't deny what blacks have achieved with the revolution. I only had to study and develop as an individual to attain what I have. It wasn't the same for my father. He had to work hard to pay for his study, to the point of making links with white masons, demonstrating his loyalty in return for their help. I have always seen things differently. I never saw things in terms of black or white, but as an individual problem, that if blacks or whites didn't study, they couldn't go to the university. If you were to ask me the economic situation of North American blacks I'd have to declare my ignorance. I know more about North American Jews than about North American blacks. When I look at them, I see individuals, like Ron Brown, the trade secretary; or I look at Colin Powell, the former chief of the general staff, whose attitudes I often see as pretty negative.

Víctor Aguilera Noriega, coffee trader

1

Under the Streetlamp

A Journalist's Story

Reynaldo Peñalver Moral

Reynaldo Peñalver Moral is one of those original, imaginative journalists who might well have been a top-rated syndicated columnist. Now retired from journalism, not only because of his age but also the lack of publishing possibilities and low incentives due to the crisis, Peñalver spent his last working years in the early 1990s writing for the weekly magazine *Bohemia.* An investigative journalist, he penned feature articles that had an avid readership. One in particular, published in the late 1970s, caused a sensation and made him a national name, when he discovered the hidden tomb of Cecilia Valdés in Havana's Colón Cemetery. Cecilia Valdés was the "mulata blanconaza" (mulatto woman who could pass for white), the protagonist in *Cecilia Valdés, or Angel's Hill,* which is acclaimed as *the* Cuban novel of the nineteenth century, and, for many, of all time. Author Cirilo Villaverde (1812–1894), a patriotic teacher and lawyer who died in political exile in the United States, recreated in the novel the ethos and pathos of Havana at the time, through a love story that crossed race, class, and family lines. Several had written about the historical grounding of the novel, but never before had Valdés's grave been discovered. An earlier famous article written by Peñalver was based on an interview he conducted with Malcolm X in Harlem, New York, in 1960. When I talked with him in 1995, he reflected on his life and that interview. (PPS)

My life has been a carbon copy of what might have been the life of any black in this country. I was born on 4 January 1927 and never thought I would reach this age. In my family, most died young, I imagine because of the poverty they grew up in. My mother, Isabel Moral, to whom I owe every-thing, was a dressmaker. My father was a construction worker. He always wanted to get on in life and went to the Higher School for the Trades for a career in the construction sector, but in the end the only job he could get was as a bricklayer.

I was born and grew up in a Havana tenement with my immediate fam-ily—an aunt and uncle, my mother, and me. When I was two, my father went to Oriente looking for work. I came to know him ten years later, when I'd finished primary school. For the whole of my childhood and adolescent years, it was my mother who looked after me. We all lived in one room. I never had a cot. I slept with my mother, or my uncle or my aunt, in the same bed, four of us in that tenement room.

It's always stayed with me, the unpleasant experience of growing up without a father. I'd see the other kids with their fathers, and mine was conspicuously absent. I was naturally close to my mother—she was all I had—and she was close to me, as I was her only child. My mother never married. Back then, many single mothers preferred their children not to have stepfathers. So she brought me up herself, always encouraging me to study and get on.

My pastimes as a kid were different from those of other kids. I never learned to play baseball, or any other game. I'd spend my time with paints, and colored pencils, and sketchbooks. I was a strange kid in that sense. I never had skates, I never rode a bike, nothing like that. I loved to read, and color, and paint. I was a fish out of water in the tenement, dreaming that one day I would be somebody. I knew that study was my only salvation. While I was growing up I saw how some kids weren't getting anywhere. Or, just as they were, their parents would send them out to work, which was almost always manual.

I finished primary school when I was twelve, just as my father came back from Oriente with another wife, from Baracoa, and my three younger half brothers. That's when I met the man I'd only seen in photos but who would write regularly expressing his concern for me. My mother's friends were constantly telling her she should send me out to work to help her in the home. She spent all her time doing things from home to bring in some money, like sewing or hairdressing. There are times I'd rather not remember how hard it was, but what's gone is gone, and, underneath, I came to under-stand life for blacks in this country, or any other country, because in reality our only crime is to have been born with a darker skin color in a world of whites.

Though my mother's friends told her to send me out to work, she always said no, that as long as she had the strength, she would help her son to become what he wanted to be. Just imagine! I wanted to be a journalist—in those days! And my father was absolutely against it. Back then, to go to high school, you had to have a suit and tie. My father was beside himself when my mother told him to help her buy me a suit for school. He refused outright, and said that if I really needed the suit, she should have me work as a bricklayer's mate on the construction site with him, where I would earn 1.50 pesos a day. My mother showed him her tongue and told him what she thought, but I said no, that I would go and work to earn the money I needed.

And that's what I did. I worked flat out all week. There I was, just out of primary school, never having picked up a shovel in my life, deep in cement, concrete, and bricks. I wound up with my hands destroyed but my morale high. My hands were bleeding so much I fell sick. I hated my father for that.

Finally, I did finish high school and then had to decide whether I would go on to senior high or journalism school. In those days, the School of Journalism was almost exclusively for whites, the children of government officials. It was tiny, in a house at the corner of Avenida de los Presidentes and Línea, in Vedado,[1] which had opened as a school for the privileged. Each year, only 20 students were selected for admission. There might be 12 who were chosen direct, and up to 100 or 200 others would have to compete for the other eight places.

I studied hard for that. I'd study on the street corner, because the lights in the tenement would be shut off at 10:00 P.M. and we only had a makeshift kerosene lamp. I didn't want to bother the others—my mother would be sleeping—so I'd go out with my books and sit under the streetlamp, much to the surprise of people who'd see me there reading every night. We lived in Los Sitios, a worker neighborhood which was predominantly black. I felt a solidarity from the neighbors who would see me and ask why I wasn't going to sleep. I'd answer that I was studying. Even the policeman, who was white, got to know me and would leave me alone. At certain hours of the night, the police back then didn't want young people hanging around on street corners, or sitting out on the street by the door to their homes. But he seemed to recognize the effort I was making, and I imagine that, even though he might have thought it strange, he must have thought it good for the *negrito* (little black kid) to be studying under the streetlamp into the early hours of the morning.

After the exam, you were told you had to wait for a telegram to be sent to your home address and, if you were successful, you then had to go and enroll. I never received that telegram, but some of the others who had also competed said that if I hadn't received it I must be among the eight chosen. Right away, I went to the school and there was my name on the list. I had made it into the Manuel Márquez Sterling School of Journalism, which was racist and classist. It was a whole odyssey. The secretary told me the telegram had been sent, but had no explanation for what had happened. My fallback was to go to the Higher School for the Trades. Many people had said to me that studying journalism wasn't for blacks. It wasn't that there were no black journalists but they were so few as for them to be practically invisible. Cuba has had, over its history, few, but very good, black journalists. My mother would be asked, supposing I did finish, where would I work? That was how I started out in journalism back in 1947, although I'd been prepared for anything. I didn't hold out much hope for one of those eight places, and I knew I wanted to study. Since the journalism classes were from 1:00 to 5:00 P.M., I also enrolled to study as a lathe operator in the trades school.

The exams for the journalism school were both written and oral. The candidate could be brilliant in the written exam but you also had to face four or five white professors and hold your own on a topic that was hotly debated. But I came through. And that's why, at the same time I became a journalist, I became a lathe operator. Then I had to look for work, because I had no contacts in the journalistic world. Black journalists were not well received in the mainstream press of the time. They'd take on a black journalist to do a social column on the black societies, not to do them a favor but to attract black readers to that small space in their publications. Many weren't on salary. Although they had the space, it would be the families who paid the journalist for the piece. I persisted in becoming a journalist against my father's will. I thought the situation of blacks had to change one day. To work as a journalist, you had to have the qualification and a track record; you had to be white or the son or relative of someone influential.

I lived in Central Havana, on Maloja Street, between Campanario and Manrique, and the School of Journalism was at the corner of Avenida de los Presidentes and Línea. That meant it cost me ten cents on the tram, when it was hard enough to earn ten cents. Every day, I'd walk the length of Reina to Carlos III, where the trams passed, and jump on the back of one to go up the hill by El Príncipe Prison. The conductors were mainly Spaniards and they'd get to know me and pretend they hadn't seen me, thinking, I imagine, that this well-dressed kid with his bag of books under his arm was taking a tremendous risk not buying a ticket. They'd tell me to get on at the back. In those four years of study, I made friends with many of those conductors!

Then in the evening, I'd prepare for my return. I'd already saved five cents, which would buy a pound of rice. I'd see the parents coming in their cars to pick up their children. Others would take the tram. I'd go in the opposite direction and wait for the right one to jump on the back without paying. There were times when I had to jump off because the police would take you in if they caught you doing that.

I finished as one of the top students. While I was studying, I was apprentice to Jorge Yanis Pujol, a great journalist who had a column called "Detrás del Suceso" (Behind the Scenes), in *Prensa libre*, which was a daily with a large circulation. He paid me five pesos a week to write the chronicles published under his name. The paper would never accept me on the payroll, but those five pesos a week were glory. We paid three pesos a month for the room we lived in, and I earned twenty. It was a fortune. We'd even had the landlord on our backs because we'd run up six months' rent owing; we hadn't been able to pay the miserable three pesos.

I was influenced by the writing of a black journalist called Pedro Portuondo Calá, who had a column on the black societies in the daily *El país*. I also followed what was happening with blacks in other countries, especially the United States. I read any North American magazine I could get my hands on, like *Ebony*, which was a magazine of the black middle class. It was one huge lie, because later I saw for myself how that was only a very small sector of the black community. And yet in a way it pushed me on to similar things, and I joined up with a group of young graduates to edit the magazine *Sociales* because there was a big movement of black societies due to the racial discrimination that existed here. There was an intellectual journal called *Nuevos rumbos* which dealt with the black problem in Cuba, but we wanted a more popular magazine, more like *Ebony*.

We also founded the Federation of Youth Societies. Since the blacks had their segregated societies—the Club Atenas (Athens), for "high" blacks and mulattos,[2] the Unión Fraternal (Fraternal Union), and others; the black societies were also very exclusive—a black newspaper vendor couldn't be a member and there were no youth programs. The forms of entertainment were very strictly coded. The "commonplace" black had to go to the Polar or Tropical Gardens where there was dancing in the open air on weekends. We wanted to found youth clubs or societies. People with spacious homes let us use them to set up our board and meet, and we held our own dances and other events.

While I was studying at Márquez Sterling I met Caridad and we got engaged. We didn't want to get married until I finished, and in fact we were together ten years before we did get married. Caridad was the sister of a fellow student at the Higher School for the Trades. We married after the triumph of the 1959 revolution. When I was studying and when I started work, I was a member of the Socialist Youth. I held several posts and even worked in the provincial office. I also collaborated with the 26 July movement.[3] As a crime reporter, I had access to the police stations, especially the 5th Station, where the notorious chief was Esteban Ventura Novo. I would find out what state the revolutionary prisoners were in and pass on the information to the movement. I worked with a group of lawyers who would present habeas corpus to get them out of the country. In recognition for my work, when the revolution triumphed I was named press chief of the Revolutionary Secret Police, and I began to earn a good salary as first detective.

In the months that followed, the Prensa Latina news agency was set up and I started work there for 300 pesos. What a difference—from the 5 I'd earned to 300! I had a different standing and that's when I said to Caridad, "Our time has come," and we were married in 1960. We'll have been married thirty-seven years, plus the ten we were engaged—forty-seven years together! It's been a good marriage. We're happy. I couldn't have wished for a better wife and mother. I have nobody else. This is my family. We have two children, Reynaldito, who is thirty-five, and Tatiana, thirty-four, who has given us a grandson we're crazy about.

In the early years of the revolution, I carried with me my idea of wanting to help my black people. When U.S. black businessmen visited Cuba to see things for themselves, I made contact with one of the sons of Elijah Muhammad, editor of the magazine *Muhammad Speaks*. He was the one who talked to me about Malcolm X. From that moment on, I was obsessed with meeting Malcolm X and learning about his organization. I kept up contact with the U.S. blacks. I received *Ebony* and *The Chicago Defender*—*The*

People's Courier didn't exist yet—and I had contacts with some black Cuban journalists who had contacts with the U.S.A., including Pedro Portuondo Calá, who organized trips to the United States for black Cuban journalists, and I went in 1957. William Portuondo Calá, his brother, was the sports journalist.

The year we were married I went back to New York, to cover then Prime Minister of Cuba Fidel Castro's visit to the UN. That was when I also met Malcolm X. It was my impression that U.S. blacks weren't interested in how we Cuban blacks lived. . . . They didn't even know we existed. I don't know whether they know more now. . . .

When I spoke with Malcolm X, he thought I was a West Indian. He was certain the island of Cuba had a white population, that there were no blacks. Now, years later, I realize they weren't in the wrong to think that, because even when Fidel went to the UN, the majority of those who went [with him] were white. And the first exiles to reach the United States when Fidel took power were almost all whites. The one who talked with Malcolm X about Fidel staying at the Hotel Theresa, in Harlem, was the Cuban diplomat Raúlito Roa, also white. So Malcolm X had no points of reference on the racial composition of our people. And yet the history is there for them to know, because we know theirs.

When I met Malcolm X, he was intrigued by the fact that I was black and Cuban. I explained to him that half the Cuban population was black or *mestizo,* that there was a tremendous mix. He was very taken. He was able to meet Juan Almeida and other blacks on the delegation who arrived shortly after. Malcolm wanted us to form a branch of the Black Muslims in Cuba. He also talked about how chain stores like Sears and Woolworth's, that didn't employ blacks, could be switched for others owned by Afro-Americans and Cuban blacks. I told him the Black Muslims couldn't organize in Cuba, because it was another kind of society, with different race relations from those in the United States, where there was an almost insurmountable physical and psychological segregation. Our racial mix doesn't allow for that, because we have the mulatto General Antonio Maceo, who fought racism in both wars of independence against Spain in the late nineteenth century, in Oriente, with black and white troops under him, in a kind of racial coexistence, more or less in harmony. At the same time, after demobilizing the Liberation Army in 1898, at the end of the Hispanic Cuban-American War, and under U.S. occupation, the black General Quintín

Bandera was reduced to being a garbage collector. The story goes that one day in Old Havana, he approached the first U.S.-approved president of Cuba, Don Tomás Estrada Palma, who liked to walk down Obispo Street greeting the populace, his car behind him. When Quintín Bandera said he was without a job, Estrada Palma threw him a five-peso gold coin. Quintín Bandera set about him with his stick. Not long after, Quintín Bandera was found slashed with a machete on the corner of Vies and Figuras streets. The press headlines of the assassination ran, "Quintín Bandera dead in Ñañigo brawl." People said it was Estrada Palma who had him killed.

But to get back to Malcolm X, instead of me interviewing him, he wound up interviewing me. I'll never forget him telling me that Fidel had to watch out for white Cubans, because they would be out to get him, that they were white "devils." I told him about that incident in Santa Clara when the private recreation centers were taken over and Fidel said publicly that in Cuba anyone could dance with whoever they wanted, but they should dance with the revolution. That was the end of the honeymoon and the true start of the exodus.

I remember I talked with one of Fidel's secretaries about him meeting Malcolm. Fidel said he wanted to meet him and the meeting took place. The photos taken on that occasion, of the two of them looking as if they're old friends, had never been published either in the United States or in Cuba until recently. The only photographer was known to Malcolm X and had been invited into Fidel's room where the two leaders met. It seems there was a lot of conspiring against the publication of those photos. Today, after all these years have passed, I think it's precisely in these difficult times for Cuba, for the Cuban people, and especially black Cubans, that we need black business and black products. For example, here in Cuba, there are no cosmetics for black women, blacks are not part of the equation. It's now that we most need a closer understanding with African Americans.

2

The Only Black Family on the Block

Elpidio de la Trinidad Molina, Jorge Molina, and Egipcia Pérez

My relationship with the Molina-Pérez family grew in stages. I first met Egipcia Pérez in the home of my old friend and colleague, Reynaldo Peñalver Moral, whose wife, Caridad Molina, is the sister of Egipcia's husband Elpidio de la Trinidad Molina. It was some years back, when the couple was preparing to take one of several vacations, all expenses paid, in the former socialist countries—Elpidio's reward for millions of dollars his inventions and innovations had saved the state-operated Cuban economy. In 1975, on the way to visit my own family in Santa Clara, I stopped by to see them at Varadero's veteran Oasis Hotel. The first time I ever visited the fabulous Varadero beach resort was en route to Havana in July 1959, when I took part in a marathon run from the east to west of the island. The marathon was to celebrate the 26 July 1953 attack led by Fidel Castro on the Moncada Garrison in Santiago de Cuba, which, although a failure in itself, has since been heralded as the start of the Cuban Revolution. Varadero Peninsula, north of Matanzas province, with its long, white, sandy beachline and lush tropical foliage, was a coveted Caribbean vacation spot and, until 1959, had been the exclusive, favorite leisure resort for Cuba's upper classes, who were of course white. The historical irony is that decades later Varadero was to become yet again exclusive, when Cuba's opening to international tourism made the modern hotels of this former enclave of Cuban-style segregation out of bounds to cash-stricken Cuban nationals. The Molina-Pérez family was an exception. On that occasion, when I asked for them at the reception desk I was told the hotel didn't have among its guests anyone of that description—this was after I had described them in great detail, especially Egipcia, whose intensely black, portly figure would be extremely hard to miss. When I did eventually find them on the beach, she gave me one of her characteristic comments: "They haven't seen us? You do realize we're the only black family around!" In January 1998, Jorge Molina was elected deputy to the National Assembly of People's Power. (PPS)

Elpidio de la Trinidad Molina

I was born on 27 May 1923 in Havana. I am married and have five children. My father was a barber and my mother a seamstress. We went through hell during the dictatorship of Gerardo Machado.[1] To survive, we boys had to clean porches, sometimes a whole house, and we'd carry buckets of water for just a few cents a day to help out the family. Things were very cheap, but it was real hard even to put together a few cents. There were six of us, three boys and three girls. I was the second oldest. During that whole period we lived in slums, in a tiny room where the family could barely fit. Only my mother really knew what we were going through, trying to make ends meet to pay for the room at two pesos a month. We lived in fear of being evicted— that they'd throw our furniture out on the street and we'd have to find someplace else to live. Those days a haircut cost five cents for children, eight or ten cents for grown men, when they had it cut, because there wasn't the money for it, not even five or ten cents . . . it was a luxury. You'd get a haircut for your birthday, or May 20, Independence Day, or October 10, another patriotic day, or for *Noche Buena* [Christmas Eve], but our Christmas Eve was pretty sparse.[2] We couldn't celebrate with pork, only pig's offal. After the Day of the Kings,[3] a long time after January 6, maybe two or three months passed before my mother would have the money to buy each of us a spinning top or yo-yo, or a rag doll for the girls. But my mother did manage to find a way to send us to school and all six of us, first the boys and then the girls, finished primary school through sixth grade. I was able to go on through seventh and eighth grades, passed the entrance exam for the Havana Higher School for the Trades, and there I graduated as a chemical analyst and an industrial chemist. When I was eighteen, back in 1941–42, I was fortunate to start work where I still am today. I worked days and studied nights, to teach industrial chemistry, which is what I wanted.

We knew that because of the color of our skin we had to study hard, because through studying we would have more of a chance of getting a job. It wasn't easy. The worst jobs were for us blacks—a bricklayer's mate, because it wasn't even easy to become a bricklayer.

Way back, when I started primary school, I'd roller-skate all the way from Mantilla to Diez de Octubre, in Lawton,[4] and back. I started to study for my baccalaureate, but that wasn't going to give me a trade. At the university, for example, the technical courses were for civil engineering and architecture. I wanted to do chemistry, and there wasn't chemical engineering, only agricultural engineering. I knew that I'd never find a job as an agricultural engineer. They were needed for the two or three soap factories there were at the time and they didn't employ blacks. I couldn't have worked in agriculture either, because the large estates were also for whites. In applied chemical engineering in the sugar industry, I wouldn't have found a job in a sugarmill. So I decided to go to trade school and graduated as an industrial chemist.

In the midst of all that, the Second World War started and some German Jews opened an emery stone factory. They moved into a house that belonged to the Alfonso family, who knew my mother, and the Germans asked if they knew of a young man who could help them. The family recommended me and I had the great luck to learn the trade. Now I'm an emery stone expert. I had the great luck of being helped at a certain stage in my life by whites who had quite a lot of power. I owe it to them for part of my education and well-being. In that sense, I can say I've been a privileged black.

The knowledge I had I gave to the revolution. When the owners went to the United States, I was left in charge of the factory with one of the sons who didn't know much about production. The son stayed and I was the technical person, because I had already graduated from trade school. When the revolution opened up the universities, I did a year's training and then studied what I'd always wanted to study and hadn't been able to, chemical engineering. But then after two years I switched to a degree in chemistry. I didn't graduate in either, but I did acquire the knowledge I could later apply in emery stone production. It also stood me in my stead when Comandante Che [Guevara] visited our factory. By then he'd already said, "Worker, build your own machinery," and we were building ours. Putting together the information and with his inspiration, we developed a whole emery stone technology for the many varieties that are used in a country's development. That helped us hold out against the imperialist blockade that started after 1 January 1959.[5] I remember when Fidel arrived here on 8 January 1959, he said in his first speech that blacks had been given the coral rock, because we couldn't visit the sandy beaches, only a bit at Guanabo. For us blacks there was Santa Fe Beach, and Biriato, which closed under capitalism; we were left with only Jaimanitas and Santa Fe beaches, which were full of sea urchins and coral rock. Today we can go to all the beaches the magnates would go to, from one end of the island to the other, without discrimination.[6]

For all that I've done for the revolution I've received numerous awards, right from the start. In 1962, I was National Vanguard of the Silicate Enterprise, which covered cement, tile, and brick for furnaces and house construction. In 1963 I was also National Vanguard. Between 1959 and 1963 I made some twenty or thirty innovations. In 1962 I was chosen as a founding member of the Socialist Revolution United Party (PURS). In 1965 it was named the Communist Party of Cuba. Up until today, I've been a member. For the merits I've been given, from 1976 to 1994 I have been National Vanguard of the Construction Workers Union. I've also been Provincial and National Vanguard of ANIR (the National Association of Innovators and Rationalizers). I have many medals and diplomas, and the highest recognition that can be given to any worker, which is that of Hero of Labor of the Republic of Cuba, since 1990. This recognition has only been given since 1985–86. There are fewer than one hundred workers in the whole of Cuba who have it. In our Construction Workers Union, there are only twelve Heroes of Labor. The rest of the unions, about eighteen of them, some have six, four . . . we're the ones who have the most.

Close to the factory, we had the Lawton Bus Terminal. The buses running at that time were GM (General Motors). The mechanics there, who were the ones who changed the brake blocks, came to ask me if I could make such a block. I said I could. I was familiar with the raw material, which was a base of amianthus and other components. I found out what they were, began to make them and try them out. The results were very good. Finally, our enterprise, which made emery stone, ceded the technology to the Ministry of Transport.

In the early days, as innovators we didn't receive any economic remuneration, only moral incentives. That changed later. After 1980, some workers received between 500 and 1,500 pesos for an invention. That was one incentive Fidel wanted to give us, because we'd received other incentives over the years; we'd been given beach houses to stay in, at Varadero and Guanabo. I've also had the honor of being on the 26 July Tribune, with Fidel. I've taken part in congresses of the party, the CTC (Confederation of Cuban Trade Unions), ANIR, and all that. Today, aged seventy-two, I calculate I must have made more than 150 innovations. Those that have contributed most to the economy of the country are those related to emery stone production. That technology isn't well known. It's saved the country several million pesos a year over the last three decades. Just calculate that before the revolution, between 150,000 and 200,000 square meters of flooring were produced, but in the 1970s and 1980s production soared to 3 million square meters. All those floors were polished with emery stone invented by me—whether tiled, granite-block, marble, or cement flooring. All the technology was mine—from street flagstones to tiled flooring in workplaces. We've been producing all that.

The factory bears the name of Juan Domínguez Díaz, one of the martyrs of the attack on the Moncada Garrison on 26 July 1953, in Santiago de Cuba. I knew him. The carpentry shop where he worked was also called that after the revolution. Now we have the factory in La Ceiba, where we're turning out all kinds of imported stone with new technologies. We've one technology left to develop, the tile grip for the machine industry—that's to say, perfect the technology. We still need it to respond to harder kinds of steel and some metals, like copper, bronze, aluminum, and different kinds of soldering. Steel is one of the most difficult metals in alloy form. There are some that have a high percentage of chromium, over 12 percent, and since chrome is an anti-abrasive, a higher percentage of chrome is added so the stone doesn't lose quality.

I encouraged my son Jorge to study refractory chemical engineering, to specialize in abrasives. He studied in the former U.S.S.R. and has been working in the factory since 1982. If it hadn't been for the Special Period, he would have completed postgraduate study specializing in abrasive emery stone production. But the Special Period and the dismembering of the socialist camp have prevented him. He could have done postgraduate study in the U.S.S.R. or in Czechoslovakia. He has some inventions, he's well trained, but this is kept quiet. Not much is divulged about this and other fields of production, because it's a strategic question. When Jorge and I went to what was then the German Democratic Republic, we visited an emery stone factory in Dresden, which the Germans told us had been bombed by the Allies. The Germans had it well camouflaged, but in 1985 it was still semi-destroyed. The bombing showed how strategic it was.

Today I'm happy to see there are as many blacks in science and engineering as there are in medicine. This is undeniably due to the revolution. There is no discrimination, either by gender or race; 52 percent of professionals are black. Among the women, there are black and white women, as there are black and white men. There is no discrimination. That problem's behind us. The revolution fought it. This is a real revolution.

Jorge Molina

There are times when I sit and meditate on all the possibilities we blacks had at the start of the revolution to study at the university and even abroad. I studied chemical engineering, specializing in tiles and refractory materials, at the leading Moscow Mendiev Institute. There was a whole explosion of students who were able to choose their study. Of the five of us in my family, four boys and one girl, there was no push that we all be engineers. The opportunity was there. I'm the second of the family. The oldest, my sister, chose another subject at the university, because she wanted to earn a qualification, not because she was interested in the subject. She dropped out and started work but then combined work and study to get an economics degree. The brother after me studied electronics to work as a middle-level electrician. He has always found work. The next youngest, right from primary school, wanted to go into the military. He was sure of what he wanted, though he isn't someone who expressed himself easily. We're a respectful and united family, a product of how we were brought up in the home. Though black, we grew up in a neighborhood where practically the only black family was ours. From the start, we had to adjust to that life; we were able to live in a comfortable house because my mother was also a professional, in pharmaceuticals. That placed us in the Havana black middle class.

I remember a story my father once told me when I was little. He was studying and already had a good salary. One day a white told him to his face, "I may be a shoemaker, but I'm better than you, even though you've studied, simply because you're black." That still holds. Recently there's been a resurgence [of racism] because not only can certain businessmen in the new joint ventures choose their personnel for their skills, they can eliminate persons of the black race. The tourism which is coming in may have certain requirements and you simply find they don't accept blacks, even when the black may be educated, speak several languages, and have training in accountancy. You can't help see it. It's there. Cubans confuse ethnicity and nationality. You see that a lot when you go abroad. I studied in the former Soviet Union. There, we would be asked our racial origin, and we didn't know what to reply, whether Bantú, Yoruba, or Carabalí. They didn't know why we didn't know, because the white Cubans, of a different racial origin, said they were Cuban.

Today those managers simply don't want blacks among their workers. They identify with you as Cuban, which is what we are, but, whether a joint or Cuban venture, management doesn't want blacks. I know of an experience of a friend of mine. One day he heard he had been promoted to a company where he would be in charge of a tourist taxi firm which had some stringent requirements. The drivers had to speak at least three languages, be 1 m, 85 cm tall . . . I added, "and preferably white." He said, "Not preferably—they had to be white." And that's happening in many areas. It's the reverse of what was applied some years back with blacks, youth, and women. In part, I'm the product of that policy in the second half of the 1980s. It became a campaign to include blacks. I was called on to administer my workplace when I was a technician because the administrator had been promoted, not only because I knew languages and the technology of the factory, but also because I was young and black. But all that was ephemeral and came to an end, and as blacks we were left to head the unions and work in construction. There are very few of us who are enterprise managers. But I was also elected to a provincial government organization—as an innovator, which was something passed on to me by my father—where the provincial administrative posts are not exactly in black hands. Yet I'm indignant when I come across a person of the black race speaking against the revolution, because I'm convinced that blacks never lived better before the revolution. My parents taught me that.

For example, during the so-called rafters crisis in August 1994, we blacks asked on the street who were the ones throwing stones and all those things—because those who were in the front line, like cannon fodder, were black. People were asking and telling us that. Were they white or were they black? People I asked would say, "What gets me most is that there were a lot of blacks who should be shot." The response comes from the observation that blacks, with all the possibilities they have had with the revolution, had no right to be giving voice to ideas that were out to destroy the revolution, and that they served as cannon fodder. Those who were out on the streets were not the ringleaders; they remained well protected. The blacks were manipulated, because they needed a body of people.

As blacks, we set out to observe how the whites live to imitate them. If whites celebrate their daughter's fifteenth birthday,[7] we want to do the same. Many black families have done that. It's hard to be black in this country. We know because we're the most marginalized, there are more and more criminals, and that's how you're seen, even if you're not.

Egipcia Perez

I was born in Surgidero de Batabanó, in the south of Havana province. My childhood was pretty hard because I lost my mother when I was very little and was brought up by my grandmother on my mother's side. My two aunts looked after me and my sister, respectively. Though I didn't know much about life, I thought everything was fine, at seven I had already had to work. My father was a fisherman and, after being at sea for two or three months, there'd be times when he'd try to make seven to ten pesos after selling the owner's catch. Sometimes he'd only make three. The fishermen had to deduct their costs—fuel, food, and other supplies. What was left was divided among them. The fishermen were poor whites and blacks of the region, while the boat owners and dealers were always white.

My aunt was a home dressmaker and when I was nine she sat me at a sewing machine to make my first dress. It was to celebrate Fisherman's Day. My aunt said I could make myself a dress if I wanted. The whites had their Lyceum Sports Club and the Spanish Casino, but no black or mulatto, or anyone with any black in them at all, could go into either of them. We blacks had the Progress Society, an old, run-down place where the sponges were cut and kept, that would be fixed up for our festivities. That's when I made my first dress.

I went to school, but since I was always ambitious and, it would seem, clever, when I was nine I was already in junior high. The director, who was white and comfortably off, and called Pelayo Suárez Orta, said in admiration one day, "Egipcia, you really study, you don't seem black." According to him, I didn't have the backward ideas of other blacks for whom it was all the same to sew or clean . . . he saw another spirit in me. He asked why I didn't go on to study. When I told my father, he said I was crazy, where was the money going to come from. I argued I would sew and with the money from my sewing I'd pay for my studies. When I told my aunt who was bringing me up and who I called Mima, she said she'd help. She was the dressmaker, and I'd do the hemming. She'd pay me twelve to twenty cents a dress, and that way I put together the money to study at Doctor Pelayo Suárez Orta's academy.

Mima told me, "You're going to Dr. Pelayo's academy, but mark my words, it's going to be hard rubbing shoulders with people who all have money." I didn't see it that way, because I never went by the color of my skin. The teacher's daughter was there, as was Laura Palomera, the daughter of the owner of half of Surgidero de Batabanó, and the daughter of Dr. Pons and Dr. Cancio, and there was I paying my six pesos a month with my sewing. I was more or less OK with my ten-cent shoes, which hung from the ceiling in the Polish shops. They looked fine with my socks, and they accepted me. A doctor who was very famous in the town even told my father, "I like the *negrita* [little black girl]," as if he were trying to protect me. I don't know what kind of paternalist help he might have offered me because I never saw any of it. Perhaps because people looked at me askance when I said I visited the home of Dr. Pons.

During one of the exams at the academy, Dr. Pelayo himself said, "You're very intelligent, it's not good for me having you here." That was because he wanted me to be passing the answers in exams to his daughter Clara and his son Pelayo, who later became a minister. That's when they started to block me.

Time passed and I finished eighth grade and went to an academy here in Havana, in Cerro, because there was nothing in Batabanó to prepare me for going on to teacher training. I was around fourteen. I had no rest: from work to school, from school to the academy, from the academy to work, and on it went. Those who went to that academy stood a good chance of getting into the teacher training school or the home economics school, one or the other. I did the exam and didn't get in because I was black. There was nothing in writing. Though I had the qualifications, I wasn't the right skin color. Yet Dr. Pelayo's daughter, the one I was to have passed the answers to, did get in. So I went to the home economics school, which was much further away and which I didn't like at all. That's when my studies came to an end. I didn't continue and went to work as a maid.

My first job was in the home of the director of my school in Batabanó, who was living close by in my neighborhood. She was called Haydée. I think her husband was also a minister. We had by then moved to Havana. That town was too poor to live in, much less to get on. So I became the nanny of a lovely little boy we called Pituco. It seems Haydée and the others in the house liked the fact that I was such a refined black woman. But the boy wanted to be carried always, and, since I was black, it was my duty to carry him so everyone would know I was the maid—in crisp white uniform. In those days, we would go on the weekend to Tarará beach, which was for whites, not blacks. I could go in because of what I was. But Haydée didn't want me always to be carrying the boy. I gradually got the boy used to the pram, or the playpen, or holding my hand, and gently taught him to speak. Haydée's husband would watch and say, "She doesn't seem black!" Always the same thing.

Haydée asked me why I had such long nails and beautiful hands. Her husband replied for me: "Because she's decent, because it looks good." Her response was, "Well, you must cut them." She didn't look after her own nails. I had to do everything for that boy, from washing his clothes to preparing his food. And people who visited the house would comment on my dress and my hands while I also looked after the boy. She hated this so much that she dismissed me one day.

I had many problems as a maid, seemingly because the master and mistress of the house wanted a vulgar black who wouldn't talk, or take part in conversation, or behave in a certain way, to justify having a maid, because when they did involve me in conversation or asked me something, deep down they didn't like the fact I conducted myself well.

With all these setbacks, I already knew my future wasn't in servitude. I decided to study, even if it was for a vocational skill. That's when I went to the trades school and met my husband of today. I was sixteen when we met, we married, and that was the end of my studies.

At the time of the revolution, I had three children and took on two new zone organizations—the Committee for the Defense of the Revolution and the Federation of Cuban Women. Into my hands came forms to be filled out by persons wanting future work. I started work in the pharmacy that was next door to my house as a sector person: my job was to report to a doctor at Lawton Polyclinic. I would write out the prescriptions and she was surprised I had such good writing and spelling. Since it was close to home, I'd go and see to the children and then go back to work. Then a course came along which interested me a lot and I became a pharmaceutical technician, and that's what I did for twenty-nine years, until I retired.

In this second stage of my life I started work as an auxiliary at Julio Trigo Hospital. There I really came up against people because my ideas were not those "of blacks." When I didn't understand how things could be a certain way, I would say so, and the directors didn't like how I would stand out above the rest. But it was simply that I felt compelled to say what I didn't understand. I had a colleague there who would say, "Never protest, because when you do it'll cost you your job." But since I didn't work to eat but because I liked my work and wanted to be independent, I went on protesting if things were not right. I reasoned that if I were dismissed I would work somewhere else.

At the time of my first job at the hospital, the head of the pharmacy was called Mario. He'd been there for many years and wanted to have everything under his control. There was a room that was never opened. One day I asked him why not. His reply was always the same, that Dr. Frías, the hospital director, didn't want anyone going near there. My argument was that it was part of the pharmacy and stockroom. My curiosity was such that one night, when I was on duty, I opened the room. What I found was that, while in the hospital there was no medicine for the sick, or sutures for operations, that room was filled with all the hospital needed. That was around 1970, when the revolution was well consolidated, thanks to the labor movement around the famous 10-million-ton harvest. We found a way to get all that out, without me being the one to denounce it, and I became the defender of justice, the leader, because I was the one to file a report to my superiors. I wasn't liked by the director and others in charge because, according to them, I shouldn't have been looking into things that were nothing to do with me. But I went on like that, always speaking out when I saw things that weren't right.

Later on I went to work at the worst pharmacy in the Víbora, one with a large personnel. I was the only black woman in my department and right from the start I crossed paths with a woman doctor who was like a whip. Customers would ask for me, not her, saying I treated them differently. The other two in charge took her side and would comment on money and medicines that were missing, saying the employees were to blame. Coincidentally, the employees were black. One day I told one of them that it wasn't the employees who were taking things: "The ones who rob here are the intelligent ones, you whites!" I was taken to a work council on charges of lack of respect. But they had to hear me out, because there I spoke about how I saw them taking medicines for their friends.

The persecution was so frequent and hostile that, in one of those cases, a lawyer told me that if I had so much as taken a single aspirin I'd go to jail. It wasn't against me as a person but as the *negra* (black woman), to say, "The black woman took such and such." But there were whites who robbed constantly and were never caught. The sad thing is that not all blacks confront these racist attitudes. That's why I finally decided to retire.

3

Issues of Black Health

Lliliam Cordiés Jackson and Nuria Pérez Sesma

Lliliam Cordiés Jackson belongs to the first generation of doctors graduating at the outset of the Cuban Revolution. She studied medicine at the University of Oriente, in Santiago de Cuba, eastern Cuba, where the population is predominantly black and where there has been much more of a racial mix. Dr. Lliliam Cordiés Jackson is currently professor of internal medicine at Hermanos Almejeiras Hospital in Havana, where she founded the first multidisciplinary group for the study of and attention to patients with hypertension. The project expanded from Havana to the whole country, and so we began our interview on a clinical note. (PPS)

LCJ: Those who have studied this [hypertension] very seriously in the Caribbean are the Jamaicans. Jamaica has a strong intellectual tradition and the University of the West Indies is one of the most prestigious in the region. There's a Jamaican researcher who has devoted himself to studying this and his work is obligatory reference throughout the area. Work has also been done in Barbados, and now in Martinique and Guadeloupe the French are undertaking long-term proactive study. It's a serious problem because blacks who are hypertensive are disadvantaged. Whites can develop hypertension but not with the fatal consequences it has for blacks. It has been scientifically demonstrated that blacks are more prone to develop lesions of the heart, kidney, and brain than whites. In 1994 we selected a group of blacks who had not known they were hypertensive. We arrived at a place and started taking people's blood pressure, telling them, "You're hypertensive, you're not hypertensive." We selected thirty blacks and thirty whites, from similar work and living conditions, and began to study the heart, which is one of the organs most attacked by hypertension, in those supposedly healthy people, that is, who had no heart symptoms. We found lesions among the blacks but not among the whites. That's been demonstrated in this country and abroad.

I don't think stress has any bearing. Stress is the same for whites and blacks. The tension and the difficulties and the drop in the quality of life [in the 1990s] is the same for everybody here in Cuba, but we blacks have genetic markers that are logically affected by what is around us. Whenever we present our findings on race, the first thing we are told is that in Cuba there are no pure races. The World Health Organization (WHO) only recognizes three races: Eurocoid, Negroid, and Asiatic. There's a demographic indicator we use for race, which is a point system based on color of the skin pigmentation and hair type. You can have fair-skinned people who are demographically black. That's how the WHO resolved the problem. We are all either Negroid or Caucasian or Asiatic.

The genetics of high blood pressure is one of the things that is being studied most right now, not only among blacks, but in all populations, because the thinking is that if the genetics can be modified, there can be hopes of improving the quality of life. The treatment for high blood pressure can be very disheartening. The patient has to be accustomed to a lifetime of dependence on treatment. So no matter what facilities are made available, the individual feels different—so much so that we try to teach people to live with the illness, not for it. They must come to terms with it.

The North Americans have developed this a lot. There it's the primary cause of death. There are some 50–75 million North Americans with high blood pressure. They have devoted time, resources, brain power, and specialized institutions. So have the French. It is said that out of every five citizens, there are four known to have high blood pressure and one who simply doesn't know. That is, there are five out of five.

I think if relations were better with the North Americans, it would be very fruitful for us all to have scientific cooperation in this field, as in many others. I personally have written to two North American researchers who study high blood pressure among blacks, Savage and Saunders. In the United States, there is an association for the study of high blood pressure among blacks, which is strong as an organization. There is also a college of black cardiologists who hold their conferences every two years. In 1992 they held a convention on hypertension among blacks in Nairobi, Kenya. They have an affiliation with Africa. I was able to receive many very interesting abstracts of the papers presented in Nairobi. We have very few links with North American medical circles, and it's a shame because they have tremendous research potential. I think that in the field of science, that lack of contact isn't a negligence of the Cuban government. When the country has needed it, it has had advice from the United States, and other places, as for example with the neuropathic epidemic.

There is a good national program for hypertension in Cuba. It is based on early detection and treatment by the family doctor. This facilitates the work of those of us who are not in primary care. I work in a hospital and so only see those whose problem is difficult to study or control in the area in which they live. Here in this country, that's something well centralized, well organized, and functioning well. I'm not speaking of high blood pressure as a social problem. I'm speaking of it as a scientific problem, because the social aspect will be resolved insofar as we resolve the health problem that we have. High blood pressure cannot be seen as a social problem.

PPS: What is your own family background?

LCJ: We are four sisters known as the daughters of Lilian Jackson (of Jamaican origin) and Juan Emilio Cordiés (of French origin): three doctors and a philologist. María Teresa is the oldest; she has two children who are doctors. She's a charming, highly intelligent woman, a bit of an introvert, but with tremendous human qualities and a special sense of humor. She's a very special person. I'm the second, and the third is Silvina, who has two children. She's a doctor in intermediate therapy at the same hospital as me, Hermanos Almejeiras. She's very gentle and clever, but very direct. Silvina is someone who vehemently goes for the truth. And Marta Emilia, the youngest, is the one who didn't become a doctor but studied literature.

When Marta Emilia told my father she wasn't going to study medicine, because that wasn't what she wanted, she didn't have a feel for it, my father asked her what she did want to study, and she said literature. "OK," he said. He went off and bought her a typewriter as a present, and told her, "If you're going to study literature, you have to be good." I think he felt good about Maité's decision, and time has demonstrated he wasn't wrong. She now heads the research department at the Fernando Ortiz African Culture Center and is doing her doctorate in that area.

There are many black people in science and medicine, at least from what I know of my generation and of my parents' generation also. In my parents' generation, for example, there was the concern to go to university. It cost a lot but people managed. Families would plan ahead long before the child was at junior or senior high. From early on there was the preoccupation with study. Blacks knew that one way of facing discrimination was through knowledge, and I saw that in my family. My father was a black doctor. He wouldn't have passed for anything but. He was a typical African, you could be looking at him and seeing a black Zulu. He was a big, tall, corpulent African, with a slow walk and persevering voice. That was my father. He was an intellectually superior man. He was one of the most intelligent men I have known in my life. And I don't think I say that as his daughter. I have also heard that from my white friends. In Paris I had the opportunity to visit one of his student friends and I was fascinated by how he talked about my father. What's more, he recognized me right away even though he'd never seen me before.

That was a great incentive for black people. Back then blacks had social organizations. There were societies where blacks could meet. There was discrimination against blacks who had no education, not blacks who had nothing. Anybody could go to the Aponte Club,[1] except blacks who couldn't hold a conversation, because they felt bad there. So, in a country where blacks were disinherited, the black class imposed a self-classification. Only a certain kind of black could go. It didn't matter if you were poor, but you had to be honest. I think that's changed. It's another generation, with other motivations and interests, and it's another kind of life. People have their minisocieties. We meet in each other's homes to listen to music, talk, and discuss issues. But in Santiago de Cuba that sense of family and society and the elders still prevails. It's perhaps remembering our ancestors, where the figure of the family elder is so important. In Oriente, or Santiago, that has remained, with all the changes of modern life. I think a lack of manners and vulgarity have homogenized the country. I don't think it's only among blacks, but blacks are a majority and that's what's seen more. The loss of values isn't only in blacks, but everybody. The government, the state, the country has come to realize that, and measures are being taken to try to resolve the problem. I myself don't think that everything's been done that should have been done. I think it's going to be very difficult. There are unfortunately two generations now like that, and a lot has to be done to restore a more formal education.

PPS: How far would you say your own thinking has been shaped by your parents and sisters?

LCJ: It shouldn't be forgotten that the family is the basic cell of society. When a man inherits genes, he inherits codes of behavior, and when you have in a family a tradition and habits of behavior, they are passed on from one generation to another. Between the generations there are points of controversy, because that's human development. But there are values that are passed on: one transmits to one's children what was transmitted to one. That's why I say a man inherits genes, but he also inherits codes of behavior: for example, honesty, honor, respect for dignity, and individuality.

My father was very open, a man with whom you could argue, and he would always leave you the possibility of what he jokingly called "an honorable way out." He inculcated us with that: you had to listen to what people had to say. He was a very open person. I have tried to pass that on to my children. And as I work with young people, because I teach, I try to pass that on to my medical students. I try to have them respect each other as individuals. I understand people have a right to be as they are, to live as they wish, to think and say what they want. I've passed that on to my family. And I've been lucky, in the sense that life has given me a wonderful family. I have marvelous sisters, nephews and nieces, cousins . . . I don't know, we're like a great tribe. I think to a certain extent that Africa hasn't left us and never will. I think it's been a big influence. Though I must say that we had an all-round education which wasn't that common. My father was no ordinary man. He had a very broad idea of life and the world. He lived in France for more than ten years. This made its mark and opened him to new things. For example, I remember that I read Voltaire when I was ten or eleven and discussed it with him. It limited me in my friendships at school, because my friends, just imagine, they were light years away from that. My mother was a very intelligent woman, with a great practical sense. My mother was like the center of the family. While my father was the intellectual center, my mother was the material center. My mother was the kind of woman who, without moving from the house, knew what her daughters were doing, what was cooking, who came and who went. I don't know how. My friends, for example, went to my house to visit my mother. They'd arrive at my house and if I wasn't there they'd wait for me.

My father never let my mother work outside the house. I don't know why. He lived in terror. It was a marriage for life. I never heard them argue. At six in the evening, she would hurry whoever was in the bathroom out, because that was the time my father would come home. We were already married and I'd say, "But how can you, Mum?" And she'd say, "No! Your father's coming and he mustn't see me like this." Whoever was in the bathroom had to get out and when he arrived she'd be bathed and dressed. She helped him. She was the one who took the X-rays, saw to the patients, and organized him at work. It had to be seen.

My mother died before him and we thought he wasn't going to survive her death. She left a tremendous gap. She was a woman who filled the place, took everything on, so ably, efficiently, and creatively. It was incredible. That's the African, the African woman is like that; she's the one who cares for the children, tills the land, goes to market and barters. That's our ancestry!

All that cultural baggage helped me a lot in the professional world. It was hard, but people get accustomed. I think that it's been hard for women in Cuba, white or black, to forge ahead in that sense, but the men have grown accustomed to treating us as equals. It depends also on the value of the individual, as a woman and as an intellectual, in the position you hold. And let me tell you that where I found it really hard was in Africa. Where it was really hard to convey my knowledge and position as a woman was in Africa. Here, people have grown accustomed. Men are used to it and pretty much live with it. That is, a woman is intellectually and professionally equal. The Cuban male has become a bit more disciplined.

PPS: And as a black woman?

LCJ: As a black woman, I think it's been that little bit more difficult, because people still carry within them that women aren't suited, should be in their place, should remain submissive. I, in particular, have an antisubmissive character, and I think it's been hard for me because I'm black and also because of my temperament, because I can be very vehement, too. I can be very direct and very exacting of myself and others. Life has placed me in positions of authority, as far as I have reached, because I have no great ambitions of grandeur in that direction. But I think where I have reached, I have done so not forgetting I am a woman and black. I think that's also important. I myself have not detracted from my condition, because I am proud of being black and even prouder of being a woman.

The opposite can easily happen and has happened to me on many an occasion. There's only one way of fighting that: demonstrating one's capacity. You have to do that, and study and get on.

I've always been careful in my relations with people, establishing a rapport which helps, especially working in medicine. When there's good teamwork, things are marvelous. But when the teamwork's bad, there are many problems that affect the work. And in medicine, the patient's the one who pays.

I've never had problems in that respect and have tried to be honest and calm, though direct, in winning over the collective. When there's something I don't like, I say so, for people to know I don't like it and to try to solve it. And when I take a stand I understand is the one I should take, I do so responsibly, to the bitter end.

PPS: Are your relations good with the men around you?

LCJ: I think the problems women in Cuba have at work are the problems of some men's capacity to face up to this. Some months ago, I saw on TV an interview with Isabel Allende, the deputy foreign minister, and the journalist asked the same question about her work relations in a male culture. She said that it had been hard for her at times to have male colleagues understand and accept her authority. But I think like her that they did end up accepting her. Because that depends on your leadership capacity and your skills as a woman at a given moment. Because you have to realize you're dealing with a whole woman, you can't divide her into the woman doctor, the woman leader, the thinking woman. She's a human being with defects and virtues who has a job to do. She has to polarize toward one thing or another at a given moment, and with time she gains in experience. And I think she does gain. There are difficulties and they are overcome.

Dr. Nuria Pérez Sesma is the youngest of our interviewees. She was born on 31 August 1969 and is the older of two daughters. Her mother is a well-known painter and her father is retired from the military. Our interview was not easy. Off the record, she had been frank and direct about race relations in Cuba. On tape, it was hard for her to articulate her feelings. But when she did, her words were charged with emotion. She had always felt her vocation was medicine; the goal she had always strived for was to study medicine at the university, and that was not an easy choice. Given the educational system established in the early months of the revolution, her parents did not have to pay for her tuition. It was her own academic merit and student record that determined whether she would get a place. In this interview in mid-1996, she began by telling me something about how the higher education system functioned in her time. (PPS)

NPS: It goes according to your student points average. That's how I was able to study medicine. My parents didn't have to pay, neither my parents nor those of any other student here in Cuba. And neither medicine nor any other area of study. I aimed for the grades which would get me where I wanted to go. In my time, it was 90 points and over, which I achieved. It wasn't only the points but also your merits as a student, especially in senior high, through competitions related to your chosen field, and the references from your teachers. I chose general medicine, which has four specialties: gynecology, pediatrics, psychology, and clinical medicine. Right now I am specializing in that. Since ninth grade, around 1982–83, I've been a member of the UJC (Young Communist League). In those days, it was hard to get in. You had to be an exemplary student, devoted to study, and take part in all the activities, recreational and political, especially political, on the neighborhood bloc, because there were verifications at all levels.

PPS: How was it for a young black woman like yourself with professional aspirations? What did it mean to you when you became a member of a political organization like the UJC, which hasn't exactly stood out for its discussions on the theme of race relations in Cuba? What was your reaction when you looked deep in the mirror and had to recognize that, while you were equal to other women of your age, you were also different.

NPS: That time meant a lot to me. It was like a prize, a glorification of my work, all my study and effort. I felt very happy to attain that and today I sincerely don't think that way any more. When I obtained it, I accepted it because I believed in the measures, the laws, and especially the values of the organization. I was fourteen or fifteen then. Now it's very different. There are few young people who want to belong to the organization as such. On the contrary, they're leaving the organization because it's not the same any more, it's belonging for belonging's sake, for the advantages of being a cardbearer. It's being abused because to get a scholarship or get on professionally, it's a requirement. I belong to the FMC (Federation of Cuban Women) and in these organizations the topic of race relations as such isn't and can't be discussed, because if you bring it up you're doubly discriminated against. You can't speak out about the race differences that existed and still exist, the priorities whites have with respect to blacks. They have more priority, in all these things, from choosing a field of study to entering a type of job or a specialized place. My field, for example, is a difficult one. We were few blacks who succeeded and are doctors today. In my class, we were only seven or eight blacks out of an enrollment of almost forty-five. I don't know about other university disciplines, I can only speak for medicine. Though enrollment is much higher than it was before the revolution, it's much less so in terms of black racial composition. We were only a few. When I was a student, I didn't feel any racial discrimination in our group, we all got on well. In universities around the world, you find your group where you fit in. Among the professors, there were those who underrated black students. I felt that in the exams, whether oral or written.

PPS: How did you deal with the humiliation that could come from those attitudes toward young people like yourself?

NPS: I personally didn't have to, whereas others among my fellow students did. You had to sit back and say, well, these things happen because of this and that. . . . You could say, well, the professor likes her, she's pretty and white, and it's not the same with the other who is colored.

PPS: But you're telling me those things didn't happen and yet you're giving me an example of someone you know. How did you react to those things, as a young woman born in the first decade of the revolution?

NPS: It depressed me, it made me feel bad, at times it made me feel inferior. I can't tell you about racism under capitalism. I don't know, I wasn't there, but for me it was a form of subtle discrimination, not overt, such as, "Because you're black we'll give you so many points, or because you're black I'll ask you this question, or you must do that. . . ." So you couldn't accuse anyone or fight against it, because you couldn't go up to the professor and say, "Professor, why do you treat so-and-so that way . . . because she's black . . . and yet so-and-so who answered the same you treat differently?" The discrimination that exists today, and it does exist, is underhanded, a sort of looking out for friends. I'm speaking of my field. Because everywhere, and especially here in Cuba, there's discriminatory networking for friends in a given field. Any specialty is hard right now, because almost all the young doctors graduating have to opt for general medicine and then another specialty. I know of examples in my class of doctors who were not good academically and sadly are in power, perhaps economic power, and even bribed the professors. And today they have a specialty. And that's how they got where they are and nothing could be done about it. Sadly, that's the case.

PPS: Where do you get hold of readings that can compensate for that kind of anguish you and people like you have had to face?

NPS: I haven't seen anything on this, either books or journals. I have attended events at Africa House, on the black issue.[2] But I haven't found any readings and I would like to. There are few texts, little information on these themes. And we need it, not only my generation, but all of us who are black and of mixed race need that kind of literature, to be informed about black communities in other countries, in the United States, in Hispanic America, in Europe, because each of those communities has its own peculiarities.

PPS: Why do you think there is this lack of information in a country as racially mixed as Cuba?

NPS: It's a very delicate issue and I think it starts with the government, which hasn't done anything in this respect. There are black and mixed-race writers who want to articulate this and don't have the possibility of doing so. I imagine that they must feel as I feel, with more experience of life and all these things, because I sense this in seminars I have attended, because they have struggled to eradicate the racial discrimination that exists on TV and radio, in magazines, and the media in general. You reach the conclusion that there is discrimination, because you watch television and you ask yourself, why are there no blacks . . . why is there no black mother in a decent role? They're all whites. You watch television and see dancers and they're white. The National Folklore Group is hardly ever on television, and little is known about them. You have to go there to learn more about national folklore. The programs on radio are modern things or classical European music.

PPS: How do you see black Cubans of your generation?

NPS: Though my people generally think much like me, there is little struggle among people of my generation. I'm not only speaking now as a doctor, but among my patients, my neighbors, and my own family. We don't fight. We're aware of the problem, that the problem's latent, exists, but we don't fight. We don't externalize the problems, it's not articulated, on radio and TV or in the CDRs (Committees for the Defense of the Revolution). But we talk about it among ourselves. A patient comes to see me and says, "Oh, Doctor, because we blacks . . . stay where you are, because look how hard it is for us as blacks to get anywhere . . . because, doctor, you know there is racial discrimination." Things like that my patients confide in me, because I am a black doctor. We have no social organizations where we could meet and talk about these things. And it exists, because the preoccupation is tangible at events at Africa House. But it doesn't go beyond there.

PPS: Do you think black Cubans, not only those of your generation, are aware the phenomenon exists and feel a solidarity when they see another in a certain position; that they are comforted, and it's a boost to self-esteem, though at the same time the problem isn't tackled openly?

NPS: We don't tackle it openly, because we're afraid to. It's true. We're afraid of the consequences it might bring, afraid of being held back by talking about the problem. I know how things like that have got around. For example, in the rectification process a few years back, there was talk on this topic, of discrimination against women and blacks, in government as in other spheres . . . the participation of blacks, women, and young people . . . that there needed to be more blacks, women, and young people. That was said, but it didn't go beyond words to action. If you look at government, there are few blacks. If you look at the mass organizations, like the UJC, the FMC, the Federation of University Students, Middle-School Students, and the Pioneers,[3] all the leaders are whites. There are very few black leaders. Take any organization with fifteen reps, and if there are one or two blacks, it's a lot. Sometimes there's one, or none.

PPS: How is it for blacks in terms of relationships among the young?

NPS: That's a hard one right now, especially mulattos. When mulattos get somewhere, they discriminate against blacks. They look for another mulatto or white, to whiten the race. That exists especially among my generation, both in men and women, but more so in the men. That's to say, it's more frequent to see a mulatto man discriminating against black women than it is to see a mulatto woman discriminating against black men. Of course, this is not the finding of any scientific study, it's only a view based on my observations.

PPS: How do you, an intelligent, attractive young black woman react to this?

NPS: I imagine this very situation in which we are discriminated against, and which values the white race over the black, is the cause of this kind of whitening. . . . Maybe the mulatto man thinks that if he marries a white woman his children will benefit more, will stand a better chance. As a black woman, this touches me close up, it hurts. I'm affected by this kind of situation, I feel it a lot, it's hurtful and damaging to me. I have felt rejection from people of my own race and that makes me depressed. I'm twenty-six years old and at this age a woman needs a stable relationship with a man, a stable home.

PPS: This kind of reasoning, do you young black women discuss it among yourselves and, if you do, what conclusions do you reach?

NPS: We don't reach any kind of conclusion. I don't know if there are any solutions to these problems, and less so in Cuba where the phenomenon is practically beginning. Years back there wasn't this problem or I didn't notice it. Perhaps now it's up close, I feel it more. We have no places to meet where we can argue and discuss these problems. And there's no motivation to create a kind of center that is attractive to people and where serious topics can be discussed. Young people are interested in other things, in videos, in games, working in the tourist industry which can give them material things—which is why an individual working in some part of the tourist industry has more respect than a doctor. Here, the one who can earn more is valued more. And any place in the tourist industry, from a simple receptionist to a bellboy, they'll be earning more than I do as a doctor, and dress better and go to places where I, as a health professional, can't go, because my salary is the equivalent today of US$12. A porter can easily earn US$6 in an eight-hour shift—half my monthly salary.[4] As a result, social relations are skewed, especially those of my generation. Now we have the *jineterismo* (prostitution), among men and women, looking for material things they can't get any other way in the society. For example, sometimes the UJC National Office gives out some tickets for the discotheques that charge in dollars and where no young worker on a regular salary can afford to go. But those tickets are given out at top level, they almost never come down to the base. And there are times when they're given to friends. I've been to those places, not because they've been given out at my hospital where there's a base organization, but because a friend gave it to me. I hate that, it's depressing. Little by little you withdraw and stop fighting. There are so many problems! Right now, I feel really frustrated. I wanted to be a doctor and I became one, because I like medicine. But this whole situation, in every sense, the economic and social problems, including the racial discrimination that exists . . . thousands of problems we have make me generally depressed. There are times when I'm alone and I wonder what the future will be like . . . is it so uncertain or is there hope? There are times when I feel tired and think I can't go on. Then I give myself a bit of psychotherapy and go on making an effort, because all that can be very soul-destroying.

PART II

The Representation of Race

Consciously or unconsciously Cuba has not wanted, out of prejudice, to take on the position of the black as an identity in recent decades; it's always been in reference to the eighteenth and nineteenth centuries. It's as if we had agreed that that was as far as the black presence should go, which meant not having to deal with the conflicts of blacks in a society that is much closer and therefore affects us all in one way or another. Directors who have done feature films for the Cuban Film Institute (ICAIC) have done them as historical pieces. The concern for the black conflict in more recent times is not there. It's like a kind of censorship or self-censorship, because it hasn't been dealt with in any other media either. Narrative is a case in point. I can't remember a single novel in the last twenty years where there is a black protagonist with all the conflicts. I think that if films were to be made along more contemporary lines, a first effect on the Cuban population would be for us to see ourselves reflected on screen. We would see the different problems facing Cubans, with blacks as their protagonists. We would not assume that black Cubans have the same problems as the rest of the population, but their own particular problems, that are still with us today, which would undoubtedly be good to see finally up front on screen.

Rigoberto López Pego, filmmaker

4

Holy Lust

Whiteness and Race Mixing in the Historical Novel

Marta Rojas

After studying for her baccalaureate in Santiago de Cuba, Marta Rojas enrolled in the journalism program at the Manuel Márquez Sterling School in Havana in 1949. Though there weren't many black students at the time, fifteen of the thirty-five students in her class were black or mulatto and came from fairly ordinary families. Two were from journalist families. Her mother was a dressmaker and her father a tailor, though both of them were knowledgeable. Although she graduated in 1953, two years earlier she had started to work for television, which was in its early, heady days. Channel 4 was recruiting students to learn on the job, and a professor chose two from the school. One was an athletic girl who knew a lot about sports and thought she could train in sports journalism, and Marta Rojas was the other. She had no chosen vocation but had a pretty face, good diction, and the desire to work in something totally new. The two took an allocution course and started out in sports newscasting. Rojas reflects on this and wonders whether, had the circumstances of her life been different, she might have continued there, even though sports wasn't what interested her. Least interesting of all was American football, which she didn't understand but had to learn to put together the news. She was very diligent—one of the powerful reasons why, almost forty-five years later, she would receive the National Journalism Award for her work in reportage. She started out by talking about her first big break in this field:

I did two or three pieces which were published in *Bohemia* magazine, while I was still a student, because of being from Santiago de Cuba. I had a neighbor, also from Santiago, who asked me to write the captions for his photographs. I always liked investigative journalism. Instead of doing simple captions, I'd research the background information. My professional career really took off by virtue of my being involved without even thinking. It was my last year of study. We had finished but were in the final process of graduating and I went on vacation to my home in Santiago de Cuba, as I did every year, to enjoy Carnival, the conga, the dancing, etc. That was 1953. While I was there at Carnival, the shooting started in the early morning hours for the attack on the Moncada Garrison and I met up with that photographer. It was a relatively small city and there weren't that many photographers. He had invited me to write a chronicle on Carnival, to send to the weekly *Bohemia* in Havana. When the shooting started, I thought to myself: "That's the end of our Carnival feature, we won't be doing it!" It hurt because I would have earned fifty pesos, which was a lot, especially for someone only just graduating. And I said to him, "Well, let's do a piece on the shooting and we'll still earn the fifty pesos," not knowing it was the attack on the Moncada Garrison, and we did that feature.

I say "we" because with him I pieced together the information like a professional. But the feature wasn't published because of the censorship at the time. When I went back to Havana I carried the article with me and took it to the magazine editor. He was very interested and told me that if I had anything else in the same vein to send it to him. I went back to Santiago. Instead of starting to work for television, I went to Santiago and covered the trial of the assailants.

The Moncada trial was when they tried Fidel Castro in court for the attack on the Moncada Garrison. It was tough. The attack itself and then the crimes committed by the army. Days after, Fidel Castro was taken prisoner outside Santiago and rushed to trial, in September of that same year, 1953.

Since I was from Santiago de Cuba, I had relatives and friends there. One of the defense lawyers, for example, was someone I had known here in Havana, at the university, and he was from Santiago. So I found my way into court and covered the whole trial, right up until October 16. I didn't have any credentials for doing that. It was a ruse. According to the laws of the time for professionals in Cuba, you had to have graduated and also have credentials in order to work. Anything else was a professional intrusion.

But, as life would have it, Santiago journalists saw me as a young woman and knew my father and liked me and never got angry because I did that without credentials. Because there was censorship, it was assumed my feature wouldn't be published and would be no more than a professional exercise. That was the truth of it, aside from people liking me.

I spoke with a lawyer called Baudilio Castellanos who was with Fidel Castro at the university and is also from the former province of Oriente. He told me, "To register as a journalist, I think it's best you speak with the magistrates, interview them, because they like to be profiled in the newspapers and all that." I knew that might be published because they weren't going to say anything compromising. I did a very short interview with the magistrates, asking them some very straightforward things about the case, how many accused there were, and sent it to *Bohemia,* which published it.

Then, when the magazine came out, I received a copy and took it to court. Since the feature was there with my name, I asked to be put on the list. So they put Marta Rojas, *Bohemia,* although I didn't work for the magazine. That list was for entering the courtroom, that's how I got in. Most of the professional journalists would leave, because they could only publish a short note and had to do other things. But my interest was to finish the feature I had started. And I had no other commitment. I didn't have to keep anyone, I lived at home. That's how I had the rare privilege of being the only one to be at all the court sessions, including the last one when they sentenced only Fidel.

Before being inclined to journalism, I wrote fiction, from when I was twelve. I even handwrote a novel, when my parents thought I was studying. The novel was called *Sweet Enigma.* It was an adolescent love story. I liked fiction a lot. My mother used to call me "Julita Verne," because I also really liked the movies. I liked the visual arts, but every day I'd go to the movies in Santiago. It had never occurred to me to study journalism. I studied journalism as a fallback. I wanted to study medicine, perhaps driven by the prestige and importance that came with it, especially for those of us who are black. A doctor had social recognition, much more than a journalist. I liked medicine, and I did my baccalaureate, but in my family we didn't have the money to keep a medical student in Havana. The medical books were very expensive, the lectures were very expensive; tuition was 100 pesos, which was 100 dollars in those years. I realized that it was going to be too much of a sacrifice for my parents. So one day, listening to the radio, I heard there were places at the journalism school. I told my mother I was going to study journalism, because I also liked writing. Journalism didn't cost so much, you didn't have to buy so many books, but rather research, go to libraries, and tuition was six pesos. That's why I studied journalism, but I always had the fiction inside.

I remember one of the first features I did at school was one which might have been considered futuristic, because in those times nobody thought about the FAX, but I wrote something about the newspapers on the television screen and such. I remember the professor, called Masdeu, said, "I'm not going to grade this feature, but I can't suspend you either. I want you to do another feature, one that is real." So I did a straightforward feature on something else.

When I wrote the pieces on the trial, I did them day by day. I noted many of the details, down to the color of someone's tie. I remember I detailed a little tree that was fighting to grow in the courtyard the assailants had to pass through. Many years later, when Alejo Carpentier did the prologue to the book on the Moncada trial, he discovered the writer and wrote about those details. Without setting out to, I put those other elements into the description of the trial.

That feature of 200-odd pages was never published before the revolution. The censorship of the press was stopped, but the magazine didn't consider it wise to publish something so long. I was by then working at *Bohemia,* because the director had asked me to work there with Enrique de la Osa. I'm going to make a parenthesis here because it's very important.

"In Cuba" was a section that approached investigative journalism Truman Capote-style, exposing something that had happened, its causes, its implications, etc. And I started working on that. Enrique de la Osa is a very knowledgeable person and I trained with him. That section helped me a lot to go beyond where others were stuck, which was the everyday journalistic piece, because we had to follow through with a whole story, whether it was political, economic, or whatever.

Then I did a 31-page summary of my 231-page feature, which is what was published. I put the original away and after the revolution a Uruguayan journalist called Gaviria came to Cuba and I gave it to him to read. Three weeks later, he brought me three copies which were selling for twenty cents each, back in 1960–61, with the whole manuscript, with no corrections or anything. That was when I went through it and cleaned it up. In the interim, I'd researched the topic more, and I incorporated other details on the origins of the Moncada, and why it had happened. That was then published by Ediciones Revolución, titled *The Generation of the Centennial at the Moncada Trial,* a very long title. That was 1963–64. Since then there have been eight or ten editions of that book, with the title *The Moncada Trial.* The edition Alejo Carpentier wrote the prologue for wasn't that one, because he hadn't read the book, but when he started writing *The Rites of Spring*—or rather having that idea, because he didn't even know he was going to write it—he was looking for things that happened in Cuba when he was in Caracas, and among them was the attack on the Moncada Garrison. He asked me for the book and was moved when he read it and wrote me a letter of thanks. So I was bold enough to ask whether I could use it as a prologue and he said, "When you publish it next, use it." When the time came, he made a few changes to it as the prologue, and there it is.

Over the years, I have worked in all kinds of scenarios. But from a professional point of view, something which influenced my life a lot was Vietnam. From the start of the war in Vietnam, I took part in solidarity movements in the United States, Europe, Cuba, all over. I became close to the Vietnamese representatives of the National Liberation Front. They invited me along with other Cuban journalists—we asked and they accepted—to visit South Vietnam, the Vietcong war zone, and I became a war correspondent. I visited Vietnam between 1965 and 1975 when they won the war. In all that time, I wrote many feature articles and two books. One is chronicles on South Vietnam, with literary elements. It had to be like that because at the time there were situations that couldn't be revealed. Places and dates had to be disguised and that gave me license to write about life in the jungle with the Vietcong. That compendium of chronicles went into a book titled *South Vietnam, Whose Strategic Weapon Is the People.* Later on, over those ten years, I did another book on the U.S. bombing of North Vietnam, again chronicles put together in a compendium titled *Vietnam Scenes.* That was very important from both a cultural and historical point of view. For the specific war situation, I had to change and recreate things. Moreover, I came to know landscapes, atmospheres, persons, psychologies, stories that culturally and historically had nothing to do with our world. Asian culture is very different from Caribbean culture, though we are all human beings alike. I saw things there you can't see in the Caribbean, and that fired my imagination. The crossing of two enormous rivers, like the Mekong, which is not navigable, the never-ending tempests, different from our hurricanes, the jungle, the austere life, everything. It's a totally different world. Any writer couldn't fail to be stimulated.

The other big impact on me was the literacy crusade in Nicaragua, where I spent the whole year in which the campaign lasted—some eight months or so. I traveled all over Nicaragua. I went down the Rama River to Bluefields to find blacks dancing to Caribbean music. The whole Atlantic coast is like that, a mix of Indians and blacks. Then I began to see all the mix, which isn't only Spanish with African, but Indian, that whole range of mix there is in the Americas. That was really interesting for me.

I haven't really had any conflicts in terms of writing fiction and journalism, perhaps because of how my professional life has turned out and how I started out, that's to say, the hard way up, when I was very young, in a very prestigious magazine and with a tough boss. That created a great sense of discipline in me and made me retain images. If I had any conflict at all, it was in how late I extricated myself to write fiction—but deep down I have no regrets. It's the time factor: the investigative journalism I like takes a lot of time, if you want to do it well. I hadn't the time to sit and write.

Between 1988 and 1989 the problems in Cuba started to get worse with the fall of the socialist camp and the dismantling of the Soviet Union as it had existed up until then. For that reason, as well as the U.S. economic embargo, many things were scarce, paper included. Almost all the newsprint was under contract from the Soviet Union. Then it had to be bought in hard currency. Hard currency is more important for food and medicine than for newsprint. There were cutbacks in magazine and newspaper publishing, resulting in a massive drop in the number of pages [column space] where I could write. I didn't lose my job, but my feature articles, which might have been a whole page of the Saturday edition, or two pages, or a series, were reduced to sixty lines. That's how I had a lot of time. And since I don't like to be without doing something, I said to myself, this is my chance.

A theme I chose for my writings was one that had been going round in my head: the *mestizaje* [race mix] in the Americas. I come from the eastern part of the country, where the mix is much greater and more diverse. There's the Cuban Creole black, of both African and Cuban parentage, and the Cuban Creole black mixed with the Creole black from Jamaica, Haiti, Barbados, etc. Santiago de Cuba is the most Caribbean city of Cuba. There's the mix with the French who arrived in waves after the Haitian Revolution. There's a mixture of French whites with Spanish whites, and, among the Spaniards, of Gallicians with Catalans. It's a big melting pot. And all those groups left their mark on Cuban culture. Some left the way of cooking *congrí* [rice with black beans], others a form of speech, or a way of serving table. For example, in Santiago de Cuba there's a custom of having soup, or consommé, with a meal, which is from the French.

My grandmother, my mother's mother, was black and born of the free belly.[1] That is, her parents were slaves. She was born in 1886. I knew her; she lived until 1958. She would tell us stories about slavery. Her sister was born a slave and cut cane as a slave in the Matanzas area. All those things stuck in my mind and I wanted to write something about it.

During the Special Period, journalists were given the chance to choose one of two courses, English or computing. I took computing, which gave me the idea of structuring the novel *El colompio de Rey Spencer* (Rey Spencer's Swing)—Rey, a Spanish surname, and Spencer, an English one—in which Lala, the computer, allowed me to play with time and gave me information about the waves of immigrants. But that isn't the first novel I wanted to write. It's the one I've just finished. I wanted to do a trilogy about *mestizaje* in the Americas set in three epochs, one around the eighteenth and nineteenth centuries, although it might have something contemporary; another at the start of the twentieth century; and a third, more contemporary one. The first, on the eighteenth and nineteenth centuries, required a lot of research. Each time I was sent to Spain as a journalist to cover cultural events, I would escape off to the Archive of the Indies in Seville looking for information on the theme of *mestizaje* in the Americas, because I love reading about history.

In a series of volumes on overseas laws, I discovered the Spanish royal *cédulas* on governing the Indies. The archive is very modern but I needed time to ground the research. I felt I needed more elements. So I put that one off and wrote the novel that chronologically would have been the second. The one I have just finished has taken more years than the first.

The novel has two provisional titles, I haven't yet decided on which. It's called *Papeles de blanco* (White Papers) or *Santa lujuria* (Holy Lust [the published title]). The novel is based on the overseas laws recognizing Spanish and white Creole *mestizaje* in Ibero-America with Indian, black, *mestizo,* and mulatto women. There was a privilege contained in a royal *cédula* of Carlos IV in 1795, which was called *Gracias al Sacar.*

This isn't to say that it didn't happen before but up until then it was a very specific prerogative in a very specific case, which is where the legislation came from. *Gracias al Sacar* is a duty set out in one of the last articles: for the dispensation of quarteroon or quinteroon, the applicant must pay 600, 800, or 1,200 *réales* [Spanish silver coins of the time]. That's to say, there was a price. For the title of *don,* it was so much, for military titles so much; the ascent of *mestizos,* whites from Indians and blacks from Indians in Spanish colonial society had its price. If a Spaniard wanted to provide a son with a black, mulatto, or Indian woman with white status, he would buy the papers and legally the son was white, though he might be our color.

What did this mean, according to my studies? In that way, the father, whether Spaniard or Creole, would guarantee the social and economic ascent of the son. The Spaniards even had laws for that—*pardo* was a mulatto of lineage, because the mulatto son of a poor white and a poor black was just mulatto, while the mulatto son of a father who was a *don* was a *pardo.*[2] And a free black wasn't just a black but a *moreno.* That was Spanish colonial society and its laws.

Free *pardos* could not practice certain professions, for example, certain positions in the clergy, or bookkeeper, or scribe; a woman could not embroider for the church, could not make jewelry, for that they had to be white. But if they had white papers, they could be scribes, lawyers, jewelers, or any other profession. It was an entry into society by the economic/work route for the children they wished to benefit—not all of them, but there were many. The Archive of the Indies is full of requests and granting of white status. Contrary to the Anglo-Saxons, in these Hispanic colonies, a drop of white made you white more than black, the reverse of over there.

It's so complex and so funny, you find incredible contradictions. And that was the novel I wanted to write first, and finally did write. I needed more detail, examples, because it's not a book of essays, I wanted to recreate the history, basing it on a true story, and so spent many years looking for ideas in characters who had existed. For example, in the history of Cuba there are various cases, like the painter Vicente Escobar, whom the books describe as "the painter who was born black and died white." A great painter of colonial Cuba, a *pardo* from Havana. He was a magnificent portrait painter. He could paint someone just by looking at him. He did many very fine paintings of captain generals. One of them wanted Escobar to go to the court to paint some Spanish nobility, but he couldn't because he was *pardo.* So he bought Escobar his white papers and he went to paint the court.

All this has a lot to do with Cuba of before, but also Cuba of today and Cuba always—especially Cuba, followed by the Dominican Republic, Venezuela, Brazil, Colombia, and others. For example, in revolutionary Cuba, when you go to get your I.D. card, the enumerator looks and you say "white" and he or she writes "white." That's enough. You're a shade light and they put *trigueño* and don't check whether your mother is black or dark mulatto. They look at your features and straight hair, and that's it.

Since the royal *cédula Gracias al Sacar,* the censuses never increased the number of blacks, of coloreds, proportionally. They began to decrease or increase those who passed for white. And it'll always be like that because of those who pass. You have to be real black not to pass, some because they want to, others just because they're seen as white. They're white on paper. Now you don't have to buy it, it's down to consumer taste.

I don't think that anomaly is ever going to change, because it's now part of Hispanic American culture. What we have to understand is that our countries are really an amalgam. In my novel I mock the elegant form of Cuban whiteness, not the passing, but the whiteness of Cubans, because it doesn't exist. I take as the novel's paradigm, not the painter I mentioned, but an individual who was the sum of that classification, a very famous lawyer called Francisco Filomeno Ponce de Léon y Criloche, second- or third-line descendant of the discoverer of Florida, Ponce de Léon. This was the son of Don Antonio Ponce de Léon y Morato, with the title of Grande de España, which was given the descendants of conquistadors, and was the most grandiose in Spanish lineage.

The son of Don Antonio—he had a son with a mulatto hairdresser—the boy was very intelligent and he wanted to help him get on, so he sent off for his papers. Much of the social and racial passing was done in St. Augustine, Florida, a Spanish possession that was a replica of Havana. In fact, it belonged to and was a part of Havana. When there were children a little confusing in color terms, they would go there and the first title they would acquire would be in language and interpretation. The elite Havana families would forget about the son of Don Fulano. When the son returned from Florida, he'd be sent to Spain for a time, or any other Spanish American possession, and come back "whitened," as a linguist or lawyer with some standing and an entry into society. He would marry white, and have other *mestizo* children, but would now be a *señor.*

That was the practice in Cuba and in other regions of Spain, but in Cuba was where it most occurred because of Spanish colonial rule up until 1898, which was when the war came to an end. In South America it ended in the early nineteenth century, but here it was only yesterday, you might say. My own grandmother, my mother's mother, was born of the free belly and lived until 1958.

And my novel deals with those things. I mock the whiteness of the *señor* I recreate, because it's not that there exists a biography of Ponce de León, but it's true that he was the *mestizo* son of the other Ponce de León and was put in the Casa de Beneficencia, the orphanage.[3] He was just named Francisco Filomeno and baptized twice, because he was baptized in the Beneficencia and was then baptized again to inherit. He was baptized as the son of the wife who had died seventeen years previously—which means a dead woman had given birth to him. That was done on paper, in Spain, and nothing happened. That's why the notion of whitening is ingrained in people, even though it's not institutionalized. Before the revolution, there was the institutional backdrop of the state and government to maintain the modus vivendi. Today that no longer exists. On the contrary, today institutionally we have what is laid out in the Constitution, equality among human beings and the eradication of racism, racial discrimination; and everybody has the same institutional rights.

There is what a Cuban ethnologist has called the informal networks—if you're my friend I'll get you in here or there—but that has no institutional backing. It seems to me that poking fun and saying "you're not white" is what hurts whites more than thinking it. And this is the first time this has been a theme in Cuban literature. I don't think of anyone in Cuba as white.

Of course, all these elements have motivated me to write a very contemporary novel which reflects life as it is today in Cuban society. My aim is to follow the same theme in my third novel, but in a contemporary setting, with that skin color on the I.D., but always poking fun. In the case of *White Papers,* Francisco Filomeno, who becomes a Spanish *grande,* with all that lineage, cannot extricate himself from his origins and (now in the early nineteenth century) he begins to fear he will have taken from him the amulet his slave grandmother made him, because he thinks that if it is taken he will lose his powers. He feels tied to the canon of his ancestors and always will be. He's a man who is neither one thing nor the other; he's a Cuban who has that umbilical cord.

5

The Dead Come at Midnight

Scripting the White Aesthetic/Black Ethic

Eliseo Altunaga

Eliseo Altunaga is a university graduate in Hispanic language and literature, a television and film scriptwriter and novelist, and more recently public relations representative for the Pablo Milanés Foundation. Created in Havana in June 1993 by the famous Cuban mulatto singer-composer for whom it was named, the foundation was dissolved in June 1995 by then Minister of Culture Armando Hart, in what has been described as a "coup d'etat" while Milanés was on tour in Spain. No reasons were ever given publicly, but many artists and intellectuals concur that the decision was rooted in the incompetence of the Ministry of Culture in dealing with a foundation that from the outset was defined as an autonomous, nongovernmental organization, and which de facto challenged the ministry's cultural monopoly. Other cultural circles insinuate that it was also because Milanés favored blacks and Afro-Cuban culture. This was very significant, in a period that was witnessing a renaissance of black Cuban spiritual and cultural values. Foundation personnel were in the main black and its orientation was toward Afro-Cuban cultural values, which Santiago-born Pablo Milanés had always espoused. It was fitting that Eliseo Altunaga—known to his friends as "the Ethiopian," given his physical appearance—should have been close to Milanés in the foundation. All of Altunaga's work is marked by the anxiety, anguish almost, of disentangling the uncertainty enveloping blacks in Cuba. His most recent novel, *A medianoche llegan los muertos* (The Dead Come at Midnight), brings to life decisive moments in Cuba's nineteenth-century history involving Cuba's "Bronze Titan" Antonio Maceo. As we were sipping coffee in his home south of Havana, Altunaga started this interview outlining his approach to a historical reconstruction of Maceo's enigmatic human profile. (PPS)

EA: *The Dead Come at Midnight* is a novel about Cuba's national hero Antonio Maceo. Maceo's mainly known as a warrior, or rather he's been given the image of a warrior, and only that, when in reality he was an entrepreneur, a man of ideas, a political figure. Maceo was a man whose political acumen made him even the idol of young aristocrats, of young whites of the Cuban bourgeoisie of the time who had differences with Spain. His general staff was known to include educated white Cubans and Spaniards in dispute with the Spanish regime. It should not be forgotten that in those years—1868–98—Gallicians, Asturians, Catalans, poor Spaniards, and other nationals were imported in large numbers, to whiten the country. In the eastern part of the island especially, there was a visible disproportion. Out of a population of some 2 million, the immigration was over 300,000. At the turn of the century, a third of the Cuban population was white. Those who were imported were helped in setting up businesses, etc. And the 1912 war of repression on blacks changed the agrarian structure of the country. Blacks who had land in 1912 had it taken away from them. The black who was liberated from slavery was totally marginalized in the republic. A physical terror was sown, people were assassinated, and the terror became engraved in memory. The fear and terror remained, as did the submission to white canon.

This intensified during the republic, and maintained a segregation—a segregation of apparent equals but a tangible segregation. There were places where blacks couldn't go. That's to say, there were places for whites where blacks weren't allowed in. There were many regulations to keep blacks out. That's why the novel deals with this problem, which I think is swept under the carpet, because the criterion was that by changing the social order, the social superorder, what's called the superstructure, consciousness, or ways of seeing, things would change. But these elements don't change on their own, because ideas don't give way spontaneously—aesthetic ideas, cultural ideas, plus their support base.

The best houses, the best schools, easy access to information, culture, and wealth were not within the power of blacks. It was always the case that for blacks to achieve demanded an additional effort within Cuban culture. Antonio Maceo was a hero, a war general, who always needed to take more care than a white general in his relations with the government. Against him, suspicions were even written. When Maceo produced the paper of the Liberation Army, the president of the republic was furious and said, "It looks like the ant wants to grow wings." He added, "Isn't he aware of his color . . . he should stay fighting."

In the novel, there's a character called Fico Castellanos who's the Cuban saccharocrat and who says that, too: "Tell him to stay fighting in Oriente." Maceo was a negotiating card, not a man who could partake of power, even when he had been a property owner, had a farm in Jamaica, a commune in Costa Rica, had drawn up a system of government by prefecture. These are things that are not known. Antonio Maceo is not known as a thinker. What is emphasized are his battles and some things are swept aside. There's a kind of cultural legacy, a historical legacy that I think hasn't been dissipated, we are lost in the labyrinth of feelings and do not go to the objective facts. History weighs down on us and, over and above sentiment and political will, determines the social structure in which the black moves. The black needs an additional effort. Often there's a chain of errors attributed to him, but they are no more than the product of circumstances in which the black takes on a certain social hierarchy with excess effort and excess elements against him.

These are the themes of the novel *The Dead Come at Midnight,* and also the present one, which is a postmodernist novel on two narrative planes: that of today, and that of the nineteenth century, 1912 and 1930. I think in this novel it is much more evident, because there are also scenes of the blacks who took part in the August 1994 demonstrations, which was unusual. There are moments when these are interconnected, directly or indirectly, which lend atmosphere, give an idea of things that happened, that are floating in an atmosphere that has remained hidden, that functions beneath the Cuban discourse. The Cuban says one thing, but does another. The black speaks but behind the rhetoric there's a world of frustrations, violence, and discrimination, but that's not said, or seen. For example, there's a white woman who lives in a building on Seafront Drive watching the August 1994 demonstrations, and when she sees there are blacks, she says, "How can they, if I gave up my creams and my clubs, if I did it, how can those blacks rally against the government that has given them power? For the first time they were allowed into public places, for the first time they could go to the beaches, they're a pack of good-for-nothings, they should be shot, they should all leave!"

But that same woman is the granddaughter of a slaveholder who sexually used a slave. She's the niece of Fico Castellanos who, in the 1912 Black War, helped a mulatto woman with whom he had a son. There's this Cuban *mestizaje* which has that mix of abolition—the idea "for the good of the black"—but also racism. There's this countercurrent: people can want socially good things for blacks and yet still be racist in sentiment. They see blacks as different, inferior, as in need of help—"That poor black needs help!"—but they continue to think of him as inferior and that's the underlying thread to the novel.

At the end of the novel, Spanish General Arsenio Martínez Campos flees Colón, which was a historical fact. Martínez Campos does not take on Antonio Maceo. Why doesn't he? "Where would Spain be if an uncouth black, a *mestizo*, does me in? Where would I be, what would become of *hispanidad*, of culture?" What I am saying in a way is that the elevation of a black in evidence as a hero and conqueror in the face of Spain would have been a debacle not only for Cuban saccarocrat thinking, or the most reactionary Cubans, but also a debacle for this country's concept of *hispanidad*.

PPS: What relationship do you see between the Africanness of Cubans and their concept of *hispanidad*?

EA: This is a complex problem. The first factor I see from my perspective is that blacks had to express themselves in a language that was not their own. The tool of knowledge and communication that blacks who came from Africa had to use was a language that was not their own. It was a language they had to learn, and adapt to, and it was what they had to express themselves in. This basic element of language was to be very important in the sociopsychological formation of the black. The first thing blacks lose is their language. The amazing thing about it is that for centuries blacks did not know their language, because they kept the original languages of their ancestors and repeated them without knowing what they meant, in Cuban cultural rituals, whether religious or forms of expression blacks had repressed until not long ago. Even after the revolution black religious and cultural forms were repressed, not only the more sophisticated forms, such as religious ones, but also musical forms—*guaguancó*, rumba, and *son* were considered immoral.

To play *guaguancó* or rumba you had to have a police permit, and it was considered, especially in Oriente, something sinful, criminal even. Even Fernando Ortiz's point of departure for studying the black was criminality. That's an important point. Another important and complex factor is that many of the Spanish nationals who came to Cuba were against Spain, they were nationals discriminated against in Spain, and with those feelings of discrimination, those Spanish nationals, especially in the nineteenth century, allied with blacks. They didn't feel Spanish. Castilians who were in power under Ferdinand VII discriminated against a Catalan as much as a mulatto. That's why many Spaniards joined Antonio Maceo, because they themselves felt the discrimination. Others are the nonwhites, like the Canary Islanders, who are totally white but African, with a culture that is neither Saxon nor Germanic, but *mestizo*.

And then the Spaniards weren't the worst. The Creoles were. The Spaniards used the black fear, used the fear of the Haitian Revolution and the white man's supremacy as an element to uphold colonialism in Cuba, the last of the Spanish colonies to gain its freedom. But this was propped up by the wealth of the saccarocracy, who were culturally superior to the Spanish, for they had studied biology, medicine, and chemistry in France; machine technology in Germany; banking in England; and sugar technology in the United States. They were very cultured because the sugar industry in Europe developed in a complex commercial and technological world, and yet on the island they were absolutely reactionary in relation to the great mass of people who were powerless.

I think the term "Afro-Cuban" is exclusionary, the idea that there was a white Cuban and a black African, when the Cuban is what matters, the hybrid meeting of European and African cultures. I would call this new entity and culture, which is marginalized, "Afro-European." Even the language is Afro-European, because beneath the semantics the rhythm is African. The change from the "r" to the "l" word endings comes from Bantú and other African languages. They are equally foreign and imported, joining the European modeling the language. There's a Cuban form of speech, there's a Cuban rhythm. The links are not only in the change in syntax and semantics but the rhythms, also to be found in Cuban music.

There's something else that's important in relation to *hispanidad,* which is that the Spaniards considered the arts in Cuba to be of a lesser nature. So for many years the artists in Cuba, those who shaped the Cuban spiritual world, were the blacks. There are things that aren't known. For example, Bishop Espada ordered all the altars of Cuba to be burned and replaced by neoclassical altars. Why? Because the blacks were the ones who carved those altars. When the San Alejandro Art School was founded, Bishop Espada fought for the arts to be considered important and blacks were immediately excluded. But blacks were the ones doing the virgins and the saints, as in Brazil. In Cuba that disappeared completely. Or did it? No, a substratum continued. The best Cuban sculpture is black—Agustín Cárdenas.[1] Where did Cárdenas get that from? There was an undercurrent that's been repressed, and it was never told in the history of Cuba that it had been repressed. That's why we might say there's no transparent Spain in Cuba. In Cuba there's only a Spanish mix. One of the obsessions has always been to seek a purity of Spanish influence in Cuba, a cleansing of the European elements in Cuban culture. But it's not like that. The black is ever present, though marginalized and hidden. Except in those areas where it is very evident, as in Wifredo Lam's painting, in the work of René Portocarrero, or in the work of Cárdenas, it's played down, and there's a perpetual quest for purity. The best Cuban painter of all time has been Wifredo Lam, son of a black woman and Chinese man . . . and the painter best known in and out of Cuba today is black, Manuel Mendive.[2]

I think there was always the obsession to marginalize the features evidencing the presence of hegemony of a culture that had an African legacy in Cuba and to take the most superficial and banal elements, the most evident, to corrupt and sell: the more frivolous aspects of Santería, for example, or the myth of the mulatto or black woman as a sexual object. There was always the attempt to emphasize the black as that. I think we have to separate out what is and what isn't considered black, which is highly complex. The emphasis is always what's most evidently black: rumba, *comparsa*, Santería. When they were doing the buildings for the 1991 Pan American Games and laying the concrete in the stadium, some of the black construction workers didn't like the finished forms and broke the linearity with curves. That's an element among black construction workers, which is much more mysterious and hidden than any being. That's hard to see. I think Cuban culture has not begun to see things in such a way. The Cuban gestures—when you recognize a white Cuban, in what way is he different from a Spaniard? What is it? It's a trace that isn't so evident and requires the will to find it. Alicia Alonso, director of the National Ballet of Cuba, has said that "what makes the Cuban is a gesture that is different." Where does that come from? What is it that is Cuban in that gesture, where does that movement come from, how can whites and blacks dance together to the rhythm of the drums at a Young Communist League party? Who nurtures that in people, and what's more, where does that drum come from? Where does that rhythm of the men and women come from? I firmly believe there's a will to deny that. Of course, now everything's rarefied with the rise of postmodernism and the incorporation of discriminated cultures into the creative cultural universe of the young who respond not to institutional but aesthetic trends, as the bearers of our country's culture, of popular culture, incorporating all the mystery and all those things in a way that you can't say there's exclusion, because it's there in their work. The Cuban visual arts of the 1980s had the mystery and all that, but they were already macerated. It's not only the traces. I think traces are a trap.

PPS: Is this perhaps a form of cultural repression that mutilated individuals' need to struggle together against these ills?

EA: There've certainly been forms of hegemonic repression, both direct and cultural. I started saying that speaking out about the forms of repression was already a problem. A Catholic priest of whatever political persuasion was recognized as a respectable person. A Presbyterian, a Baptist was recognized as a respectable person, but a Babalawo was not. The Babalawo was considered almost a criminal. Nobody in a given institution could put on any document of importance that he was a follower of a Babalawo, no matter whether the Babalawo was the spiritual father of 10,000 or 100,000 Cubans, black and white. Even if the Babalawo was doing transcendental social work in the community, institutions within the power structure took a negative view of the Babalawo. In the same way, from an aesthetic point of view, having a mother with a flat nose, thick lips, and short kinky hair wasn't the same as being the daughter of a mulatto woman. A minister didn't put a black woman with short kinky hair and a flat nose in his office; he had a fair-skinned woman there. These are forms of repression. Being white and fair and Germanic gave you a social merit the other didn't have; being black and flat-nosed with kinky hair meant having a lot against you — and still does.

I could give you the example of people living in neighborhoods like Kholy or Nuevo Vedado and people living in marginal neighborhoods, or in slum areas, who are for the most part black, when those living in the other areas are white. The habitat in which you live comprises a system of relations, a system where the young know each other, a system of how they are valued, independently of having the same access or same rights and obligations before the law, but not society. It isn't the same for the youth whose father has a car as for the youth whose father goes on foot or by bus. His effort is greater, his is a whole other world of reference.

That's the world my novels are about, not only a world of traces, of folklorism. Why is it mainly black women who are going with Europeans and why are they considered the most erotic when they come from the least favored sector, with less access to money, to the dollar? Until 1994, or until Mariel in 1980, the majority of people leaving for the United States were white, some 90 to 95 percent. It's after Mariel that there's an exodus of blacks, and in 1994 there's a mass of young blacks who leave for lack of an alternative, because they can see no light at the end of the tunnel, and if they see it they think it won't last and won't ever be for them . . . and because on top of everything else, in the United States there have also been changes for blacks. That's another problem. Blacks in the United States today have access where they didn't in 1960–70. Cuban blacks know that and emigrate. There's the whole power structure, too. There's a meeting of the unions, and the leadership is 90 percent white. . . .

PPS: You just mentioned the events of summer 1994 in Havana. Can you go into your view of what happened?

EA: Blacks of other generations one way or another used to see, or still see, the revolution as an important leap forward in comparison with the situation in the 1950s. Blacks at the grass roots took the change of the revolution as a promise, a hope for their situation. And although many measures mainly favored the middle class, blacks were an active part of the revolution. There was a feeling of gratitude to the revolution for having realized some of the ideas that hadn't been seen crystalized by black struggle, whether by black trade union leaders, the Liberation Army, black associations, or even the House of Representatives when they had access during World War II. The revolution was linked to the efforts of black leaders like Jesús Menéndez and Aracelio Iglesias,[3] who were discriminated against and repressed by the Creole state, and whose struggle the revolution took on. I think it isn't the same with the younger generation. They grew up during the revolution, and don't feel a gratitude but rather perceive a link of equality and yet don't feel equal. They feel they're not equal, because there are masses of young blacks who live in overcrowded places they'll possibly never get out of, and if they do it'll be in twenty or thirty years when the best years of their lives are behind them.

I wrote an article about that. I think there's a dual manipulation: one, that blacks can only be living in slums or living in this society and not leaving; and two, that if they could reach the United States they'd have the things they'd always dreamed of having. The power structure painted the U.S. way of life as unattainable. Ideologically, the United States was the worst place in the world, but from the viewpoint of the conduct of the middle to top bureaucracy, those who had a videocassette, a car, a good house with air-conditioning, films that they passed around among themselves, music that was played . . . all that pointed to the U.S. way of life as the model, in which blacks also played a role, because blacks have been incorporated into the image. I think that group on the one hand sold the image that it was bad, but on the other had a lifestyle, conduct, and aesthetic model, a mode of functioning that was the American way of life. The reasoning was: "To have a car, a cassette player, which is what those in power have, I can get that by taking to sea, and leaving." Besides the desperation, the other reasoning was: "I don't have access to that." The ideological model was one of sacrifice, but the other's son had those things, without sacrifice. There was a contradiction between what was put forward and what was done, which is part of the double standard that was so criticized by young artists of the 1980s, black and white. While those factors continue, society has changed, and there are now whole sectors that have been displaced, and former bureaucrats who are now part of the masses. They are taxi drivers, craftsmen, caterers . . . there's been a social upheaval that has brought change. I can't say the same now as ten years ago, when there were sectors crystalized where everyone was basically white, or white-skinned, though *mestizo,* which is what Cuba is as a whole.

PPS: The year 1996 marks the fall of the "Bronze Titan." How do you see Cuba and Cubans and the racial problem in these fateful years of the end of the century? Is it really a problem?

EA: I think, and I may be wrong but I'm as yet to be convinced I'm wrong, that the only possibility in the face of neoliberalism and the economic changes the country is having to undergo, given the international situation, the development of communication, and the life of the nation, the Cuban nation, if it is to be a nation, is to recognize itself or perish. Harry Belafonte said to me, "It's better that you choose who you want as friends and which models you want, rather than waiting for the door to open, because then the avalanche will be so violent there won't be time to think."

I think that the negation of any of the components of Cuban culture and the obstinate desire to marginalize a component that has been forged, wishing only to select four or five features—music, poetry, Santería, rhythm—as what is black in Cuban culture, weakens that culture terribly. I think they have no alternative but to look at themselves in the mirror; if they want to perpetuate themselves as a nation, the members of that nation must recognize themselves as black as much as white.

What is black in Cuba resides in the spirituality of Cubans and is expressed in their food and clothing, in their way of seeing the world, speaking Spanish, using music. I think the black is what makes Cuba different from Spain and from Europe. It's what the black put in the pot, it's what the black changed. I think that the Cuban black is not African, nor is the Cuban white European. I think the Cuban white is black and that the Cuban black is white, and the idea of a *mestizo* society is the only one that can save the nation. I think the Cuban has a white aesthetic and a black ethic. This is where the struggle lies. There is the idea that a man who looks in the mirror and won't recognize himself for what he is, is weakened by that. I honestly think that one of the ways Cuba can be salvaged as a nation—when all economies are the same, money is the same, commercial values and cultural cosmopolitanism are the same—is recognizing it is black.

6

Todo en Sepia
An All-Black Theater Project

Elvira Cervera

Her full name is Tita Elvira Cervera Batte, but she is known simply as Elvira Cervera, radio, television, and film actress. She was born 4 January 1923 in Sagua la Grande, only three months after radio was first heard in Cuba on the afternoon of 10 October 1922. Consequently, the radio receiver was part and parcel of Elvira's childhood. She still remembers the family listening to the fights of the legendary black Cuban boxer, "Kid" Chocolate. When I first met her in the Havana winter of 1995, she described what had drawn her into the performing arts. Her father, a construction worker, would rub cooking oil on his hands and arms to loosen the lime before bathing. While he was doing this, he would have his daughters read to him, maybe one of Aesop's fables. Then they would reflect on the moral of the story. Thus Elvira formed the habit of spending her free time reading out loud. She realized she had potential, took part in a competition, and won. She remembers with irony how the studio broke out in laughter because "the *negrita* [little black girl] had won a perm," but she decided right there and then she'd be a radio actress. In 1995, when this interview was conducted, the seventy-two-year-old veteran black actress had just launched Todo en Sepia (All in Sepia), an all-black drama project designed "to break the apartheid that prevents the black actor from taking on roles of world theater," proposing "to create a show for actors . . . to document, analyze, denounce and reject the evident limitations on the dark-skinned actor professionally on the Cuban stage (theater, cinema and television), with casts of only black actors." That evening in her Havana home, she reflected on what had led her to take this step. (PPS)

So, blacks learn to read and write, become educated and cultured, and then find culture is denied them. In this, the mass media play a very important role, imparting a general vision, a mass subliminal vision, which is constantly lacerating the self-esteem of the black, both as actor and spectator. Blacks are constantly being told they are neither beautiful, nor feeling, nor able to interpret the classics, and that a romantic couple has to be white and fair, and so the black couple is merely picturesque—as is the noisy, funny, laughable black with no developed character. And I ask myself, how can this be after so many years when all the progressive movements in this country have held up the banner of black struggle and proclaimed that when the left took power the black would be revindicated? Suddenly I find that revindicating the black means home, food, and clean clothing, because what I'm asking for seems to be excessive—because what I've been demanding for fifty-seven years, including thirty-six years of revolution, is to see the black problem as a national Cuban problem. How can you use the black as a banner all these years and the moment you're in power all the talk is of blacks redeemed: "because they were starving to death and now they're not," because they're economically OK, or because they're in the professions, which is true, when blacks were conspicuously absent before, such as in banking or as drivers. . . . But is that black revindication? That's not in the spirit of Martí's thinking. As Fidel said in "History Will Absolve Me,"[1] on José Martí's centennial, it was as if the Apostle were to die all over again. But this time it seems that this is effectively going to happen without these issues of black revindication being resolved. We know the problem is complex and not easy to solve, it's not solved by laws, or anything drastic, but it does have to be established as a problem. That's all I want, that they stop being ostriches sticking their heads in the sand each time they're told there's a black problem, simply because they don't want to deal with it.

Raquelita Mayedo is the moderator for *Contacto* (Contact), a prime-time television program. All the blacks who appear on *Contact* fear the word "black" and are incapable of being up-front. I've never been on *Contact* . . . . I was called to do an interview for *Teleavance* (Previews). *Previews* never does interviews. It was a way of seeing what I would say in the interview. They don't want things said up front. And for me that's skirting the issue.

I have a letter I sent to historian Vicente González Castro, on the forty-five years of Cuban television, for which there was a very good and interesting gala not long ago. I wrote, "I once read that history was the service record of the winners and since I have just heard that you are writing about the 45-year history of Cuban television, I'm sending you the daughter of the losers, those who didn't win the battle." And I wrote about the blacks, the losers, those who didn't win. I gave their names, and in such a way that the director had to say, "You've presented such a convincing case, there can be no disputing it." I can give you the example of Natasha Díaz, and a top-rated actress, Susana Pérez. The two started out with the same novel, by Cirilo Villaverde. They both got off to a good start, because it was clear that they were both talented, and also attractive and young. Now they're older. Susana has acted a host of romantic novels which have allowed her to develop and demonstrate her talent. The other has had only secondary roles. You have to ask why the two have developed so differently.

A bit of history is needed here. When Comandante Jorge Serguera was director of the Cuban Broadcasting Institute, he started to recast Cuban television. Anyone in the institute in those days can tell you how he brought in former military service recruits. "You're a man?" he'd say. "Then come to put an end to these *maricones* [queers] we have over here in TV." Some of the young men had talent—and not all of them, it should be said, were "men." But that happened. A very good actor, Serafín García, told me the other day that his grounding came from the volume of programs done by those, like him, who were recruited from military service. Then there's the case of an actor who is older like me, well, perhaps a little younger, Jorge Prieto. I exaggerated when I said Prieto is an actor who for 364 days was sitting out on the bench and on day 365 was given the part of Jesús Menéndez.[2] Even today the in-jokes are the anticommunist Jesús Menéndez he did. There was no acting. For an actor, to act is tremendously important professionally; it is in the exercise of any discipline, but especially in the performing arts. While the military service kid gets thirty-two serials, plus all the other programs he did, another who has had no acting gets a figure like Jesús Menéndez. What I say is that those who brought in the military service kids prioritized discrimination against homosexuals over the struggle against racial discrimination, because blacks were never given the opportunities those kids had.

That's the argument I put to the drama director, who was very pleasant and receptive, but spent an hour and a half trying to convince me that I not call my project All in Sepia, and that it not be with all black actors, which was to combat one error with another. But you can't have happening to black actors what happened to poor Jorge Prieto. He couldn't do such an important part well, because he'd been 364 days on standby. With All in Sepia, we want to give them what others have had.

And if TV programming and films made by the Cuban Film Institute (ICAIC) have all fair-skinned casts, what right have they to tell me not to do it with all dark-skinned ones? What is it they want, an aesthetic explanation? There is the aesthetic explanation, but the other, the social, is that blacks should have the opportunity to work, that is not there in the current stage apartheid—and I include the thirty-six years of revolution, and incredibly in this year of the centennial of José Martí's death. That's why I won't be on *Contact,* why all the hullabaloo about not having me talk—and why that good lady, who was very kind, helpful even, spent an hour and a half trying to convince me I should not do All in Sepia, unless I gave it another name and integrated black and white casts. In the first place, we'd have to do what they do, which is a caricature, that's to say, giving lead roles to blacks and having the whites play maids and slaves, but I don't want to get into all that. I think, like Sara Gómez, that this has to hit home.[3]

Revista Prometeo (Prometheus Review), Year III, February-April 1950, published in Havana:

Elvira Cervera was the great theater promise of the recently created GEL Group. . . . The tremendous personality of this black actress made its mark on an audience hovering between being skeptical and amazed, and, of course, unaccustomed to the experience.

Black theater, which in other countries, North America for example, has made great stage contributions, is a novelty among us. With the drive of those who are starting out, GEL Group made its debut with *Before Breakfast,* O'Neill's difficult monologue that actress Marisabel Saenz made famous.

O'Neill was the trampoline for Elvira Cervera's stage revelation. Audience surprise and skepticism turned to admiration and a final burst of applause for the actress. But if this is Elvira Cervera's stage revelation, it's nowhere near her first theatrical part. A proven radio actress since 1938, when she won the Martínez Casado's contest on Radio Progreso, she has since consolidated her artistic prestige with her full, rich and deeply moving radio voice on CMQ Red Wave and RHC.

Why do I have a right to say what I do? Because I started out in 1938. There was no TV, of course, but there was radio . . . and I faced fierce racial discrimination. I remember a Spanish actress like Pilar Bermúdez objecting to a Cuban actress like Marta Casañas because she had kinky hair. She said, "How can they bring that woman here, with that curly hair showing she's *mestiza*!" She was a Spanish woman who was opposed to a presumably mixed-race woman being an actress on Radio CHIC, as it was called. At that time, on Mil Diez (Thousand Ten), the Popular Socialist Party station, there were two of us who were black. One was a very good actor, dead now, who later became a comic actor playing tame TV blacks, with Garrido y Piñero, and all that . . . a black actor talking *bozalonzón* (slave talk or black talk). That was in 1943, when people were coming back from Europe, talking about Paris and Picasso and African beauty.

A year after I graduated from the Havana teacher training school, Thousand Ten radio station went on the air. That was one of my more interesting experiences, and where I chose to channel my career. I had won a prestigious contest, in which many performing artists took part, the majority of them going on to brilliant careers. It was also a station with a difference, with social concerns, sensitive to popular aspirations. My link with Thousand Ten was the great sugar leader, Jesús Menéndez, who was married to my cousin. The two of them were very good friends of mine.

I signed a radio contract with minimum wage and with no great enthusiasm on the part of management. We were the two blacks among the founding cast. On more than one occasion we were interviewed by the party paper and the point was made that Thousand Ten employed black actors. In the case of my fellow black actor, he fitted the bill perfectly. One of his first parts was a vernacular character, Cicerón Toruga. Television still hadn't arrived but later that magnificent actor, who is now dead, did prime TV comic slots interpreting a philosophically tame character, though he did it charismatically.

I don't think I personally fitted what was expected of a black. My stamp was not marketable as an interesting and exotic product. I was an ordinary young black woman whose only merit was oral expression and being able to interpret with feeling the parts I was given. I had the basic conditions for a radio actress, the kind of conditions that launched many white or lighter-skinned actresses on brilliant careers, but I was evidently of no interest to anyone. Maybe they were bothered by that "fine" young black woman who "played whites." My good pronunciation, my deep yet ringing voice, and a certain perfectionism of language, all obviously went against me. Possibly unconsciously, it was thought that the color of my skin should condition my way of acting. I bear the personal limitation evidently atypical of blacks: I like all kinds of music, but I have no aptitude for singing or dancing. I was in my element in radio drama, interpreting authors unknown to me but who wrote in a language in which I was a perfectionist—Alvarez Quintero, Benavente, Ibsen, Molière, or García Lorca.

I only remember two regular parts on Thousand Ten. One was offered by the late actor Eduardo Casado and consisted of a delightful narration of stories by Guy de Maupassant, Somerset Maugham, and others, adapted for radio. The other was presenter of the radio news slot *Doctrina y acción* (Doctrine and Action). Not long after, the main presenter, whose voice identified the station, was signed up by one of the big stations. They tested for her successor and I'm told that when they heard my recordings I was singled out as the best. Even so, a few days later a white actress and presenter of debatable talent was given the job. Now, with hindsight, I think that, although Thousand Ten was a station proud of its progressive ideology, it also felt obliged to its few sponsors, who wouldn't have been pleased by the presence of a black voice regularly identifying the name of the station.

Disillusioned, I decided to leave the station and go into primary teaching. Among those I told about my decision and the reasons for doing so was my friend Jesús Menéndez. A few days later, Lázaro Peña, then a House representative, a person I didn't know and with whom I had no political link, came to my house and brought me a rural teaching post which I gratefully accepted.[4]

The little rural school was rife with difficulties for pupils and teacher who had to travel long distances. Yet for me it had its charm, like the peasant child's readiness to help and the possibility of teaching something that might be of use. But their work at home or in the fields held them back from coming to school and conspired against my efforts. There was a very blonde little girl who didn't come to school often, but when she did seemed to enjoy class. When she didn't come over a number of days, I went by her shack to find out why. She was on her own, looking after her little sister, because the rest of the family was off at the coast charcoal burning.

Those rural schools were an unforgettable experience. During the week I was a practicing rural teacher. On Saturdays, I'd attend the Faculty of Pedagogy at the University of Havana to consolidate my teacher training, with the intention of competing for a primary teacher post nearer to the capital. Long before that happened, I had gone back to broadcasting for minor stations. Meanwhile, I spent my days in the rural areas, on local transport, on horseback, crossing streams that became rivers during the rains, cutting across farms whose gates I couldn't always manage to close on horseback. It was hard and made my nightly presence in the broadcasting studio almost heroic.

I remember one peasant whose gate I left open more than once. When he knew I was leaving for another school with better conditions, he was waiting for me on the path and shouted for all to hear: "Teacher, we'll be seeing whether the one who comes isn't as dark as you!" I stopped my horse short and when I had him face to face shouted out loud, too: "And we'll be seeing whether she, like me, can shit on your mother!" He never expected that kind of reply and I never expected I would ever say any such thing to anyone. But I didn't regret it and I don't to this day.

After my state of depression from leaving Thousand Ten and the unforgettable experience of working as a teacher with peasant children, I returned to the stage. The music station Radio Progreso, known then as Progreso Cubano, changed its programming from only music and I began as the protagonist of a radio soap in which I was one of a couple of lovers. For almost ten years I worked that show, along with others for the same station, with record audience ratings for such a second-rate station as Radio Progreso back then. Radio had become a commercial success. As audience ratings went up, powerful firms were more and more interested in buying air time. The first slot chosen for this was precisely my soap, *This Is Your Life*. We were immediately laid off and two stars put in our place. On one occasion a director desperately wanted me to take the part of a black slave whose speech was broken. According to him, I was an all-round actress. Curiously, all those years he'd been directing adaptations of world literature in which he'd never offered me a part.

My prolific time on Radio Progreso won me the affection of listeners that has lasted to this day. Already back then artists relied on big sponsors to promote them in the written press—photos, interviews, favorable reviews, and write-ups in dailies and specialized journals. I was never in sponsored slots and so what audiences knew and felt about me I'd had to earn myself.

Jesús Menéndez was assassinated on a weekend, which was not a working day, and I was able to go and meet the body as it was brought into Havana Train Station and accompany the cortege to the Capitol Building and funeral. Even so, I missed one day of classes, which was unusual for me, and I was taken aback by the virulence and obscenity of the anonymous aggression I received from people accusing me of being a communist.

I was married then to Enrique Alzugaray, a magnificent black actor poised to go far. He worked for various radio stations and when television started all he could get was a secondary part in a comic slot. He eventually emigrated to Venezuela in search of new horizons.

As I mentioned, I'm a founder of Cuban television. Early on, I had a lead role in a piece written by Manuel Moreno Fraginals, author of *The Sugarmill*. The part was Doña Giomar. Later, I worked for the Ministry of Education playing the black woman in the biography of Baudelaire. My work for Cuban television has been very varied, but, as programming increased, it became more noticeable that blacks were being typecast for the color of their skin as the historical figures of slaves or of pauper families. In the early days, there were no black presenters. The work I did for television was always with other visuals and my background voice. Once, a well-known soap company called me for a test. The tests were done with commercials read on camera. When I was finally accepted, I was given a script to follow. I was to be on camera washing clothes in a washtub. The jingle was sung praising the virtues of the soap. Needless to say, I didn't accept.

I think my bouts of rebellion like that, and the statements I'd make in the few interviews I was called on to do, earned me the reputation of being a communist, which I wasn't. I don't know if my inconformity was equated with communism or if I was simply being punished for being so bold. Whatever, my communist fame limited me a lot in my work. Paradoxically, years later, my denunciations of racial discrimination earned me more names and I kept coming up against hurdles in my professional career. That's why for ten years, between 1970–80, I decided to stop acting.

I've always thought that my great drawback in the media has been my continued determination to break with stereotypes. I never held back, as many other blacks did, from referring to racial discrimination as something we all had within us but that few referred to publicly. I could never stand paternalisms of speech such as "I had a nanny who was black" or "my best friend was black," or such praise as "black and ugly but really intelligent." They were often well-intentioned people, but racist all the same. I wasn't easy to deal with and for many really hard to understand.

It's unquestionably objective to point out how minimally dark-skinned actors are employed in our country, except in what our bitter humor has called the *negrometrajes*.[5] It's hard to find black actors on our television in nonvernacular comedy, in detective series (as police and not criminals), in world theater, or adaptations of major novels. You only have to switch on the TV or go to the cinema. What's happened with ICAIC? In the early years of the revolution and in the context of the struggles for freedom, the woman was the axis for the film *Lucía* by Humberto Solás: three episodes with a Cuban woman protagonist in three historical periods, the last characterized by the actress Aleida Legrá, who is a *mestizo* woman. Nearly thirty years later, woman is again the central theme, this time during the revolution, in *Transparent Woman:* five episodes on women directed by Hector Veitía, Mayra Vilasís, Mayra Seguda, Mario Crespo, and Ana Rodríguez. There was not one black woman. Nor on television, as in *A Bolero for Eduardo,* whose bevy of beautiful women only go so far as a *mestizo* woman. The black woman has no place in the established canon of beauty. After thirty years! How can that be?

In the early 1940s, I remember as a fifteen-year-old going to the meetings of the Constituent Assembly when Lázaro Peña and Juan Marinello[6] spoke of laws like those of the revolution, making racial discrimination a crime and setting the sanction to be applied to those promoting racial discrimination. What would have been the sanction of those television directors if that had gone through? What would be the sanction of Alfredo Guevara, director of ICAIC? And you start seeing films in North America, where there is a sanction, with Eddie Murphy and Whoopie Goldberg, Morgan Freeman and Oscar-winner Denzel Washington, and blacks playing all kinds of roles. In the home of the baddies! And in the home of the goodies, we're discriminated against. Does that make any sense? Again I insist, are they going to let the year of the centennial of the death of Martí go by without analyzing this as a national problem? Because we all know that if you don't establish a situation as a problem, you'll never find a solution. That's why I don't appear on a whole lot of things, I'm evidently not an official persona grata, and why I was really surprised when I was invited to the gala celebrating forty-five years of Cuban television.

You don't have to be unpleasant or angry, but you do have to be graphic for people to get what you're saying. I've met with silence. Neither Mayedo nor Rosalía Arnaís [deputy to the National Assembly and TV anchor woman] has answered me. I said I was never invited on their programs, but I thought that whether they agreed or not they would stand to gain by having me on. I didn't get a reply either from Sergio Corrieri, former actor, protagonist of *Memories of Underdevelopment,*[7] and the current president of ICAP (Cuban Institute of Friendship among the Peoples) when I approached him about All in Sepia. Very few people have responded. One is Juan Allied, one of the few black majors of the revolution, who was very receptive, understanding, and clever. He had Nivaldo Herrera, the first and only black director of ICR-T (Cuban Broadcasting Institute), meet with me. But I didn't convince Nivaldo, who is himself antiblack. How could I convince him? And I had visits from MININT (Ministry of the Interior), playing cops and robbers, asking me what it was I was saying about the race problem and all that. I protested about that.

I also had a very amiable meeting, I think despite everything it was amiable, with Carlos Rafael Rodríguez, who, when I was young, was one of the regulars on "Doctrine and Action."[8] I said, "You won't remember me, but I was the presenter . . ." and he said, "I do remember you. I remember the presenter very well. But let me tell you I don't like the tone of your letter because it's full of misgivings about the revolution," which is true. He sent me a letter to my house, "but you're right in what you're saying." I'm so stupid that when Jorge Serguera called me and said, "Let me see the letter from Carlos Rafael," I gave it to him and he never gave it back to me. I was stupid enough to give it to him. So I don't have that letter from Carlos Rafael Rodríguez.

Whenever I have discussed the black presence in the dramatic arts in Cuba, it has always been pointed out to me that characters should be played corresponding to our physique, skin color included. That obviously limits our scope tremendously and eliminates us from world theater. At the same time, the fierce racial discrimination for years in our country maintains its presence in such arguments justifying the minimal participation of blacks, limited to works on slavery and other picturesque-type themes associated with blackness. Being black is the bane of any black Cuban actor.

I think there's a residual sub-esteem of canons of beauty, of mental approach, which ends up being prejudicial to those who do not have the necessary conviction to place the black actor on a par with other actors, while considering themselves free from prejudice. This explains the generalized attitude of ignoring the existence of the problem, attempting to silence the voices or denunciation, twisting the concepts as "inopportune," "complex," and "inverse racism." Ignoring the problem as if it didn't exist, pretending it will be resolved of its own accord, is a kind of complicity evidencing a lack of conviction, regarding not only the actor but also the black man and woman.

7

Tackling Racism in
Performing Arts and the Media

Alden Knight

The first time I heard the name Alden Knight, it reminded me of King Arthur and those Knights of the Round Table. It was in the early years of the revolution and I had just arrived in Havana to study English and North American literature at the University of Havana. Alden Knight had also come from the provinces, but in 1956. Born in 1936 to a family of West Indian immigrants in Camagüey, he had grown up in Guantánamo. From an early age, he liked playing the parts of the people around him. His interest was to reflect people in Guantánamo he knew well. Almost six feet tall and with a baritone voice, as a young man he was called on to declaim poetry. When he did, people said it was as if he were acting. In 1959 he was almost twenty-four. With the new openings for poor, rural, and especially black people, he was discovered by the late famous actor Alejandro Lugo, who wanted him to play the popular Havana figure José Terezo Valdés. Alden wasn't that familiar with Havana slum culture, which was quite different from that of towns and cities down the island, and his ability to improvise came from declaiming poetry. He had no background in the theory or practice of acting as such. When I was starting out as a radio journalist at the Cuban Broadcasting Institute (then ICR, later ICR-T), I crossed paths with Alden Knight, who was then taking acting classes. This interview was conducted in May 1995, on a balcony of the Hotel Neptuno, looking out over the sea. Savoring an enormous Havana cigar, Alden Knight reflected on those years when ordinary people, who previously would have had little chance of social mobility, were being trained as the new generation of actors and professionals.(PPS)

I've always been asked to play ordinary people. And I'm satisfied with that. I think it's the biggest thing to feel you can play people you love, and even when I've done other parts, characters of other social strata, I've always injected that sense of ordinary people, blacks, people who sweat and toil.

I didn't really want to be an actor. I saw black actors used in things that really didn't interest me. As a declaimer, I could do as I pleased, express what I wanted. I would take a poem by Nicolás[1] and say what I wanted, and it didn't have to be Nicolás, it might be a poem by Félix B. Caignet,[2] or by the English poet Kipling, or the German Brecht, or anyone, but I said what I wanted to say with my physique and my voice; it came from within. As an actor I had to wait to be called to represent someone in their canon, and I wasn't always interested. From Alejandro Lugo's proposition of TV work, I started out in acting. It felt good. I assimilated well the Stanislavsky system. That was how I started out in this world. Of course, as a young black actor of twenty-four coming from the provinces, Havana was very hard. There were few opportunities, and when there were they wanted you to change your image. For example, I can tell you one anecdote that happened to me in the Salón Rojo of the Hotel Capri. Anido, the director of the floor show, saw me on television and wanted me on the show. "It's great what you do, I love it," he said, "but your image is very aggressive, you have to perm your hair like Nat King Cole." Straighten my hair! I told him I didn't like Nat King Cole's straightened hair. What would my folks back home say? They'd be laughing at me. He replied, "But Nat King Cole's a world figure and he has his hair relaxed." "That's all well and good," I countered, "but he lives there and I live here." And he ended the conversation: "Well, if you don't you can't be in the show, because you look ugly."

Later, when Anido left, I did work at the Capri, but in other things; it was a different culture and mentality. And I didn't relax my hair. But aesthetically it was hard. Then I started to work in television and often playing leading roles, but they were always about marginal life. That changed bit by bit. Cuban society already had blacks in other spheres. It had before and had even more after, but TV continued with a false, assimilated aesthetic.

When my son was seven, he was asked to play my son in a crime program in which I was a criminal, an important role, but a criminal all the same. And my son, who was always outspoken, asked me in front of the director: "Dad, why do they always have you play the criminal—because you're black?" The director turned and drew me aside and said, "Your son's right, you know; you'll play the police in the next series." *Movil ocho* was a weekly program that was always different, with different characters to play. That was 1968–70. Jesús Cabrera, the director then, changed things. I played the policeman and sometimes other quite diverse parts I was given, and not only on that program. I did "Oedipus Rex" on TV and "The Three Musketeers," and I wasn't the only one; there were other black actors like Bertina Acevedo and Erick Romay. Programming began to change as ordinary people began to clamor for that truth my seven-year-old son had made the white director see—which was a mind set in which he didn't see; for him it was normal that a doctor had to be white and a shoeshine black. Out on the street it was different, but this wasn't reflected on film. Cinema barely changed and TV was limited. There was an evolution, but the momentum hasn't been kept because not everyone has the same ideas. We have to create, in Cuban culture, in Cuban arts, directors of all ethnic backgrounds and all kinds of thinking. That's where we fall down, and in recent years there has been less work for black actors on Cuban TV. I don't know why. Perhaps the kind of programming being imported is influencing our own TV. When we did series like *Horizontes* (Horizons), the people of Cuba were on screen, in all walks of life, with all ethnic groupings. Lately, that isn't so much the case. There are no black TV directors. There are black producers, but they don't decide, there are no black presenters, there's no collective of black actors in current programming, and so Cuban TV is white.

It was like that when TV was set up, but with the 1959 revolution I became an actor because I was called on to change that image. I was told, "We have to change that image because it's a false TV image." Erick Romay, Bertina Acevedo, and myself, we were called on. At least there began to be a change in feature programming. Now neither feature nor news programming reflects the ethnic composition of the country. That's one of the reasons I'm not currently working in TV. It's not that I've stopped wanting to, I'm just not asked.

In the first place, we're not part of TV and radio. We're under the Ministry of Culture. ICR-T as an independent body requests the actor according to programming needs. Those programs like *Zumbí en las montañas* (Zumbi in the Mountains), by Abraham Rodríguez, or *Horizontes* by Ramón Brené, that period when we were part of ICR-T and actors almost ran production meetings, that's all gone. We're no longer part of that. There was a separation, maybe thought-out maybe not, but the end result was a rupture between actor and TV. We're no longer part of TV and can't make demands on TV, we have to go through other channels, and by the time they reach TV or get lost on the way . . . nothing gets done.

Elvira Cervera gave a magnificent paper at a theater event, precisely because she wanted to found a black theater group, to do a whole range of work from Shakespeare to Eugenio Hernández.[3] All kinds of theater. A place wherever and whenever there's a foreign or national director who wants a black actor can turn. It's not simply about doing black theater, but about us being able to develop as black actors. Elvira Cervera proposes something I wouldn't have agreed with a few years back, because I had always fought for an integrated theater, like our society, but you realize you have fewer possibilities and you have to have a place where you have those possibilities, as she puts it, "where the magnificent, the mediocre, and the bad can work" because "the *caras pálidas* [pale-faced][4] magnificent, mediocre, and bad can always find work and develop."

I think this imbalance has developed since the actors were separated from ICR-T. Since we separated, there's no direct channel for making demands. When we were in ICR-T, and I was on the union, we had a say when they were doing the casting. "Who's going to do what? He's got a lot of work, what about the other. . . ." The possibilities of the actor and also the ethnic representativity were taken into account.

And here we ask ourselves a very difficult question. Has racial discrimination been eliminated? In our Magna Carta, racial discrimination is proscribed. But can discrimination against women be eliminated by decree? Can discrimination against homosexuals be eliminated by decree? Can discrimination against blacks be eliminated by decree? No, it can't, it has to be through awareness and first it has to be recognized that there is discrimination. There has to be an awareness that the problem exists, it has to be said and confronted, because when you say there's racial discrimination in Cuba, you're told there isn't. Yes, there is! When you go for a job in one of the new enterprises that are being set up, they're looking to see whether you're black or white, whether you look good. Looking good, of course, means you look white. Because foreign businesses have other needs and outlooks, and we're assimilating them in a humiliating way. We're losing what it is to be Cuban. There's really no awareness.

I've spoken out in meetings where the top leadership of the country has been present. When you say, "Because the black . . . ," they look at you as if you're saying a dirty word. They're incapable of dealing with this present-day problem. They put blacks on the menu only as slaves, so people go on thinking of us only as slaves. You can't deny the U.S. series *Roots* is good, but there are those who say they like the first part best, they like the part where Kunta Kinte is the slave, when they cut off his foot, instead of the other part where a society is being formed. I don't know to what extent that part holds true, but in this country, my country, I have the example of my own family. I come from a family of Jamaicans settled in Cuba. They chose to come, and were poor, black, and foreign, discriminated against on three counts. Plus they were peasant farmers! Yet they worked hard. In the 1960s, my eldest brother graduated as a doctor and is now a well-known cardiologist. I've never seen that on TV, and I said so at one of the recent meetings of UNEAC (the National Union of Writers and Artists of Cuba), with the top leadership present. And I repeat what I said: I put my family as an example, not because it's the best, but because it's the one I know best. I have an older brother who's manager of an agricultural machinery plant in Guantánamo. He worked at the U.S. naval base and when they started putting pressure on him, he left and came over to Cuba. My sister is principal of a secondary school in Guantánamo. Then there's me, and I'm known throughout Cuba as an actor. My other brother is head of an electrical engineering section of a fertilizer plant in Matanzas. And the youngest is a building engineer and officer in the Revolutionary Armed Forces, in Guantánamo.

I've never seen my kind of black family represented on Cuban TV, a family that made a concerted effort to move on, from living in one room to an apartment to a large house, through its own efforts—nothing was ever handed to them. I don't see the black Cuban intellectual represented. They've never put the blacks of the Club Atenas (Athens) on TV; it's as if they never existed. Where are our writers, who are writing about our lives? Do they exist? I believe they do. Is their work accepted? That's where the problem lies. I graduated as a TV director and when they were going to give me a play to direct, the scriptwriter was told, "Don't give it to Alden, he'll pack it with blacks." I don't know where that guy is now; he's no longer at ICR-T.

Bearing in mind the large number of Cuban whites living abroad, I can't say what that might mean sociologically, but I do think that, despite everything, we have confidence in the country's future. Like it or not, here the

Cuban black can shout his truth. The black emigrés don't do so well because the discrimination is stronger. The first Cuban emigration was of the white capitalists who discriminated against the black. When a black emigré arrives, he's helped less than a white emigré. That's a fact. The Cuban knows that, but also loves his land. When the Africans were brought to the Americas, some committed suicide as a way of returning to Africa, but the Cuban black has that love for his land, which stays with him even when he's abroad. I have met Cuban blacks and whites abroad. They both cry, but the black feels it more. I don't know if it's a satanic love for the land or what, but there is a confidence that one day his truth will be listened to, because that truth was preached all the time, not by blacks but by the leadership of the revolution. People feel they can say things. They won't always be listened to because thirty-five years in the history of a people is too short to wipe out a whole legacy. But people feel they can say things, and will say things, and will have to be listened to. One day it will not be a sin to speak of whites, blacks, and Chinese, because you don't see Asian ethnicity on TV either, and to speak of the black, because the black came as a slave, lost his name, lost his identification and took on the American, of this continent. I, at least, as a Cuban black, feel I can say what I want, wherever I am. Sometimes I'm listened to, sometimes not; or I'm listened to, but it doesn't go in. But the truth is out there, and, despite the differences I may have with people, I know they respect me. They can hate me for what I say, and they might hate Elvira Cervera and Asseneh Rodríguez for what they say, and Tito Junco, because he's outspoken on radio and TV, too. They can hate all these actors but they go on being outspoken: there are always those who are more submissive and want to get places and give in on certain things . . . because they know that if there's only an opportunity for one out of five they'll have to fight for it at the others' expense.

All our work has its impact on life. We should be looking at the links between all of this and the summer 1994 riots. I'm no political analyst, but those who are should be examining to what extent the disorders were an index of inconformity on the part of the black and *mestizo* populations. I don't know whether it was provoked by someone or if what was going on around them was what caused people to react in that way, where there were many who might be considered white but the great majority were visibly black and *mestizo*. Why? In the new social structure we have had to adopt there is much more discrimination against blacks. The black feels hit, feels little represented. When he goes to hotels, when he watches TV, he sees he is not part of current moves forward. And that makes you feel rebellious, because you're only represented as the lowest, the worst, as in the case of the *jineteras* (prostitutes). In the international press what is most commented on is that the prostitutes are only black and mulatto women, and when I see young black women with middle-aged or older men, I reflect and say to myself, "OK, take her, so you know what it's like!" What I mean to say is that I don't criticize the women.

The play I'm rehearsing in at the moment is about a mulatto *jinetera* and a leader. I play the leader. There's a whole defense of what it is to be a *jinetera,* which was not understood here. Some are lucky enough to become wives, though they continue to be thought of as prostitutes, especially those who are not white. Black and mulatto women have more trouble finding work, whether from a Cuban or a foreigner, because, although they're qualified, they're not seen to be the ideal choice. They're not the right Western type. Then there's a rebelliousness, which I think is a contributing factor, because, even when those so-called antisocial elements shouted "down with this" and "down with that," and threw stones at dollar shops, they were placated when the revolutionary leadership went down there, they were with them. There's a moral there, a message.

I don't perform Nicolás Guillén's poem "Tengo" (I Have) any more, because I think "I Have" is the sum of what was achieved in this country for the blacks, for the poor, and which has now been lost. I have said that when "I Have" can again in all honesty be performed, then we shall have achieved again what we had by the late 1960s, which were years of poverty but equality.

When you're poor but equal you have the right to the same spiritual and material enrichment. Many of those who felt they were being left out [in 1994], many of them said, "Hell, Fidel's here. Now let me tell him a thing or two. . . ." Fidel realized why they'd protested. It's the case that, in large measure, the Cuban black, as in 1868 and 1895, contributed 80 percent of the fighting and the bloodshed. That's not to deny whites were there, too, but its groundings were the rebellion of the black, whose awareness was of being American in the Americas and Cuban in Cuba. White awareness gained through black struggle. The revolution gained through the social clamor of black suffering, and when the revolution gave blacks what should have been theirs, blacks supported the revolution. How can that idea be allowed to dissipate with the same people in power? So yes, blacks are the backbone of the revolution, but they also protest.

On reflection, I think that the North American blacks who have made it should not become part of white society's discrimination against the dispossessed, the poor, the blacks, and the *mestizos* of this continent and think they are the only ones who have power, the only ones with a right to exist. It's true that talent can open doors, but there are those with talent for whom the doors are shut tight. I would ask the well-off North American black not to be egotistical and think about the millions of dispossessed who should be accorded a minimum existence, value, and recognition, and not to shy away from any struggle for dignity, wherever it might be. I had had the opportunity of talking with well-off North American blacks, some of whom identify with the struggle of our black people, others of whom don't. When Sidney Poitier and Harry Belafonte came to Cuba, they each took different stands. Harry Belafonte was for struggle and when he was in ICAIC he asked, "Why is there so little black representation on Cuban TV and film when I see out on the street people are much more integrated?" Sidney Poitier didn't say anything about that and when he was asked didn't answer. I had the impression he didn't want to lose what he had and Belafonte didn't mind losing if others could win what he had. That was what I saw. What can happen is, as the old saying goes, "But you don't seem black." And you start to feel distanced from the poor black because of everything that goes in your ears. And you start discriminating against yourself. But why poor? As actors we have to reflect life and its contradictions. There's enough theater and film that reflects only power—power propped up by those who have no power. We have to reflect people below.

None of this will change without greater participation and influence at the national level. I think there has to be a revaluing of blacks nationally. We continue to be the poorest in the country. I think culture is of vital importance in a people's awareness. The African cultures that were brought are of fundamental importance, but alongside with the origins must go the current achievements of our race. Yes, our ancestors brought the *orishas,* but did it stop there? No, they continued to advance. That question should be formulated for Chucho Valdés and his group Irakere, the band Adalberto y su Son, [and the band] Juan Formell and Los Van Van—musicians who are more than just musicians.

We have to show that evolution. We mustn't stop in slave times, for if we do we'll continue as slaves today. Many artists have a goal which I share, which is to go from the roots to the present, and with a vision of the future. It's important for ordinary people to have a sense of how far we've come and where we're going. The mass media (radio, television, cinema, theater, painting) all need to express what was, but also what is and what we hope will be. The past we know. The future we want to see is what we need to express. Each and every one of us, artist, musician, painter, journalist, this conscious stratum of society, must do everything possible in this regard, because if we stay in the past that's how we'll be seen: not only as black, but as nonachieving blacks. The world changes, years have passed since the first slave reached this continent, and as the years pass and the world changes, things have happened that need to be reflected on, and almost never are.

That's why I refuse to go on playing the role of the slave, not because I deny slavery, but because from that we reached this and people can't go on seeing you and me as slaves, because people who see you as a slave will treat you as a slave. That's why, in the arts, in music, there have to be the achievements. That's the mission of the black artist, who is in the majority, and whose stamp is the whole nationality of the Caribbean. The Caribbean is truly what it is because there is that mix in which blacks are a tremendous part. So demands have to be made on those who hold the reins, who are still the whites . . . and when the black reaches that position, he becomes white. Not white because, as someone once said of Nivaldo Herrera, when he was president of ICR-T, "He wound up marrying a white woman!" So what? I'll marry whoever I want. What I can't do is deny the black, or stop being black. He married a white woman because he wanted to. He's been with her for twenty years. The problem is that he didn't allow blacks to occupy their rightful place. If you want to marry a white woman, that's your affair. Because nobody criticizes the white man who marries a black woman. You marry whoever you want. Or are we going differentiate in all that craziness? Love is beyond all that, in my opinion.

The problem is through our work reaching where we can. Because it has reached out. When there are equal rights for intellectual capacity we can attain what we want, and that's what we have to demonstrate. That's what has never been reflected in Cuban cinema, or Cuban shows. It's not there and we have to demand it; not because we're against the system, we're demanding it in support of the system, because if I say yes to everything and no to nothing, as the Pablo Milanés song goes, love dies. You have to create the conditions. It's like a cog. If two cogs have worn smooth, they slide and the car won't move. There has to be opposition to advance.

I think the revolution has to understand when people protest, and not from enemy ranks. The enemy isn't the one protesting from within. You clamor for that for which you shed your blood and die. You clamor that you revalue what you taught me. I think those who have made it should not forget, afraid that what they have might be taken from them. You can't forget those who haven't made it, whether white or black. Artists must reflect in their work the past we have left behind, the present we have attained, and above all the future to which we aspire. Futuristic work is very important for people to gain awareness. That's what we constantly call for in theater meetings. And when I say theater, I'm not referring only to theater as such but also film and TV. Because when you listen to the symphony orchestra and see equal numbers of blacks and whites, the music is the same. We need to take that equality in music, which is the soul of peoples, into the performing and visual arts.

In my world of the performing arts, I see more opposition because it's what reflects the achievements and shortcomings. When you see a Gonzalito Rubalcaba or Chucho Valdés playing, your spirit's in the music. But when you see a Harry Belafonte or a Sidney Poitier in character, you're seeing a man. And in *The Defiant Ones,* which was important in its time, what you see is a girl who is frightened when she sees a black man. And it cuts you as a black man. Why, if he was the one who helped her? What's a truth in the United States, and a truth of discriminatory humankind, wounds, because the white girl is frightened simply because he's black. So the black boy who sees that program, and others who put themselves in the same place, don't want to be black. And they want long hair. My grandson says, "I've long hair," because that's the canon of beauty. To be intelligent, you have to have straight hair. No way! We have to create the image of a flat nose and thick lips as beauty and people like that falling in love, and that we're intelligent, that we're teachers, that we go into space. Art has to create that, so when you're home you see that normality. But if what's seen is that if you're black, you're no more than a slave, well, the slave who didn't want to be a slave became a maroon. Today's maroon is the criminal, protesting oppression by turning criminal. Maroons were the criminals, which is why they were hunted down with dogs. Was the maroon to blame?

8

Poetry, Prostitution, and Gender Esteem

Georgina Herrera

Georgina Herrera read little when she was a child, but now literature is her vocation. A poor home gave her no incentive. She barely had books. Even so, when she only nine she dared show her poems to her school principal, who doubted their authencity. She was born in Jovellanos, Matanzas province, on 23 April 1936. Her father was very strict, in keeping with the times. She came from a united and fairly stable family; however, feeling a lack of love from her parents, as a girl she was both vulnerable and sensitive. She even thought she must be illegitimate and that her mother didn't love her. By the time she was fourteen and had lost her mother, there was virtually no communication between the two of them. That was when she began to send her poems to various publications in the capital, and she had the good fortune to see them published. When she came to Havana to stay in 1956, she began to visit the offices of the dailies, bringing along her poetry. By the time of the Cuban Revolution in 1959, she had established good relations with several journalists. One of them, the poet Joaquín González Santana, took her to *Prensa libre,* where she was serious and constant in her work. She started to give poetry readings, though not many, recognizing that it wasn't her forte. Looking back over the years, Georgina realizes why she always insists on putting first her relations with others, trying to make them the best possible—precisely because this is something she hasn't always managed to achieve. When she reflects on her mother's world, she concludes that she and her mother should have talked more, and they didn't. She also remembers a love relationship with someone who died young yet left a deep imprint on her life. More recently, she suffered another devastating loss when her daughter died in a tragic accident. Georgina thinks yet again of many things that were never said between mother and daughter. Her first book of poems has no title, only the initials GH. It was precisely in talking about those years after her first book of poems that we broadened out the conversation, from what she was cooking and writing, at one and the same time, to the substantial changes in her poetry writing. (PPS)

GH: The theme's the same. I really like writing about insignificant things. Big exotic flowers are lovely . . . but I like the little ones, those nobody pays much attention to. It's the same with basic, everyday events. That's why things that for others pass unnoticed are what shape my poetry. I do many things. I write for radio; for many years now I've been writing shorts and soaps. One day I hope to put some of them together and publish them in book form. I also write plays and I'm writing some short stories to be read.

PPS: In terms of your literary themes and ideas, do you think of yourself as a feminist writer?

GH: I don't think of myself as feminist, but very feminine. All my poetry bears an undoubtedly feminine stamp. There's a kind of poetry in Cuba that women are accustomed to write, which is to talk about the men with whom they have been in a relationship, and I do that. I say it all, I don't hide it. Sometimes you have to dig deep in the poetry of Cuban women to know what's being said. I don't think I have anything to hide. That's why I say I am feminine, not feminist.

PPS: In addition to the feminine, how do you bring being a black woman into your poetry?

GH: I think being both black and a woman have made their mark on my poetry. Being black has sensitized me, because I have been marginalized, subtly, but marginalized all the same. I have become very conscious and very proud of being a black woman.

PPS: Has it been over time or has there been a particular experience or phenomenon that gave you that awareness of being a black woman?

GH: I think it's been an awareness over time. I began to read and remember things from my childhood. My family lived in a very black town, where most people were black. I remembered the stories my great aunts used to tell about the slaves, about my grandmother who was a runaway slave. That used to have a different effect on me. But as an adult, I began to be really aware of being black, of knowing where I came from, of where my people came from, how they were brought, how they lived, and what they passed on.

My grandfather was born a slave. He was freed when he was a boy, but my great-great aunts had been slaves, and they told me about what was done to them as slaves, including some stories I imagine were all true, like the one about the sugarmill that was razed to the ground because the slaves worked Good Friday and the master was very cruel. All that strengthened me. I realized that the black woman had always been in the shadow of the white woman and that she needed time and space apart.

When I began to write for radio, I did historical programs, and women were always on a second or third plane, if there at all. Then I started doing my own research, directly with the sources, not based on documents or books. For example, a friend told me about the rebellion of the Alcancía sugarmill, in the Jovellanos area, and about the consciousness of blacks, and I said to him, "But what did the women do in that rebellion?" His answer was, "Yes, them too, but . . ." Because I wanted to know if there were also women in that rebellion. It's always the same.

Once Rogelio Martínez Furé gave me a very lovely piece for a program called *Grandes momentos de la historia* (Great Moments of History), and said, "It's about an African warrior queen." When I began to read about her, how her father had risen up against the Portuguese, I said to myself, "This is more than a radio program," and that was when I wrote the poem *Canto de amor y respeto para Doña Ana de Souza* (Song of Love and Respect for Doña Ana de Souza). I'm still working with this theme. Whenever I do historical programs, there are always women involved.

PPS: Are you working along these lines in relation to Cuba today?

GH: Let me be sincere on this. The topic of Cuba today is hard and I'm a bit apprehensive. I'm out on the street and people talk and I take notes. It's so hard: there are times when I'm looking for some papers and come across things I've jotted down some months or weeks back, and it's as if they're talking from another galaxy, another time. It's like magical realism.

Right now I'm writing a lot about women. I have a series of poems about black women. I'm preparing a book which is called *Siete mujeres* (Seven Women) and is about African women or women of African origin. I don't know when in the next millennium this little grain of sand which is my literature will have its day, but I know its time will come. I'm working with some of the *orishas,* like Yemayá and Oshún. I have a vision that is totally different from the one in which the saint seduces Oggún, the god of metals, with honey. It's a wonderful story of a woman who really existed and Oggún was simply a warrior who left traps and wouldn't let anyone go to get food in the mountain. People were dying of hunger and Oshún tricked him, seduced him with her beauty, but so her people could eat. That's a different vision, even though she used her beauty and sexuality to achieve it. I'm working on all this in my poetry.

As for Cuban women today, it has to be recognized that they were given every possibility for their emancipation—study, maternity care, day care centers, work. But up to a given moment, and all women know that. It's gone backwards. The time came when the Federation of Cuban Women stopped short and was only offering cleaning, cooking, and embroidering, when other things were happening in the world. Out in the world there was the vision of gender as a philosophical category for the study of women. It was a mistake to pit women against men. That wasn't the problem, but rather the conviction of the two hand in hand, which is how many of us think this has to function. But women have dropped back a lot in these times of shortage. It's the case that women weren't emancipated before, but they had the protection of men.

Then women started to work and to do everything in the home. That's why many women have stopped working. It's alarming the number of women who have stopped working. They say that now, because of need, women are working outside the home again, but there was a moment when it was tremendous how women stopped en masse. Now women know they are not emancipated, that men are predominant in many things, that it takes time. A revolution passes laws, but there are many subjective ways of subverting the revolutionary order as well. And that's what has happened.

I'm part of a nonofficial women's organization, of women in the media, called MAGIN.[1] It's called MAGIN from "iMAGINation," intelligence. Since it's a nongovernmental organization, it has gained a lot of prestige nationally and internationally, over and above the FMC. When I joined the group I gained this vision of gender in a way that opened my horizons for approaching the women's problem. If I had known this years ago, things would have been different. Intuitively, I acted in a given way, but that's not the same. One thing is empiricism and another the truth. That's why as women we are very stimulated by MAGIN, but up until now it has no legal status. We receive a lot of material on Latin America, on women there's a lot of material, on the differences, for example. Women thought we were all equal but we're not, we're talking about differences. I'm fascinated by MAGIN and what it's doing.

For example, I was rapporteur when racism was discussed at one of the meetings we have every other month. It was discussed whether there is racism or not, especially in the media, because Cuban TV looks totally Scandinavian. But it wasn't only the media. It was everything. There were those who had other points of view. There were two white psychologists who said there was no racism in Cuba. The ones who said they weren't racist demonstrated they were with their language—*pasas* (nappy hair) for the naturally curly hair of blacks, *bemba* (thick lips) for the mouths of blacks, all that terminology, and yet saying they weren't racist! There was one who had married a black man and said, "I've two girls, and one has 'pasas' and the other has 'good hair.'" At the end, we reached the conclusion that we were all racist, from one point of view or another. It was a very good discussion, well conducted and respectful. I gathered all that information and wrote something for the next issue of our magazine. It's hard to publish an issue, but now and then we do, and sometimes we do fliers for an activity.

I have a TV program which is called *Te lo cuentan las estrellas* (The Stars Talk). There's always a woman who in the broadest sense of the word is the star, because she shines, whatever her walk of life. We have had from professionals to housewives. There are five sections. One of them is Legend, and there we had the African queen I mentioned, whom I used in one of my poems, Zdinga Bandi N'gola, daughter of N'gola Kiluanji, the first king who fought against the Portuguese. To reach an agreement with her, they demanded she take a Portuguese name, hence that of Ana de Souza. MAGIN is very recent, although we've quickly realized all the possibilities it has, how to make the most of our discussions. My next novel is called *Los días pequeños* (Small Days), which is about the process of a girl who goes off in the literacy campaign right up until the present day, how the family shattered in pieces as they all went their own way, and from a gender perspective.

PPS: When did you decide to write novels?

GH: Not long ago, because I liked writing stories for radio, because they reach a wide audience. We receive incredible letters from all over. People like what I do, so much so that we have to do repeats. But I realized that the radio world isn't the same as literature. That's why it's so urgent to write books. Right now it's harder to publish, but even so the literature needs to be written.

PPS: Race and gender coincide in the resurgence of prostitution in Cuba. What is your vision of this problem?

GH: Ever since Cuba has been Cuba, there have been blacks and whites in our country. The whites always had the power, have always been better placed. Those who left Cuba at the start of the revolution because they had everything to lose were the whites. The blacks stayed. Now, whites are the ones abroad who can help their families—because now it's allowed, they're no longer traitors, or anything like that. Blacks are still the most marginalized, despite all the possibilities they have had. We laugh sometimes when we hear that a family member has sent for so-and-so because the relatives have died and there's an inheritance. The whites still get their inheritances, and all the blacks have is that they went to die in African countries because they're black.

So it's logical that blacks still face more economic privation, and, in the case of the black woman, who is also exotic and attractive, she has the most difficulties. Whites help each other out a lot. With the bankruptcy of the socialist camp, chains of stores were opened that we call "shoppings," because you can only buy there in dollars, and all the whites who were in power in government started placing their people, their families and friends, and almost no black women. And so black women were the first to go into *jineterismo*. Needs aside, they know they're attractive. It's a means of survival, there's no doubt about that.

The position of MAGIN is very interesting, because we say that the women who go into *jineterismo* must hold themselves in very high esteem. To assimilate that she will go on living and come out of this chaotic situation, she's a star. The FMC has a completely bourgeois concept of moral values. All this started very sportily, but then grew tremendously when girls saw that others could get food, clothing, and shoes with the foreigners who come to Cuba, in exchange for sexual favors.

The phenomenon has spread like the plague, especially in the cities and in the major tourist attractions. The *jineteras* have another kind of education, they're not your vulgar prostitute, though some are. So it's accepted at home. Here next to my place lived a young woman who was a member of the Young Communist League and was sleeping with any foreigner who came her way. Finally she met up with a Spaniard. The mother, who's a party member, would come by my place. One day she saw a broom I had bought at a "shopping" and she showed it to her daughter so that she could buy her one. I hadn't bought mine that way, I'm too old for that, but the daughter wasn't, and the mother knew the daughter could get dollars through her *jineterismo*.

I think everyone has a right to seek a living any way they can, especially when there's inequality. I see it here in the building. There's no food. It's diabolical because even if you have money you can't get it. You can't be spending so much money every day for pork or mutton, because the price is very high. With the two or three pesos you'd normally have, you can't buy a thing. Today I'm cooking because a neighbor lent me a cup of rice, because I gave the pound of rice I had left for the month to another neighbor who was without and said she would pay me back, and hasn't yet. You see how wretched it is. So a girl who knows she's attractive takes advantage of it. And the foreign men know what it's about. I have friends who tell me that if they were twenty years younger they wouldn't think twice about going out on the streets.

That's why MAGIN concludes that for a young, intelligent woman to go out and give her body to bring food home for her family and for herself, she has to have very high self-esteem, she has to be very sure of what her values are and what she's going after. That's the thinking of MAGIN.

The economic situation is very chaotic. They say we're in takeoff, that it's getting better, but people continue to have more and more needs each day. There's a ration card for underwear that hasn't been available to buy for five years. If you can't get it on the ration, and you don't have anyone to send it to you, what are you going to do? You've no alternative but to go out and get it—while there are others who do have them, because they're the daughters and relatives of another kind of woman who has it all.

PPS: Are you and others like you in literary and media circles reflecting the problems of today's Cuba in your work?

GH: I think it's a historic moment we're living through, but a lot of people are afraid. I did a radio novel recently and told my supervisor, "I'll write it my way and don't call me in to criticize it. Take out or put in whatever you like. It's your responsibility." I was quite cautious, and she didn't take out anything. When I heard it on radio, I jumped for joy. I surprised myself with the things I'd put in it, things that aren't really allowed. Any criticism you make is against the homeland and socialism. And that creates in you a great feeling of anguish and despair. In the final analysis, I don't have trips or anything else to lose, but it does create in you that feeling of anguish. It's a fear. There are times when we meet as writers and all concur that we should each be writing and keeping it, because the things that happen are tough. Drama can't go on in the same way. Events and characters are much tougher. This is the moment for great theater and a great novel, but what happens is that people soften it for it to be accepted. I don't think anyone dares venture to write the novel of Cuba today. And even if you really were to do it, what would you put, who is to blame, what are the roots of what's wrong? You can skirt round things and talk of this functionary or that, but it's a whole system that hasn't functioned!

PPS: To what extent has this whole situation you have been describing been anguishing for you as a woman?

GH: I'll be sincere in my reply. I would have been extremely anguished if my son Ignacio were here in Cuba, or my daughter Anaís, who died a few years back in a traffic accident, were alive. That's the egoism of a mother. Nothing can happen to me, I'm not going to be doing great things for anything to happen. Ignacio and Manolo [Granados],[2] who are both outspoken, and are the ones I love most, are safely out of it. I do feel down. I would have wanted this to be something better. You realize how I'm lowering my voice, almost to a whisper. That's a reflection of the situation here.

PART III

Race and Identity

My work is part of the light, perhaps all the light of the island. People illuminate this land, this magical world that accompanies me, of dreams and realities that make it easy to understand difficult things in life. From an artistic point of view, everybody has that color. Each human being might give it his or her very own form and meaning, or something maybe others discover. I think the color and form, the general landscape nurturing that inner world, is in my work and people relate to it. Much remains to be done in Afro-Cuban culture. I never thought of my own work opening doors, but rather people themselves having the opportunity and courage to open doors. It worries me that things are done in poor taste, perhaps using elements from a painting, to sell cheap on the tourist market. That's bad. I also know many people have taken this path of the *orishas,* this magical world of ours, of our identity, our *mestizo* culture—some because they get drawn in, others maybe because it's the fashion, but, well, I'm one of those who believes that, though it might take a long time, all that's bad will come to an end. Two years ago I was in Ouidah, Benin, and I had the honor of being invited to restore the temple of Jebiozo, of Shangó. It was a wonderful encounter with the people, the roots of that whole world of color and cowries of Arará culture, which is the same in Cuba. Now and then my work has been used in Cuba, in events, in a very interesting experiment in textile design, but little more. I would love to see a huge mural or stained glass of my work in some hotel or place of prestige. I'd like to be there and I'm not. It's all very complex. We can have endless objectives and each takes a different form, a color that might convey to me a sentiment. And so I imagine there are many people who really love my work and I know there are many who are maybe not interested, but it's important I go on painting for my people.

Manuel Mendive, artist

9

Africa, the Caribbean, and Afro-America in Cuban Film

Gloria Rolando

Gloria Rolando was born into a modest home on 4 April 1953. From when she was little, she would listen to her grandmother's stories of slavery. Her grandmother lived to the age of ninety-six, long enough for her first-hand oral testimony to make an indelible mark on her granddaughter's future career as a filmmaker. Today Gloria Rolando feels the urgent need to speak of her origins, of her roots as a black Cuban woman. She asks herself how, coming from such modest origins, she could have become a filmmaker and believes that the educational policies of the Cuban Revolution opened avenues for the less advantaged in society. In 1959, at the time of the revolution, she was the only black girl at a private religious school—though not for long since revolutionary policy was for public lay education. The story of how she went to that school might in itself be a film script. Her grandfather was working as a cab driver in New York and met an English woman who had separated from her husband. Gloria herself doesn't know whether it was only the need for spiritual comfort that led the woman to go to live in Havana, where she founded the religious school. Rolando attended thanks to her English lady benefactor, pious grandfather, and shoemaker father. When the school was closed, Gloria went into the public school system. She and her sister studied piano, and her brother, German. She later enrolled in history at the university. As a student, she did agricultural work combined with study. This gave her experience of rural Cuba, for which book learning is no substitute. She was selected for the Cuban Film Institute (ICAIC), although filmmaking had not even occurred to her. At the time, in the 1970s, there were no film schools. People trained in the industry on the job. Her first promotion was to the Latin American Newsreel team headed by director Santiago Alvarez Villafuerte and her first piece of research was on music. This interview was conducted in November 1996, when Rolando was on a speaking tour in the United States. By then she had two documentaries to her credit as director—*Oggún* and *Los hijos de Baraguá* (My Footsteps in Baraguá)—and we started talking about the making of these two documentaries. (JS)

GR: It's incredible to me that many people should think that *My Footsteps in Baraguá* was a project that came after *Oggún*. It was really a project I dreamed of doing many years back because, when I hadn't even thought about doing *Oggún*, I'd been working on an idea of doing something more recent on the Haitian migration to Cuba. There'd been Cuban productions on Haiti, more than any other Caribbean country—Tomes Gutiérrez Alea's *Cumbite* (1964) and Humberto Solás's *Simparelé* (1974). I know the Haitian singer Marta Jean-Claude, who has lived in Cuba since the early 1960s, and I know her children because we studied together, and Haiti has always interested me a lot.

In the 1980s, I worked with director Rogelio Paris on a documentary on Cuban culture called *La huella del hombre* (Man's Trace). We traveled all round the island for Cuban culture. One day we arrived in Ciego de Avila and one of the things that came up as an important and interesting part of Cuban culture was a small Haitian community, which of course we filmed. It wasn't a filming I particularly liked: a group of children watching the group of Haitians, very distanced. I can see that sequence now. I said to myself, "I'm coming back." In those days, I was only assistant director. I went to Santiago Alvarez, the first director I worked with, my friend and mentor. My first job in ICAIC was working with him on *Tumba francesa,* which was also my first script. It would have been great if I had continued along those lines, but other things and the very dynamic of ICAIC diverted my interests. I did everything I could to interest Santiago in the Haitians. It was two years after when I made contact with the people in Ciego de Avila, and that's how I started.

I put it to Santiago when ICAIC was doing some forty to fifty documentaries a year, when the resources were there to travel, which is how we did *Haití en la memoria* (Haiti on my Mind). When we were in the sugarmill towns of Ciego de Avila and Camagüey filming the old people, not one of whom is alive today, I came across some West Indians. I didn't know that was what they were. I heard them speaking English, went over and asked an old, very black man where he came from. In that accent of his, he replied, "Ah, from Jamaica." I realized then there was a whole other history out there. I started researching on my own but never had any backing for the idea. Later, I remembered from the Cuban culture documentary the group La Cinta (Maypole), which subsequently I was able to film, and they told me they too were the descendants of Jamaican immigrants. So for various reasons, I started to get into the theme, but I was never able to see it through, because I'd be told it was the same thing, when I felt it wasn't.

That's as far as it went, and I started work on *Oggún,* my first serious piece as director. It was about someone I knew because I live in Havana, I had heard him sing, I knew he was very respected. Actually, it wasn't originally my idea but the idea of Pedro Betancourt, who was then stage designer and artistic director of the National Folklore Group. One day he came by my house and said, "Why don't we do a documentary on *mestizo* Lázaro Ross?" My response was, "Well, we can do it but with what resources? I'm not a director or anything." We went and interviewed Lázaro, and between interviewing him the first time and my battling for it to be done in ICAIC, which it never was, and getting financing from Videoamérica, three years passed. Three anxious years trying to get someone interested. In that time, Lázaro had even retired from the Folklore Group. Then things started happening. One fine day, at a Casa de las Américas prize-giving, talking as I always did with everyone I could about the project, I said to Altunaga, "There's this idea I've been working on for ages." His response was, "Well, we're starting up a private video company called Videoamérica and we're interested in Afro-Cuban themes." And there, at Casa de las Américas, under that Latin American tree of life, the documentary came into being. That was the start, and I have to thank Altunaga and other colleagues in Videoamérica for taking up the idea, because nobody was showing any interest.

JS: Why do you think ICAIC was never interested?

GR: Up until then, I had really put forward very little. I presented the script for *Oggún* when there was very little chance of it being taken up. It was a big project and what was being required was a ten-minute documentary, filmed outside, without lights. But I hoped that the topic would be interesting and new enough to grip people—because everyone in Cuba knows Lázaro Ross, especially in film circles; whenever they want a Yoruba chant, he's the one, with that unmistakable voice of his. That was what I hoped but it didn't help. I wasn't even short-listed. But I knew it was culturally important and fought hard for it. The documentary did get made and was filmed on video with quite a lot of resources. But it has never gone anywhere in Cuba. *Oggún* is known outside of Cuba, especially in the United States but also other places, including on tour with Lázaro, and people have shown great interest, but very few people have seen it in Cuba. It was produced to sell in tourist places and, from 1991 to this year, 1996, it has never been on Cuban television—and Lázaro is still alive.

That aside, what has it meant for me? It was a whole learning experience. It's a very ambitious first documentary to direct, involving fiction, music, a *tambor* ceremony, none of which is easy. But I wasn't fazed. I had two good friends who were behind me from the start—cameraman Raúl Rodríguez and scriptwriter José Manuel Rivera, as well as a good sound technician. We worked closely together. Imágenes del Caribe (Caribbean Images) didn't exist then, but that was the basis of it, and even Lázaro was surprised when I invited him on location with the whole universe woven around the *patakín* (legend) of Ochún and Oggún. I was afraid that it might end up looking ridiculous, presenting Ochún, the goddess of love, naked. When you're working on these things as cultural products, you also have to bear in mind they're not archival material but living things that people venerate.

I was working with the history and representation of two deities that are very alive and highly respected. What would be the reaction? I wanted to recreate the fantasy and also the beauty. My aim was to make an aesthetically pleasing documentary that would show the internal beauty of that religion. The altars were filmed with lights and the same care, the same dedication, as we filmed Lázaro himself, as a modern-day griot, the wise man in that tradition, not something folkloric, because he not only sings, he has feelings and a history, and it was important to me that he had that history. But how was he going to tell the story? There had to be a context, which wasn't in a studio or in a house seated on a white wicker art deco chair. The African in all our Caribbean world is very close to nature, is in dialogue with nature, and so the setting for telling the story was at the foot of the silk cotton tree, which is a sacred tree, for Cubans a point of confluence for all that came from Africa. There at the foot of the silk cotton tree, he narrates the legends, the *patakines,* of which there are many. I was giving voice to him, showing the universality of the values of that culture from Africa, specifically the Yoruba tradition, as a philosophy and way of life.

JS: One of the parts that moved me was Lázaro himself telling the story of his life as a child, discovering the Afro-Cuban world, the black world of Cuba, because he was initially brought up sheltered from that. How has it been for you as the first black woman filmmaker in Cuba since Sara Gómez with themes evidently connected with the African, Cuban, and Caribbean black heritage?

GR: Not only because of my color, because I'm black, but where I have lived and what have been my roots. I've always lived in Havana. I grew up in Chinatown. I now live in Old Havana but always used to live in Central Havana, surrounded by all the world I think one does approach through that window, like the child in *Oggún,* and can't always explain. Because not all blacks in Cuba have been linked to African religions. Many of us have been and continue to be Catholic, not orthodox, but believing in the Virgin of Mercy, the Virgin of Regla, and the Virgin of Charity, in Santa Barbara,[1] which has been the Cuban Catholic religion, and of course the Virgin Mary and all that.

I wasn't a child who had been brought up in that context. I would see the images, and later on I discovered I had family members who had been initiated and were involved in all that. But I had been at the Amadeo Roldán Music Conservatory, playing Bach and Mozart, from when I was eleven to eighteen. In those days, in the 1960s, they taught some Cuban music, the *danzón,* some rumba perhaps, but not black, African music, much less Caribbean music. I didn't even get that in the university, but rather after graduating in 1976, when I have to thank the Film Institute, which enabled me to move around a lot and discover things, working on documentaries.

In 1979 CARIFESTA was held in Cuba and I first saw a steel band and heard a lot about the plantation world. Suddenly, all these figures in Latin American history that had seemed isolated to me came together, and I was fascinated. The seeds had been sown.

Casa de las Américas has been important to many of us as Cuban filmmakers, and it certainly has been to me. It was at the Center for Caribbean Studies, whose director was then Nancy Morejón, that I started to learn about that world, in talks given by Nancy herself—before even traveling to the Caribbean. That would come much later, because first I went to Germany, Africa, Spain, and a host of places—even the Sahara Desert, with Rogelio Paris, to film the Cuban doctors—before deciding what it was I wanted to do or where my own history lay. When I did decide to make *Oggún,* I felt more grounded. Through literature, I began to discover the value of oral tradition. Lázaro was that for me, which is how I came to *Oggún.*

Now, with *My Footsteps,* I feel very committed. I felt very driven when I did travel to the Caribbean, which in itself was incredible. I'd spent about three months in the United States between 1990 and 1992. When I returned to Cuba, a friend from Trinidad and Tobago invited me to a four-day television conference in Barbados. It's amazing how four days can change your life. When I went back to Cuba, I had the project *La tierra prometida* (The Promised Land): the old lady I met in Barbados singing *danzones* to me, and showing me her records of Antonio María Romeu, and all that. It was like a bridge, putting that together with what I had found with the Jamaicans and the Haitians. She had family in Cuba but had gone back, while others had stayed, and I came across other Cubans who also lived in Barbados but had family in Cuba. I couldn't do anything at the time but in 1993–94 I was invited to Jamaica by CARIMAC.[2] I talked with lots of people and began to see the significance of that whole story of those who went to work on the Panama Canal.

I had no resources for the project, which was big—filming in Cuba, Barbados, Jamaica, and Panama was crazy. It was too big, but sometimes you have to do that to go out and find what you can get. Between the trip to Barbados and the trip to Jamaica, I started going round the eastern part of Cuba with Antonio Romero, my friend and assistant on this venture. By the time I went to Jamaica, I talked about who was what and where and a community called Baraguá, and they were fascinated. Time passed and I wasn't able to get anything done. That's when I decided to launch a national campaign, among friends, to do *My Footsteps.* At that point, all I had was the camera which had arrived. Lazarito, who lives in Miami, gradually got together the monitor, the cassettes, and between March and July 1995 the money, anything, to do the research, write the script, and produce the documentary.

JS: *My Footsteps* is a very gentle documentary. Can you tell us a little about your integration as a Cuban black woman filmmaker into their community?

GR: I arrived in Baraguá with the support and knowledge of the local municipal authorities, but I really didn't know anybody, except La Cinta. I arrived and was put up by the director of the group. In such places, there are always people who command respect, who take it upon themselves to represent the community, and I was taken in from the start by the family in the wooden house that is in the film. I began to live the life there, talking to people I would interview, the oldest ones. I went to the Seventh Day Adventist church on Saturday morning; I became an Adventist on Saturday, then Episcopalian on Sunday. I shared their lives, I ate the food they prepared, and little by little interviewed people.

Of course, I already had a base. On previous travels, I had interviewed people in Guantánamo. I was really looking to see whether I could find in Baraguá the history many had in common, that is, telling the story of Baraguá but at the same time allowing me to use their testimony to narrate a process they had in common with others. I got talking with people, letting them get to know me, becoming part of their lives, eating with them. I dressed in a way that fitted in, I had my pigtails, which was different, but I liked what I was doing a lot, I was interested, and it was a relationship of love and mutual understanding. They'd ask me if I was a "descendant," why was I interested, perhaps I had a grandfather. I said no, but I knew their story, like that of their ancestors, was important for the history of Cuba. They asked why, if it was important, had no one been interested in them before. Nobody had ever gone there before.

La Cinta had been filmed many times, as a tourist thing, but what was behind it? It was the same as with Lázaro: yes, there was the dance and the music, but what else? I knew that it was important to find people with that history in Panama and from Panama never going back to their island of origin but on to Cuba. Like Stanley Holding, for example, with a family from Montserrat, whose father went to Panama and then Cuba. The fact that he told me, "I remember when I was a child that my mother would give me money to take to the post office to send to the family in Montserrat." What did that mean? What had happened to the family that had remained there? I already had something of a notion from Jamaica, where I'd talked with Rupert Lewis,[3] and with other historians. People had few alternatives; the world of the plantation gave them little option.

So Cuba was the promised land, and for them, Baraguá really was, despite all the divisions. And my project kept growing. The story of Baraguá summed up the history, the music, many things. The big challenge was how I was going to get all that in one script. Who was going to narrate it? When I left Baraguá, I went with a mound of interviews, and it was when I reached Havana that I began to assimilate it all and find a way of telling it. In Havana I had met some people who were from Baraguá and talked about it so affectionately, and I thought, why not take the voice of one of those people visiting Baraguá? I was never really going to be able to go in depth into the history of Baraguá, and there were people who had left and would go back to visit their families for the festivities of August 1. So I went with the angle of those who would go back to visit.

That was how I found a very personal way of telling the story, bits here and there, a narrator who suggests, reflects, feels, recounts, and wonders— "I never knew when I was a child why granny was so sad when someone spoke about Panama, and it was the time when all the men in the family went off in search of work and money." Always looking for that personal touch and of course in the voice of a woman. . . .

JS: Perhaps that's why it's gentle and not hard, because it's a very hard history, too.

GR: There's something else. It rained every day when we were filming. The skies there aren't like the Cuban skies, they're gray, but Raúl, the cameraman, said we'd film the rain and see whether it would come in, and it did. We had those rainy sequences which later blended with the passing of time, and gave a sense of things forgotten, things that change. There's a part when the narrator says, "I don't recall when at home they stopped talking about going back, but I always knew that those who were waiting died without ever being able to see us again." When I wrote those things, I cried, because it was as if I were possessed. I think I was. I think you had to really feel the history they were passing on to me. It wasn't easy to find someone who would talk to me about the discrimination, their suffering, but I think it has been implicit in their longing and separation.

And I found those separations in the literature. It was George Lamming's *In the Castle of My Skin* that gave me the idea, and that's why I dedicated the documentary to Nicolás Guillén, for his poem *West Indies,* and all he loved about the Caribbean; to George Lamming; and to Rex Nettleford, because I met him at that Caribbean event, and I remember the interview of him talking about his theory of how a Caribbean man walks and feels the music.[4] They were all key in helping me discover the Caribbean without ever having visited it. I traveled to Barbados when I read *In the Castle of My Skin*.

JS: It's striking how you dedicated the documentary to three Caribbean men, and you talk about a generic Caribbean man, yet you're a woman of the Caribbean (taking Cuba as part of the Caribbean) and you chose the voice of a woman to tell the story of the community. Can you comment on this, thinking also of the few women filmmakers there are in ICAIC and the poor representation of black women in Cuban film?

GR: *My Footsteps* is narrated by a female voice, a woman, and the two threads are two women, two old women: one from Barbados, Miss Jones, and the other, Ruby Hunt, from Jamaica, the two countries from which there was the strongest migration. And then there's Cuba. The narrator is also the daughter of a Jamaican father and a Barbadian mother, which was very common. The silk-cotton tree symbolizes the two. It's the voice of those women who suffered, who worked, who came as small girls, who are now part of Cuba, who are black, who were maids and servants, but are part of a whole historical process, and who had to have a voice. That was my objective, in reality, and that's what's so fascinating about documentary making: these things grew. I had met Miss Jones when I was doing the research, but I had only seen Ruby, not interviewed her. So the idea of the two old ladies grew after the filming, when I had to rewrite the script.

That's the advantage of documentary: everything changes, because reality is even richer. I went with a script, but it was open to what presented itself. I'm really glad I had that approach, and the team also. We filmed everything in eleven days. We had no time for a pre-shoot. I had no lights. I never managed to get lights, and I knew that black people absorb light. We had to perform miracles. We made something called a boom light. We put a lightbulb on the microphone, made a photo-flood, and lost a lot of footage because of the reflection in people's glasses!

JS: Going back to imperfect cinema?

GR: Absolutely! Trying not to have the camera break, as it is now broken, and asking all the while, why, if this is what I want to do, is everything so uphill? Because I simply didn't have any support from ICAIC, they weren't interested in what I was doing; but that didn't mean I wasn't going to do it. The presence of the black man and woman in Cuban cinema is irregular because no directors, except Sergio Giral,[5] set out to develop a whole theme and characters in either features or documentary.

JS: All men, I take it?

GR: Men. I think if Sara had been alive, she would have done it, but she set out to do a very controversial couple, in a film I respect a lot—not because she made it, but because the reality of that couple was a reflection of Cuba.

JS: You're referring to *De cierta manera* (One Way or Another)?

GR: Yes. . . .

JS: Tomás González, the scriptwriter, has written about the early discussions between Sara Gómez and himself as to who would be the actor and actress, and Sara says, "It'd be too much" for a black woman to be accepted.[6] It's striking she felt that a lighter-skinned person was needed to make the point.

GR: I think that at this stage we should be able to have a black couple with all their conflicts. Why not? No present-day Cuban filmmaker has felt the personal need to do that. I won't speak for feature films, but documentary is much more interesting as regards a black presence. I'm not underestimating Sergio's films but am speaking in relation to various directors who have included a wide variety of figures. That's why I so admire documentary and why it's extremely important in Cuban filmography. You find incredible facets in Cuban documentary, and that presence is there in different themes by different directors. Documentary has reached into society as well as history, and I am one of its products. For the last twenty years, I've worked in nothing but documentary.

JS: Reflecting on this same point, if reality is such that documentary reflects the black population a lot more, why not feature films, too?

GR: I think there's also a consensus, an idea, that there are no black actors. If there aren't, or if those there are, are no good, then they should be looking to train them. I can't speak from personal experience because I haven't done a feature film, but I think it goes beyond that, to the very conception of a character. It doesn't even figure when the character is being written. It's as if that's another world, cut off from the filmmaker. So the character is born, grows, and is enacted in white Cuban society.

JS: Do you aspire to fill that vacuum?

GR: I aspire to do what I can. I'm working on video, not even film, and I don't know when I ever will. I have many desires and dreams. A lot will depend on help I get from abroad, not because of discrimination in the industry, but because the only projects right now are those with financing from abroad. And there's little documentary being done—from the forty-five to fifty that used to be made, there are now only two or three. Many are not making anything at all. But, as the title of a Cuban documentary goes, "we have no right to wait," and I can't wait. What am I going to do? I'll do what I can.

10

Crafting the Sacred *Batá* Drums

Juan Benkomo

From various parts of West Africa, cargoes of Congo, Carabalí, Arará, Mandinga, and Lucumí slaves were brought to Cuba. They brought to the Caribbean their language, religion, dance, music, and instruments to celebrate their beliefs and their traditional festivals. An early manifestation of African art in the Antilles was the crafting of those instruments by men skilled in their making. And the drum, more than any other of those musical instruments, became the collective, tellurian sound of a race determined not to disappear. The *batá* drums didn't take their shape and sacred form until the nineteenth century when—after the Fula destruction of the Lucumí capital in 1825— major shipments of black Lucumí came to Havana and Matanzas, bringing with them the *añá*, or personal and religious conditions, to be *tamboreros* (sacred drummers). The *batá* drums exist nowhere else in the Americas outside of Havana and Matanzas, though there are some drums that are similar, especially in Brazil, where there was also a strong Yoruba influence. In Cuba, the *batá* drums are linked with *orisha* worship. There are three drums, with hides at each end, played in horizontal fashion on the player's lap or hanging from the neck. The use of two hides of different diameter and the drums' variable height gives them a rich and melodic tonality. The largest and main drum is the Iyá (the word for mother in Yoruba), which has a sharp, grave sound. The Itótele, or medium drum, is grave and sometimes the bass. The Okónkolo, the smallest, is high in pitch, like a cornet. The drumhead is tightened or loosened by hide strips round an hourglass form. Small and large bells adorn the sides of the Iyá, for additional sounds. A ritual preparation of a resinous substance is also applied to the larger drum hide to absorb some of the vibration and give it a sharper timbre. According to Yoruba belief, there is an *orisha* in all three, but especially Iyá. Therein lies its secret, or *añá,* and the strict ritual of its making, which requires animal sacrifice for the drum to "feed" like the gods, abstinence of the players, and consultation with sanctified hides that speak the Lucumí language. The secret of making the sacred drums of the *orishas* has been passed on from generation to generation, to our time. Juan Benkomo has inherited the secrets and is today a maker of *batá* drums. For him, drums can laugh loud like Ochún; be delicate like Elegguá, god of the paths; or go into a fury like Changó, god of lightning. They are like men: they eat and love, they can joke, they can be cruel, weak, and strong. When I talked with him in the intense Havana sunlight outside his home, Benkomo was devastating the trunk of an almond tree that believers in the town of Palmira, Matanzas province, would consecrate to Argayú. From this would come the Iyá. Without interrupting his labor, Benkomo agreed to share with me some of the drum secrets that can be told. (PPS)

JB: Argayú is the father of Changó, the man who carried the world on his shoulders. The syncretism is Saint Christopher, but the *orisha* is Argayú. First we pray to the wood to be offered to Argayú, we ask the wood, we give it coconut, and then start work. This is almond. The *batá* drum should be made of cedar but, since this one is going to be for a set *orisha,* which is Argayú, it's being made out of almond—hammer and chisel, and then hand-finish, nothing electric. It's for a *tambor* ceremony to present *iyawoses* (initiates), who will lower their heads on the Iyá. This drum has to come into being by hand, not on a lathe. That's how it has to be. The sacred instrument has to be a hand instrument. In this case, it is just the Iyá drum. When it's the set, I ask the wood who it wants to be. It can be in three portions, and I ask it who wants to be which portion. There's a part of the wood that wants to be Iyá, another part that wants to be Itótele, and another that wants to be Okónkolo. We give the coconut to the wood, before starting to work on it, and then begin to make the drums.

I think that to make this kind of drum you have to have an inner love— I mean as lived. You can't make a drum any day and any hour. When you make a drum for a ceremony, it's not you who's doing the work, it's the dead who are working with you. And when the dead want to work is when you can make the drum. If it was up to me, I'd make a drum every five minutes, but there are times when no matter how much I want to, I can't. The drum comes when the dead want to work. If the *eggú* doesn't work on the wood, it doesn't happen, because the dead do the work, I'm only matter, I'm not the one doing the work. I can make you a drum in six months or in twenty-four hours. It depends on how the dead feel and work. They say it's not easy. I think it is, but not everyone's born for it, and so not everyone can make a drum.

I learned on my own. One day I just made a drum. I remember it was totally deformed. When I put the hide on, it wouldn't tune, and I paid close attention to the physical details of the instrument until . . . well, I've been making these drums now for over thirty years. And they say I'm not that bad making them, everyone likes my drums. I never play the drums. I give them open to the Olú, the Babalawo, who comes to get them. I give him the hides, the rings, and the Babalawo performs the secret ritual to put the *añá* in the drum; from then on it's theirs. I haven't asked much. What I'm interested in is them doing it and, as they say, the link is Benkomo, so they come here and I make the drums for them, which is as far as it goes. But I do ask them what the drum is for. When it's for musical purposes, I do it in two days. A drum for religious purposes takes a month. That's the physical making, without introducing what is contained within. That's down to the priests, the *orosaín* and the Babalawos, who are the ones to give voice to the drum.

Right now I'm preparing to make a series for Grand Canary. I'm going chisel in hand, with some *irú,* and we're going to see what can be done over there, in that other *ará* close to Africa. But for now we're doing this, doing what we can.

Without the love, this can't be done, because without love the tradition is lost. Now it's become a business. The new generation's generally after the greenback dollar that moves everything. I make them, with or without that money, and I often make them to give away. People come who need a drum and don't have the money and I offer them a drum. That's not why I say I work for the love of the art, because I have to keep the children, a woman, and economics is basic to life. But you shouldn't mistake money for love. There are many who have commercialized the religion and its attributes. For me, the drum is a sacred thing. The drum is an *orisha.* It has its birthday, it eats, it has to be initiated with coconut. It has a life of its own. There are days when, to play the drum, it has to be asked if it wants to play, because if it says no, it shouldn't be played. There are times when it's tired, when it doesn't want to work. And so we go on. Up to now, here is Benkomo, seeking to keep alive that tradition I don't know who gave me.

PPS: Have you always been the same Benkomo?

JB: No! In 1972, I was head of salaries at CUBATUR, the tourist enterprise in those years. I lost my job for religious reasons, because I wore a bead necklace. That's to say, twenty, fifteen, ten years back, it was denigrating and a crime to be religious in this country, because you didn't have access to certain jobs, you couldn't be in certain social and political circles. But then, after religion was discussed at one of the party congresses, religion's become a fad or way of life.

Now you'll find whites in this country are Santeros and wear their bead necklaces. The new Babalawos of today wear their necklaces but it didn't used to be like that. It's become the fashion. I don't think everyone should be initiated as Santos, that's not the way it should be. What's happening in our country is a social phenomenon. If you were religious, you couldn't be in the party. And if you were black and religious, it was a double crime. I'm talking from my heart. I'm not exaggerating. You can go by Cuatro Caminos market, just two blocks from the house here, on Monday morning, or any morning, and see all those *iyawoses* going round the market. And you ask yourself, what is this? Before, you'd be hard put to see one *iyawo* going round the market. The *iyawo* has to go one day, though, in the oracle of Ifá, some are told not to; but most of them do have to go—I see them every morning.[1]

What's true is that Santería is on the increase—though the *orishas* were always venerated in this country, what happened was that their worship was repressed. To be singled out as religious was to be socially ostracized. You'd get up to speak at a work meeting and they'd tell you, "You can't be a party member because you're a Santero" or "because you're a Babalawo" or "because I saw you dancing at a *tambor* ceremony" or "because I saw you in church." There was a witch-hunt against the religions here and now it's just the opposite. Everyone's religious. Now everyone wears a bead necklace.

I think it's good when you wear a necklace, not around your neck necessarily, but in your heart, which is where it should be. Because I don't wear my necklaces. I wear a chain and "feed," or worship, my chain. Because there are so many people out there with bead necklaces that it puts me off being with them. In times when you couldn't wear the necklaces, I wore mine. But now that everyone has them, I've put mine away and wear the chain. The world's upside down. The whole thing's crazy. They say people like forbidden fruit and maybe that's what's happened. Forms of religious expression were prohibited for so long that, with the opening, people have cast caution aside. Even at the party congress, delegates were talking with their necklaces on the outsides of their shirts. I ask myself, what is this? Now there are people whose skin color is white saying they have a grandfather who was a slave, that their grandfather was black. Now they say they're black, when before they said they were white, that their grandparents were Spaniards. Now they say their grandparents were black Africans.

I'm from Cayo Hueso. I was born on the corner of Trillo Square in 1944. They were the times you'd come across Chano Pozo on any corner. You'd find the big *timberos* and *congueros* in Cayo Hueso. I've lived here in Jesús María for twenty-five years, here at the corner of Carmen and Vies Streets, making my instruments for a quarter century. This is my workshop, here where you see me standing at the door. This has been my workshop over all these years. I'm known for it, since I'm outside and have never hidden what I do. The big problems I've had were because I was seen doing these things, when these things were simply to promote culture from a social and religious point of view, and everybody knows me for that. This is a very religious neighborhood. Here's Jesús María Square. In her time, you'd find Digna Guerra, director of Las Jardineras *comparsa,* over there in those apartment blocks. You'd find the late Evaristo Aparicio, "Picaro,"[2] who lived near here; I've got his drums hanging here. This is a very noble, religious neighborhood, where there's culture at all hours in all parts, singing, dancing. . . . This here is Amalia neighborhood.

I first realized I was Benkomo when I was sixteen, at art school. That's where I wanted to be and where I met with big difficulties, where they demanded membership in the Communist Youth. Since that wasn't in me, because I was religious, I ran into great difficulties and had to develop my culture outside school, in the marginal neighborhoods of Carraguao (El Cerro), La Timba, Colón, La Victoria, Cayo Hueso, and here in Amalia. From drum to drum, dancing behind the *comparsa,* I've always been one for popular movement. I haven't been able to have many things I'd liked to have had because of how I've been. When you're a man and religious, and people say it and know it, politics doesn't enter into it. In this country, politics is a mechanism for getting places and having things. But I'm an apolitical individual, and in my youth that was a big taboo for me. I've come up against big hurdles because of being apolitical, though I've always been a sociable kind.

That period in the mid-1960s, when blacks couldn't let their hair grow because they'd have problems, were accused of practicing "negritude" and would be thrown out of scholarship programs, there were also those who latched onto the revolution and from those positions showed their racism and hatred. I tell you, here in Cuba there have never been whites, but they believed themselves white because their skin was that little bit lighter. I was OK until 1980. That year I was accused of being involved in Santería. The year 1980 was the Mariel exodus, the egg-and-tomato throwing, those eggs and tomatoes we now don't have. They'd throw whole crates of tomatoes, and now a bottle of tomato puree costs ten pesos. And an egg—they're seven per person on the ration every fifteen days—costs about eight pesos. Just imagine the cartons of eggs and the money flying in those times.

I was always against all that. And today Olofi has punished us, because we now need those eggs we threw. Right now. What are we going to eat today? There's yellow rice and that egg is what I now need to eat with the yellow rice that's listening to the conversation. Boy, we'd have made a tremendous yellow rice and egg. You could even pick them up from the ground, because they'd fall without even breaking!

Many stayed here playing a role that wasn't for real, but I always go by the new generations. I'd sometimes see how the police would repress the youth and I'd think that when I made a set of drums it meant fewer youth to repress, because the sound of a set of drums means three players, one singer, and a number dancing. So the drum is social prevention. Now they look after me a lot. The revolution looks out for me. I'm the spoiled child. The president of the People's Council comes and sits here and says, "We've got a children's cultural project we're doing next to here, in the 'House of Iroko,' by the silk-cotton tree over there." We're going to do lots of things, especially for the new generations, because what would I do if I didn't, if I drank it all in rum? It's better to spend it on children in song and dance, and I'm often much happier giving a set of drums to a group of children than selling them, because it's my work that's out there. Right now, I'm restoring the instruments of the Music Museum and advising the musical instrument factory.

Much of this work is without pay, though sometimes I might charge, because I do it out of conviction. Here in the museum I have a contract and they pay me for the instruments I restore. But, for example, would you believe that the musical instruments factory is right in the heart of Cerro and the children at the Culture House right there in the municipality don't have a set of *batá* drums to play. And when a drum is broken, they have nowhere to send it to be fixed. Because it's all dollar shops [shops that will not accept pesos, only dollars], and where are those kids going to get dollars? You have to sit and think. And so I'm building my own workshop, a bigger workshop. When I come back from the Canary Islands, I plan to bring back money to make a bigger workshop. We'll see how it goes. . . .

11

Grupo Antillano and the
Marginalization of Black Artists

Guillermina Ramos Cruz

Guillermina Ramos Cruz (Havana, 1948) developed an interest in Africanist themes in Cuban art soon after graduating from the University of Havana in art history in 1978, when Grupo Antillano (Antilles Group) was established. The following year, when the major Caribbean arts festival, CARIFESTA, was celebrated in Cuba, she was covering it as a journalist for several Cuban publications. Since then, she has curated exhibitions and appeared on Cuban radio and television discussing these themes. In 1993 she traveled to Venezuela to lecture on Cuban art and cultural identity at the Ateneo in Caracas. A second visit to Caracas was to organize the exhibition *De los ancestros símbolos y atributos* (Symbols and Attributes of the Ancestors), featuring Cuban painting and sculpture paying tribute to the island's African Caribbean heritage. For her, Antilles Group was instrumental in developing a dynamic art movement rooted in the history of the African diaspora in Cuba and the Caribbean linked to the revolutionary present. She began our interview by reflecting on those years. (PPS)

I began working on the theme of *africanía* in Cuban painting back in 1978, when I joined Grupo Antillano (Antilles Group) and started researching the African roots in greater depth. I was, of course, familiar with the theoretical grounding to the anthropological work of Don Fernando Ortiz and the work of master painters Wifredo Lam, Roberto Diago, and Mateo Torriente, and I pursued this up until the present.

Although there had been other groups of a similar nature, Antilles Group was different from the rest in that it was a group of artists who wanted to take up that theme and develop it much further. In effect, it was a cultural movement. Exhibitions were organized with a conceptual unity as a way of broaching the history, and present, of the African diaspora in Cuba and the Antilles, although each artist expressed this differently. There were also lectures on identity, in a dynamic sense. We had moved on from slavery and the middle passage. Now we were offering a concept from our optic: the flora, the fauna, the strength of African culture, and how this translated into the revolutionary context.

The driving force behind Antilles Group was sculptor and engraver Rafael Queneditt Morales. Africanist Rogelio Martínez Furé was its main theorist. Others were sculptors Rogelio Rodríguez Cobas and Ramón Haití Eduardo; painters Arnaldo Rodríguez Larrinaga, Leonel Morales, and Angel Laborde; and the late Manuel Coucerio Prado. Two other artists who joined the group were Miguel Ocejo and Pablo Toscano, both of whom had been in Grupo Orígen (Origin Group). They also took up the theme of the Caribbean, and the two later joined forces. They were intensive times for Antilles Group, as it became a national movement. While he was still alive, Lam met on various occasions with the group, which also involved Manuel Mendive, and recognized the work it was doing. I was fortunate enough to interview him and he saw it as very positive that there were those in the art world who were approaching that theme with new forms.

There was also some official support. We had exhibitions in the Caribbean—Suriname, Barbados, Guadeloupe—and took an active part in CARIFESTA in 1979, here in Havana. And yet, as the group strengthened, there was a certain reticence to accepting the group as a movement with Ministry of Culture support. Initially, the group was well received; it gained in strength and had support from figures in intellectual and artistic circles. The problems started later when the group advanced a more profound vision of what it was striving for. At the outset we had asked for the house of Don Fernando Ortiz; that was our goal, for the group to meet there and develop its work.

At that same time, well into the 1980s, young graduates of the Higher Institute of Art set up Grupo Volumen Uno (Volume One Group), with a trans-avant-garde vision of modernity in contemporary art, in opposition to Antilles Group, not because the latter wasn't modernist in concept, but because Volume One Group undermined all the African roots to maintain a universal modernity beyond cultural identity. In fact, it wasn't only Volume

One Group that was upholding an artistic universality based on a vision of "the other," because the Western European aesthetic had been the paradigm for generations before and for the personal originality of individual artists for whom the issue was not identity, which was the cohesive force of our group.

After Volume One Group was set up in opposition to Antilles Group, certain Ministry of Culture art advisers and critics started a public debate arguing that the theme of identity had been saturated in Cuba, ever since 1927 when generations of artists had taken up the theme. They argued that the roots with which we identified were spent. There could be an identity from the Hispanic root, or an identity from the peasant world, but we were clearly identified with an identity from the African root.

It should be said that there was support initially, and then a series of incidents began to atomize the group. On one occasion, a North American art critic from New York interviewed me on all the artists' work. It was for a New York publication, but it never came out. That and other things led me to the conclusion it was always being kept quiet. In 1982 I had a forty-five-minute TV art slot interviewing guest artists and showing their work. On one of the programs I invited artists from Grupo Raíces (Roots Group), founded by Miguel Angel Ruiz Silva, who is very knowledgeable on Cuba's African roots. After the program was recorded, it never went on air, since the recording mysteriously went missing.

In the 1980s art world in Cuba, there had been groups of artists coming together to work on a particular thematic vision, one of which was Grupo Indoamericano (Indo-American Group), set up in 1983 and headed by Jesús González de Armas, who had been researching and working on Indo-American culture. This was the context in which Volume One Group achieved international recognition with Ministry of Culture backing. For its part, Antilles Group never folded but did lose its support, while Roots Group was totally marginalized.

Many might ask why we needed official recognition to continue working. The answer is very straightforward. Official recognition implied backing to organize and take part in national and international events. In those years there was a certain silent opposition to Afro-Cuban themes.

In late 1989, postmodernity in Cuban art was successful in Paris, New York, and Madrid, but then the theorists began to take an interest in the art with African roots, because the theme was of interest to international foundations. All that Antilles Group had started to do was taken up by other artists who had realized that what was of interest at the biennials and in big galleries and museums of the West was the imagery of Cuban religious culture. A subtle and complex story began to unfold, which was an incursion into black culture without the Afro-Cuban artists.

An artist who has remained faithful to that legacy is Manuel Mendive. From the 1960s to the present, he has surmounted hurdles to become an established Cuban artist of international repute, developing his own Cuban art aesthetic, one that is intensely original and grounded in his African ancestral spirituality.

All this interest in the Afro-Cuban came at a time when UNESCO and other international cultural institutions prioritized the African presence in the Americas. In Cuba, the Fernando Ortiz Foundation was created, taking up the important legacy of Ortiz as an ethnologist and historian who, from the early decades of the twentieth century, contributed to an understanding of African roots as fundamental to a definition of what is Cuban. But why, precisely at the time when we had our project, in 1978? The foundation was headed by the writer Miguel Barnet, with the backing of the National Union of Writers and Artists of Cuba (UNEAC). Our Antilles Group, and all that came after, is there as a valid antecedent, but also as a lost battle.

There is something else about how the arts evolved. Some artists, including those in Volume One Group, started working on Indo-American culture—José Bedia, for example, took the prize at the Havana Biennial in 1984 with a North American native Indian piece. Now Bedia is in the United States and is incorporating into his work elements of the religious culture of Palo Mayombé, in which he says he had been initiated. And so, over time and outside Cuba, the majority of these artists who started out with a contemporary vision, influenced by North American trends, have been taking up Afro-Cuban themes derived from Cuban popular religious culture.

Those who were in Roots Group, headed by Miguel Angel Ruiz Silva, are almost all abroad. The only one in Cuba is Miguel Angel Ruiz. Tagle went to Paris to lecture on Afro-Cuban culture and later settled in Mexico. Roberto Manito is working in Canada.

I have tried to follow the work of Cuban artists who continue to work with their own explosive metaphor. I reviewed the *Errant Avantgarde, Generation of the Eighties* exhibition in the Euro-American Art Center in Caracas, Venezuela, in March 1994. The artists were Gustavo Acosta, Julio Antonio, José Bedia, Consuelo Castañeda, Humberto Castro, Arturo Cuenca, Florencio Gelabert, Quisqueya Henríquez, Ibrahím Miranda, Alexis Novoa Vian, Ciro Quintana, Rubén Torres Llorca, and Juan-Si. Since the art world has continued its course in Cuba, there are artists here who work on the African presence in the Americas but have not had the possibility of taking part in international events, like Nancy Sesma Muñoz, who paints and sketches, as well as doing craft work and installations.

That's why I am struck by the fact that, when there is no cohesive movement of interests, affinities, and concepts, there can't be work that transcends as a social force, for black people to feel strong by what they see represented in the art. As an art critic, I have come to the conclusion that in Cuba a group of people with a position that might change social concepts is not liked or welcomed. There's an old adage in Cuba that's become very popular, which is that whites don't like blacks in positions above them.

Those of us who are researchers, critics, and artists, who have remained in Cuba and continued in this line, are isolated. When this kind of work is done in isolation, with no close relationship between individuals working in similar directions, it does not transcend at the social level. That is what has been happening here, which has meant that many of us have spent many years working on this alone. I think that in Cuba it isn't accepted that people can meet and take a stand that might express another level of analysis with regard to the black in Cuba, and very much so regarding the problematic of black intellectuals and artists in the Cuban cultural field.

Many researchers, historians, artists, and musicians who for years have worked in this direction have been ignored or excluded when institutions such as the Fernando Ortiz Cultural Foundation are set up. Those who work on these themes who are white are considered ethnologists or anthropologists, but if they are black they are considered religious or Santeros and never occupy their rightful position.

I graduated in 1978, and I do believe I have experience. . . . I don't want to stray from the interview, because an individual experience can be anecdotal and we are conceptualizing here. But I know that here in Cuba there have been attempts to disactivate what might amount to cohesion, especially of those who have been historically marginalized. There have been situations that are highly significant. What many have wanted to do among their own, in their own country, they have had to achieve on their own abroad. Caridad Martínez, a mulatto ballerina with the National Ballet of Cuba, broke her pearl mask and created her own ballet in Mexico. Nicolás Reinoso, founder of the first-generation Afro-Cuba Group, is playing his music in Uruguay. Novelist Manolo Granados continues to write in Paris. And there are many others who found themselves on weak ground, without the backing they needed, and decided to change context.

There are times it's like going back to square one, when the black is satirized on stage or on television, as if we were back in the times of Víctor Patricio Landaluce, the nineteenth-century Spanish painter who satirized the black but also left a historical presence of the black in his painting. Nowadays, a black is satirized with deformed speech. There may be aspects in which the concept of identity has evolved, but at the social level we're still in the nineteenth century when the black was satirized for not speaking good Spanish. In my everyday life, I'm alarmed at times by the things I see that haven't changed.

I'm currently working on the theme of identity, but since I know Cuba, I'm interested in Venezuela, Brazil, black Peru, and Caribbean art. I think blacks in Cuba have a lot to give. I see my individual problem generalized. Whether in UNEAC, or the University of Havana, or in a gathering of intellectuals, I don't see criteria whereby blacks are seen as equals, as musician Juan Formell[1] would say. There are certain subtleties that do not translate literally, but there are many things that are said between the lines, translated by racial prejudice. And there are many omissions. I think that one of the most terrible things in Cuba has been the omissions. I didn't know about the black Cuban writer Gastón Baquero. I was never told, and it was in Venezuela that I had to find out who Gastón Baquero was—a mulatto writer, considered to be one of the best Spanish-language poets of this century.[2]

I think the black continues to be marginalized at the intellectual level. I think this because I live it. My proposition is that we need to unite because we are all dispersed. I don't think the theme of identity is closed. On the contrary! My grandson tells me, "I'm a free mulatto," because that's what he sees and hears on television. "No," I say, "you're black!" I don't want him to be a black with a slave mentality, but a black with a self-perception that is not exclusionary. And that's how things are. At the moment, we are excluded, marginalized, and out of context. I don't mean politically, I'm speaking of self-denial. When I recognize who I am, I can act. But when you see the obstacles, you see it as a denial of self, and then you exclude yourself, and go someplace else.

Perhaps it might be possible to bring all that presence together. I believe, and am pleased by the thought, that if I am black here in Cuba and feel I have strength, then so also can I can be in Brazil or Martinique. The point is that I not lose the vision of who I really am.

12

A National Cultural Identity?

Homogenizing Monomania and the Plural Heritage

Rogelio Martínez Furé

Rogelio Martínez Furé was born in 1937 in Matanzas, the second major city of western Cuba after Havana, and one that received major black cargoes of Arará and Lucumí slaves during the nineteenth century. The Yoruba, or Lucumí as they are known in Cuba, were among the most culturally developed of the African nations, for the rich liturgy of their belief systems, their sacred instruments, music, song, and dance. Like Havana, Matanzas has a rich cultural tradition of African origin. That world was without a doubt what led Martínez Furé to specialize in the history of African civilizations and their influence on Afro-America. The author of major works on the culture of Africa and the African diaspora, he pioneered the study of African literature in Cuba. He is also a founder-member of and adviser to Cuba's National Folklore Group. My mentor of over thirty-five years and a veritable torrent of knowledge—who better to outline his concept of the Caribbean, Cuba, and the polemic concept of *afrocubanía*. (PPS)

RMF: I believe there is a Caribbean civilization, in this region of the so-called New World, which is complementary to the realities of the Caribbean civilization of our African ancestors. The autochtonous indigenous population was almost totally exterminated and substituted for African forced labor wherever the plantation system of agriculture took hold. There was, then, a rupture of the different African civilizations, from western, central, or eastern Africa, which became syncretized with elements of the dominant European cultures—Spanish, English, French, Dutch. Out of that synthesis emerged the typically Caribbean civilization.

On each island, in each territory of our geographical area, particular national cultures emerged according to the economic, historic, geographic, and political realities in each of those places. That existence of national cultures does not, however, deny, but rather reaffirms, the existence of a civilization throughout our region.

It has a very defined profile, distinct from what is called "Latin America"—a term created in the mid-nineteenth century which I have always rejected because I think of it as alienating, a term that conceals the complexity, richness, diversity, and plurality of our historical experience, our historical heritage. When we say we are Latin American, I ask myself, where is the Indo-American element, where is the African element, where is the Asiatic, Chinese, Arab or Hebrew, where is the Hindu or Indonesian part of our America?

So how does Cuba fit into this Caribbean context? I don't think it has to, because it has always been a fundamental part of the Caribbean. You can't say it was integrated a posteriori into a concept of the Caribbean. On the contrary, it's been part of the Caribbean from the start. We shouldn't forget that Cuba was the second island visited by the Spaniards, that Columbus reached Guananí on 12 October 1492, so if any country forms part of the terrible history of ours, it's Cuba. The ethnic makeup of Cuba is typically Caribbean. First, there is the Arawak, Taino, and Siboney presence. Then there is the Iberian presence, but from the south, especially Andalucia, Castile, the Canary Islands, Extremadura, peoples and cultures that are in themselves very mixed, the product of Europe plus Africa and the East. As for the African components coming here in the early sixteenth century, there are many Guineans, Sudanese, and Bantu.

All the conquest campaigns began in Cuba. It shouldn't be forgotten that Hernán Cortés left from Cuba on his expedition to conquer Mexico and soon after came the slave trade and slavery. Cuba is one of the first regions where the extermination of the Indo-Caribbean population began. The ideas of the French Revolution and of the great Haitian Revolution come into Cuba, and the struggle for freedom in Cuba goes back to the early sixteenth century. The slave regime in Cuba is one of the most prolonged in the New World. We were the next-to-last country to abolish slavery, in 1886, and Brazil in 1888. From the sixteenth century up until the nineteenth century, our history is one of slavery and of Spanish colonial rule. Our people's tradition of struggle, therefore, comes from the maroons and their settlements, and the conspiracies of the nineteenth century. These are characteristic features of our Caribbean reality—in addition to the extermination of indigenous peoples. But it so happens that the awareness of being Caribbean has not been homogeneous in all the lands that belong to this Caribbean civilization. That depends on the degree of intellectual maturity, assumed ethnic awareness, and in Cuba there have of course been many aware of our Caribbeanness, as there have in Jamaica, the Dominican Republic, and Haiti. But the Caribbean is divided. One half is of absolute evasion, alienation, and not wanting to recognize the fact; and the other half is aware of its creative potential, virtues that can be built on and defects to be overcome—of becoming what you are, as Goethe said in the eighteenth century. I think many of us in the Caribbean have become what we are, aware of our origins, of our problems, and we take on that reality with all its defects and all its virtues.

In the case of Cuba, I think that when Fernando Ortiz first used the terms "Hispano-Cuban" and "Afro-Cuban," he did so in an attempt to clarify, classify, and study in greater depth his observations of Cuban reality. He said that Cuban culture is in a constant process of formation. Those parts of Cuban culture which are predominantly of Hispanic origin, he called Hispano-Cuban: for example, the country music form *punto guajiro,* the tradition of string instruments, colonial architecture. Those other parts of Cuban culture which are predominantly of African origin, he called Afro-Cuban: for example, *orisha* worship, rumba, *son.* Cuban is the synthesis, he said, of European antecedents, principally Hispanic and French, with African antecedents, fused on what remained of Indo-Cuban cultures, and enriched by those brought by the Chinese and others.

Don Fernando always said that it should not be thought that the African was grafted on a preexistent Cuban culture, but rather, on the contrary, the Cuban came of the fusion of African and Spanish, plus other elements. But there are some who evidently choose to forget this. They say "Cuban" and "Afro-Cuban," as if Afro-Cuban is something else and Cuban is chemically pure, Hispanic, or white. That's when you find the biggest mistake of all, which is to talk about Cuban music and Afro-Cuban music, when most of the genres known throughout the world as Cuban music have been created by those of African descent. In the final analysis, it's Afro-Cuban music.

Habanera, danzón, danza, contradanza, son, rumba, conga, cha-cha-cha, mambo, *bolero*—they're all the creation of Cubans of African descent, of blacks and mulattos (*pardos* and *morenos* as they were called in the nineteenth century). In all those genres there is a synthesis of the musical tradition of European origin, mainly French and Spanish, with those of African origin. That means you can't say Cuban music and Afro-Cuban music. That's a huge mistake. It's the same nonsense we see and hear with Latin jazz. In the first place, there's no such thing as Latin jazz. What's called Latin jazz employs the rhythmic and melodic base of Cuban Lucumí, Congo, Arará, and Abakuá tradition. It's called Latin jazz, but why not Afro-Cuban jazz or simply Cuban jazz?

That's to say, the terms are used erroneously and I don't believe innocently, but rather to conceal the true roots of our cultural forms. That's why I always insist that there's too much talk about roots, about the antecedents of Cuba and of other world cultures. That's fine, it's right we should try to trace our cultural traditions or ancestors, it's important to know where we come from, but it's as or more important to know who we are.

I think there's been enough insistence on roots and we should exalt the outcome, what we are, because we are a mature culture. There is, of course, no homogeneous Cuban culture, which is why I also think it's a mistake to speak of a national cultural identity. There is no one national cultural identity. In all countries of the world, there are multiethnic, pluricultural identities. In all countries of the world, pluriculturalism is prevalent. What we must accept is the plural heritage, not homogenizing monomania. In Cuba there is no one cultural identity, there are diverse national cultural identities, or, to simplify, there is a multiethnic, pluricultural identity. A mulatto Cuban from Baracoa, the descendant of Haitian emigrés in a coffee-growing area, is not the same as a black Cuban descendant of Arará from the province of Matanzas. a sugar-growing area, or a fair-skinned Cuban from Pinar del Río, a tobacco-growing area, the descendant of Canary Islanders. They are all Cuban, but there are differences in food, speech, psychology, religious beliefs, and phenotype. I believe it is important to accept plurality and free ourselves from that monomania, according to which we're all the same. As a great Chinese thinker said, the garden is beautiful because there are white, yellow, and red flowers; how boring a garden with flowers that are all the same color.

The problem lies in accepting what we are critically, not idealistically, believing ourselves to be the world's navel. We must cast aside chauvinism and xenophobia, and not drive a wedge between our differences, because we might well fall into one of two camps which are for me erroneous. The first, a negative type, is to say, "We are that which makes us different from other people" and the other, mimetic, whereby "We are like other people." I think there are elements in common and elements which differentiate us, the product of our historical experience in a specific island called Cuba. But the concept of national identity has changed dialectically. Each epoch has its identity. In the times of Domingo del Monte,[1] the meaning of the word "Cuban" was not the same—because we know that in 1835 a Cuban was of the white population, whilst the majority in the country who were black and mulatto were excluded—as in 1875 after the outbreak of the Ten Years War, or in 1895 with the War of Independence, or the very concept of Cuban in 1912 with the war of Evaristo Estenoz and Pedro Yvonet;[2] nor is it the same after Fernando Ortiz wrote on his anthropological research findings and Guillén published his books of poetry, or Amadeo Roldán and Alejandro García Caturla[3] composed their great symphonies inspired in the tradition of music of African origin in Cuba, in the 1930s. Neither is it the same in 1959 as in 1980 or 1995.

The concept of Cuban has been enriched dialectically. I always say it's like a river current whose waters are constantly replenished but the river is constant and ultimately flows into the ocean of humankind. I think it's illusory to be seeking always what makes us different. It's good to accept differential traits, not in an antagonistic sense, but simply as a particular face, as Nicolás Guillén would say, but not forgetting that we are all part of the human species.

PPS: Of your published work, one stands out in relation to the theme we are discussing: *Diálogos imaginarios* (Imaginary Dialogues).[4] Are there points you would have dealt with differently, were you writing that book in recent years?

RMF: I wrote those essays in the early 1970s and I've been revising them for a second edition to be published here in Cuba, but my experience of life has demonstrated to me the validity of what I wrote back then. The magazine *Revolución y cultura* ran an interview with me titled "Folklore y seudofolklore, modas y modos" (Folklore and Pseudofolklore, Fashions and Forms), which I see as a continuation of *Imaginary Dialogues*. That's to say, it goes into greater depth on certain aspects, related to problems I foresaw back then with respect to using traditional popular culture as a commodity. I saw it coming, that popular patrimony had to be treated with care, because people who had neither respected it nor been part of its expression were, when the time came, going to take it up in a commercial way. I developed a concept that's being very much quoted, which is that of "pseudocultural *jineterismo*" (prostitution).

Look at what's happened with Cuban religions of African origin. There's a whole parasitic layer calling themselves priests, or Babalawos, or Babalochas, who are simply prostituting traditional Cuban religion. Santería for tourist leisure. It's very dangerous. And I warned it would happen. You invent a pseudofolklore that, instead of exalting the positive values of popular traditions, simply presents the most superficial, the most deformed, and of course that negative attitude to our cultural heritage leads many people, who were already prejudiced where popular culture is concerned, to reaffirm and strengthen their rejection of popular culture. Because we all become an exotic landscape, which is terrible. Cuban culture or Caribbean civilization is comprised of natives, not the product of cultures with universal values. We are not exotic landscapes and, I repeat, we have to reject that self-exoticising vision to attract leisure tourism.

I think *Imaginary Dialogues* definitely has a relevance today. I intend to continue working with those concepts and coming down on all that I see as depredating popular patrimony. In the same way that there is a struggle against those who are environmental depredators of the Amazon, and of marine fauna, it is equally valid to struggle against those who would depredate traditional popular culture. It always has been and always will be valid, as with any other cultural manifestation. In short, if I were to write *Imaginary Dialogues* again, I think that, except for some minor updates, it would stay the same. My opening sentence is: "Here I am, sitting in the shade of the 'ravenalas'. . . preoccupied by disturbing thoughts: Zionists' expansion in the Sinai, deaths every day in Santiago [Chile], unending fratricidal war in Ireland." I would simply have to change the places and say, "I continue to be horrified by the fratricidal war in Ireland, the struggle in the Middle East, the war in Chiapas, the wars in Sri Lanka, the ethnic wars in Ruanda and Burundi. . . ." That's to say, we continue to confront problems whose seeds were sown decades ago, problems for which nobody has come up with the solutions, because the will isn't there to accept plurality.

PPS: It's hard to have you reflect on your own grandeur, but how do you see the relationship between you, as a cultural wizard, and your work, which is like balsam?

RMF: I think you always have space—I have through my work—to be a link in the chain of transmission of past culture to the present and future. It's not me as an individual that matters, but my wish to contribute to a process of feedback. I gather what I can of oral culture, thanks to the trust of old people who are truly living libraries (in the words of Baa, the great Malian thinker), to help the people of Cuba understand their historical heritage—and peoples of other countries, because I have been fortunate enough to work not only in Cuba. I have traveled to almost fifty countries of all continents where I have been asked to speak on this topic. Because it is not only a concern of those of us in the Caribbean; I have found it throughout Europe, Asia, Africa, and the Americas. Right now, the more aware in all countries know traditional cultures are gravely endangered; there are honest persons who wish to salvage that which is salvageable of the positive values that are the legacy of our forebears. That's why, wherever I'm invited, I speak of pluricultural identity, the need for each individual to accept the plurality of no culture being the center of the world. As the wise saying goes, "God the Father spread beauty and ugliness, good and evil, among all people on earth." When we can accept the other, who is different, and feel the same love and respect as for ourselves, that will be a first step towards working together to salvage world patrimony. I think we have work to do, not in offices but out among the people, for our peoples to be aware of their popular traditions, to have a critical appraisal of our realities, in all countries, in all peoples of the world. If we play our part, I believe that we, as the researcher, the anthropologist, the folklorist, all have a role. I am aware, for example, that if so-called folklore groups do not play a much more active role in cultivating an awareness among our peoples, they will become simple showcases of a pseudoart and artificial art forms to entertain the tourists, which is not the function or role or objective for which they were founded, which was that of helping people take on their heritage, free from that inferiority complex, conscious that they are the creators of cultural forms that have universal value, as is any painter or writer in any rich city of the so-called First World.

This is why my work has been very varied. In 1962 I founded the National Folklore Group with Mexican Rodolfo Reyes, and a large part of my life has been devoted to field research and conceptualizing shows as one of the artistic directors and the folklore adviser of the company. The shows are not only for the theater but out among the people who are the creators of popular culture, both traditional and contemporary. That's one of my activities, but I've also taught for forty years, at all levels, from peasant children in the Sierra Maestra to the diplomatic corps, the university and the Higher Institute of Art. I have lectured in universities in Asia, Africa, Europe, North and South America, and the Caribbean. At the same time, I have written my books. For over three decades, I have studied ancient and modern African literature, and translated it into Spanish. I have also collected Cuban oral tradition, especially on our African antecedents. I am a singer and composer. I have worked in all the dance and theater companies of this country—Modern Dance, the National Puppet Theater, the Popular Art Theater. I have worked with painters and sculptors. That's to say, my ambition and my desires have always been to act as a sort of catalyst. I have had the privilege of living Cuban libraries—some now dead, those eighty- and ninety-year-olds—entrusting me as the keeper, as the Paleros would say, of their treasures of national patrimony, which are what I wish to share with others, not only in Cuba but the whole world. So I can't say I'm this or I'm that. I inherited from maestro Fernando Ortiz science, conscience, and patience. There's an African proverb which says that "lies bear flowers but not fruits." You can be firm in struggling for the values in which you believe and never abandon the battlefield to your enemies, because when you do, the battle's lost. For me it's wonderful when I go on television and the butcher calls me, and the old man in the bread queue talks to me, the housewife, and they say, "Rogelio, I saw you on TV, I agree with what you said. . . . You're right. . . . It has to be said." They're telling me they got the message. I'm referring to a program I took part in for Culture Day, when I talked about cultural identity and said there's a multiethnic, pluricultural identity, and I referred to OCHA-TOUR, where people pay money to go on a tourist trip of Santería houses. What's that?!

13

Grounding the Race Dialogue

Diaspora and Nation

Nancy Morejón

Nancy Morejón and I were together at the University of Havana, in the School of Letters, in the early 1960s. We would read our poems to each other and to fellow student friends, and we'd delight in the urban treasures of Havana back then, the libraries and bookstores, before descending exhausted on the Coppelia ice cream parlor, to work at our writing. There was a time when we were so close that almost every day we'd stroll hand in hand back to her place, in the heart of Los Sitios, one of Havana's famous popular neighborhoods. There she lived with her parents in a narrow little house crammed with books, family photos, and school diplomas. I can't remember when it dawned on me that it was no coincidence we'd arrive just at the time her father Felipe, a cigar maker, and "la China," her mother, were about to sit down to eat. The invitation was impossible to refuse. To their delight, we would tell them stories about what had happened that day at the university. I can recall now Camila Henríquez Ureña translating the classics directly from Greek and Latin, because she didn't trust the translated versions, and Mirta Aguirre, with her passion for the life and work of Sor Juana Inés de la Cruz; she, more than anyone else, taught us the secrets of how to write good verse and throw out a bad poem in good time. I found Nancy Morejón's knowledge of French and French Afro-Caribbean literature as contagious as her smile and sense of rhythm. Night's intimacy became a complicity that has lasted to this day, despite some heavy political and literary differences. Since those early days, we have been together on panels and poetry readings in the Caribbean, Europe, and the United States, and she has been a guest in our home in Havana and London. But I was specially delighted when she finally agreed to this interview in 1996. A year later, her views on the *chavacanería* (vulgarity) of Cuban bands, creating a negative image of blacks for tourist consumption, appeared all the more timely. At the summer 1997 World Festival of Youth and Students, La Charanga Habanera was publicly criticized, and subsequently apologized, for a performance that was considered indecent and denigratory to women. (PPS)

NM: The ethnic factor, it has to be recognized, is fundamental as the twentieth century, and the millennium, draw to a close. The experience of the Eastern European countries is a lesson. We cannot speak of utopias, of social change, or anything else, without reference to that basic turnaround which threw into question a whole philosophical thinking and political practice. And yet, I think that in Cuban history, the race question is one that is a shared universal experience, of our neighbors to the north, of our neighbors to the south which are the Caribbean islands, but one that in us has been extraordinarily linked to the search for a national identity. If we take, for example, the work of Juan Gualberto Gómez, the close friend of José Martí, who helped found the Cuban Revolutionary Party, we can see how crucial this is.[1] All of nineteenth-century journalism was marked by the ideas of Juan Gualberto Gómez—which were integrationist, naturally. The journalistic thinking of Nicolás Guillén[2] also stemmed from the thinking of Juan Gualberto Gómez. And in that vein my own poetry has always been linked to the phenomenon of nation.

While I respect the concept of diaspora, the concrete experience and reality of the African diaspora, I believe that diaspora cannot in any way be divorced from the phenomenon of nation. That is, a black from Panama, whose ancestors might have come from the contemporary world of Barbados or Martinique to build the Panama Canal, cannot lose sight of the fact that those ancestors from Martinique or Barbados were in turn the descendants of slaves transplanted from the sixteenth century on, in the context of the whole colonial edifice of the Americas. That's undeniable.

I say this by way of explaining that I think there are a number of black and mulatto women writers in whom this phenomenon fluctuates. They may evidence lesser or greater awareness of the phenomenon, as the full

Cuban citizens they feel themselves to be. One woman who is older than me, and who for me demonstrates this well, is Georgina Herrera. Her poetry is very varied, there are times when the phenomenon is apparent and others when it is not, but the literary merit is undeniable. Another woman who comes to mind, earlier than Georgina, is Rafaela Chacón Nardi, whose mother was Martinican. I see the Caribbean in lyrical, poetic form in the work of Rafaela, but not in race terms. Then there are younger women poets, like Soleida Ríos, who definitely do not express a nationality through race. I think we're all very different. And that's just speaking of my experience in Havana, in the heart of the city. I don't know what's happening in this respect in Matanzas, where there's an interesting poetry movement; so far I haven't met anyone working on this theme. But there must be in Santiago de Cuba, Camagüey, Pinar del Río, all over the island. It would be pretentious on my part to say that I know all that's being done and published. One thing we have to overcome when we come out of what we've called the Special Period, are the shadows of communication, which has nothing to do with the power cuts, but with the rupture of a whole language of civilization. The gas shortage is real and its effect has been felt. We have to recover that and I think there'll be surprises in store, marvelous writers. People don't stop writing despite the great drawbacks of not being in the technological world. As Cuban intellectuals, writers, and artists, we have had to move multiple obstacles and I think we've found an essentially human form of expression living in an age of technology without it. I don't think that detracts from our work. But there are undoubtedly limitations.

I'm not so concerned all these things should be reflected in an anthology. I am concerned about the absence, or invisibility, of the historical phenomenon. Tomorrow there may well be some strange admirer of José Antonio Saco[3] deciding that no Cuban woman poet celebrating her blackness should be part of the Cuban nationality. It could happen. The problem is not that there be an anthology recognizing this, but that there be literary output; that it be revealed twenty or twenty-five years later matters less. In that sense, I'm not pessimistic, because I think that, for example, it's there in the arts. There's a painter called Belkis Ayón who's doing very good work, or another painter Reynaldo López, who studied with Roberto Diago, as his disciple and friend. The work of Reynaldo López lies between that of Wifredo Lam, of Diago, and the work of Agustín Cárdenas. Reynaldo López is a man who has been doing extraordinary work now for thirty years. Afro-

Cuban myth is a primordial presence in his painting, which is very personal, lyrical, devoid of stereotypes. I think that stubbornness of his, painting how he wants, not what's in vogue, has had its price. I think he has paid a price for his purity of expression. His figures, the animals, all bear the trace of the African man and woman in Cuba.

PPS: It's evident that the theme of women concerns you, but also that of blacks in Cuba today. What do you see as the biggest obstacles to blacks developing intellectually on a par with the rest of the population?

NM: I think the stereotypes have prevailed. For example, in the sports world. We open a magazine, and there they are. In Cuban sports you find lots of black men and women, mulatto men and women, and whites. In the world of music, it's exactly the same. But the question's been raised as to why there are no black Cuban swimmers, when Cuba's an island. Water sports are the least changed. Not so long ago, the whole Havana seafront was in commotion. Speedboat races were the city sensation and people took part quite spontaneously. In those sea-related sports, you won't find a swimmer, anyone, with that phenotype taking part. I believe, fanaticism aside, that blacks have a traumatic relationship with the sea. We came by sea, and it would take a huge psychological study in each and every family, on the fear of the sea in blacks and their descendants. I think the proof lies in the phenomenon, which is yet to be analyzed. There's also no black chess player, though the black's around and in other sports. I think it's not so much that there's been a collective consciousness to perpetuate the stereotypes, but rather the image in the mass media and certain propaganda. Wherever there's a chicken thief, or negative social behavior, the associated image is immediately black, or at least mulatto. I think there's a whole legacy of the vernacular stereotype that remains within us and hasn't been wiped out.

For the black image to be funny, the black has to have little education so as to fit the vernacular stereotype. It's the same in the United States. They created the minstrel stereotype that was challenged and exploded in the 1970s. We're still confronting those stereotypes. I think we need far more profound dialogue, one that is more rigorous and grounded, with regard to race, and which has to be tackled head on, because there's a resurgence of racism worldwide. Naturally, in each part of the world, it has a name: Turk, for the Mediterranean world; Muslim, for the Arabs; and in our world, the

Indian and the black. I think it's a phenomenon of the end of century, of the millennium, for which we must seek an urgent response, because there's evidently a resurgence. I think it's fatal that it feeds on a larger racism that has mushroomed since the demise of the socialist countries. We thought that nations and collectivist societies had resolved their historic ethnic problems. And that wasn't the case. That's why the ethnic factor is basic. It comes in many stripes.

I think art has to be autonomous in relation to these phenomena. Naturally I express myself on these topics as a Cuban writer, not a social scientist. I can't be asked to be the social scientist. I don't have that vision. I may be wrong about many things, but that's how I express myself. I think there are many battles yet to be won. I think we have traveled in a good direction, and that should be recognized. The popular masses have won a space where the *mestizaje* Guillén spoke so much about, and which has been so important to me, has gained ground. I think that's important, but there's another space that has to be won, which is historical reflection, knowing more about our history of slavery and the black and mulatto population of Cuba. I think there's a lot we don't know about our own history, because, although we've been a heroic country on many fronts, we've not been systematic in teaching our history grounded in the heroic values we have so systematically upheld all these years. We need to know a lot more. A man like Juan Gualberto Gómez, there are perhaps some—not my generation—but maybe a 15-year-old today doesn't really know who Juan Gualberto Gómez was. That's serious. It says a lot about moving towards the future without looking to our roots. I see these issues as fundamental to the history of the nation and I don't like to exclude, to see things exclusively through my own individuality and experience. There are many others to which I'm not privy and on those I can't speak. What I can say is based on a wider experience, from TV and radio.

PPS: What do you see as the art forms that are in the media playing a negative or positive role?

NM: Thinking about the stage, the actors' world, when we see black and mulatto actors in this country have to play slave roles or roles where the social behavior of the black transgresses the law and social custom. If I'd been an actress in this country I'd be really hung up because it's impossible to see a black character functioning normally in contemporary Cuban society. It's practically impossible. I think that's really a result, a consequence of those stereotypes that have remained over all these years. And I think there's a conformity. Fortunately, my vocation was always for literature, and also theater, with the visual arts in a very second place. But if I'd been born wanting to be an actress, I don't know what would have become of me.

PPS: And in the case of music?

NM: There's been a very rich continuity. I think that music expresses most our *cubanidad*. But I think that right there's a whole other stereotype. It goes with the bad black, the vulgar black who talks and acts bad. There's a word used a lot, which is *chavacanería*, that I think all Cuban blacks and mulattos get accused of one way or another. It's hard to find it leveled at someone whose skin isn't dark. Show me if I'm wrong. That's how it is. There have been many times when my personal dignity has been very scarred, and it's heart-wrenching, I've often felt very alienated. I'm against that *chavacanería*, as it's called, but I see that behind the adjective there's a rejection of the black, or that stereotype we hang onto, of the black ogre, the uneducated black. And yet it's the only vision, and there's a passivity: that is, I take that image, which is the image they give me of myself, and I accept it. That image is uncritically produced and reflected on TV.

PPS: Who produces it, the music, for example?

NM: Some black musicians ride the stereotype, because it sells. While rejected, it sells, it's a success, among blacks as well. So the black is seen as stupid, as someone who talks bad, who sweats and shouts and gyrates, and behaves in a socially inferior way. And I have to accept that canon, because I've been told over and again it's my canon. That person is my color, and there's no escaping it. The worst thing is rejecting the type. We all suffer from it, and it needs to be studied. Fanon said that a society is or isn't racist. I think that all Cubans, all those of us who live here and belong to different races, have an obligation to confront this problem, whatever color we are, because it's a problem of nationhood. It's of vital importance to us, as the Indian question is to the Guatemalans, the Mexicans, and the Peruvians; or in the United States, where the very term "immigrant," as Patrice Lumumba said, has racist connotations—the immigrant is assumed to be nonwhite, is always colored and disadvantaged, not only for entering an unknown territory in search of gold, in the majority of cases. The one who arrives is always different, the other, it's the "otherness" that is still questioned, and that's why it's such a hot issue in big European metropolises of our day. After the fall of the socialist countries and in the United States, this phenomenon of migration is key.

So I think there has to be a big antiracist campaign and we have to study racism. We're on the brink of a philosophical rethinking of countries of color, of the emerging cultures, in postmodernist language, of the periphery. That periphery is condemned always to be immigrant and other, the otherness of European.

PPS: To what extent is the economic factor influencing this?

NM: I can safely say I think never as much as now has there been such a visibly strong black and mulatto presence in middle positions that are sometimes more important than those at the top, because they are closer to reality. And yet, we haven't been able to recognize this publicly because the topic is taboo, and we haven't established a corresponding image of that progress. The progress is undermined by the stereotypes. We have major figures in many areas, economic, political, and cultural, who have worked and sacrificed to get where they are and who must always confront that stupid or criminal image. And that's where the problem lies. That's to say, a great ballet dancer, a black Cuban ballet dancer acclaimed abroad, sees his image reduced because the image representing him is Boncó, the comic black on Cuban TV. Whatever he does is equated with that stereotype of the uneducated but wily black, whose speech is deficient and yet he's supposed to be funny. And there's the extraordinary contradiction, because that individual has a family, a setting, a child, and the children too have a particular image. It's admirable how the actor does it, because he's a great comic, but it's of another age. It's how the figure has been treated in vernacular theater. It can be very funny but behind him there's a noise, a terrible colonial rumor, of values that are supposedly against those we have fought for.

PPS: Is it that the Cuban black has not completely decolonized?

NM: I wouldn't say that. The Cuban black has been part of the epic and everyday life of this country. It's more the absence of dialogue in relation to this, the incongruence between what we've achieved and the poor or distorted diffusion of the progress we've made. The mass media are stuck in their language and those images. When it comes to the image of the Chinese, which is taken to be a minority, where are the Chinese? Where do they figure in the national imagination, in the collective memory of Cuban humor? The Chinese are a case in point. Our stories always poke fun at the Chinese. I refer to things we haven't been able to change. It's not easy to create an awareness that goes beyond this. It's also a phenomenon of the collective unconscious. We make jokes on the basis of old canon, that should be spent. I say the prejudice is spent but not dead. That's what we have to work on; there's a lot that needs to be done and learned.

PPS: The themes of family and black woman are in your poetry. What are your reflections on your own treatment of the Cuban black woman and black man in your literature?

NM: I repeat what Fanon said, a society is or isn't racist. We all have our weak spots. We are all party, blacks included, to racial prejudice. It's not the domain of whites only. It's been a fatal experience for us all. And so I am part of that phenomenon. That gives me an authenticity but also limits me, because, feeling as I do part of the phenomenon, I may not perhaps pronounce judgment. When you're going to express something, you do so from your own standpoint, and that has its risks. I think this is terrain that can be better expressed in prose. Poetry can hint, sum up, give a swift brush stroke, but hasn't all the elements of a novel or short story. Unfortunately for me, I've never had a passion for the novel. Maybe in my old age, that I already see coming, I might try, out of a love for those themes, not the genre, but because it is the genre that can serve me well. I might try. . . . I have tried but it hasn't worked. Narrative requires a discipline, a maturity, and sacrifice which I have for many things but not that. It's not really the genre where I could unload these things, memories of my neighborhood, how I've always perceived the race question, which has been hard.

NOTES

Introduction

1. For recent conceptual debates, see "Race and National Identity in Latin America," special issue coordinated by Helen I. Safa, *Latin American Perspectives* 25, no. 3 (May 1998); Richard D. E. Burton, *Afro-Creole: Power, Opposition and Play in the Caribbean* (Ithaca: Cornell University Press, 1997); Gert Oostindie, ed., *Ethnicity in the Caribbean* (London and Basingstoke: Macmillan, 1996); Anthony Bryan and Andrés Serbin, *Distant Cousins: Latin America and the Caribbean* (Miami: North-South Center, University of Miami, 1996); Darien Davis, ed., *Slavery and Beyond: The African Impact on Latin America and the Caribbean* (Wilmington, Del.: Scholarly Resources, 1995); Michel Rolphe Trouillot, *Silencing the Past: Power and the Production of History* (Boston: Beacon Press, 1995); Ronald Segal, *The Black Diaspora* (London: Faber and Faber, 1995); Michael L. Coniff and Thomas J. Davis, *Africans in the Americas: A History of the Black Diaspora* (New York: St. Martin's Press, 1994); Anthony P. Maingot, "Race, Color, and Class in the Caribbean," in Alfred Stepan, ed., *Americas: New Interpretative Essays* (New York and London: Oxford University Press, 1992); Rupert Lewis, "The Contemporary Significance of the African Diaspora in the Americas," *Caribbean Quarterly* 38, nos. 2 and 3 (1992); Norman E. Whitten Jr. and Arlene Torres, "Blackness in the Americas," *Report on the Americas: The Black Americas 1492–1992*, NACLA, 25, 4 (1992). For the Hispanic Caribbean, two comparative studies in Naranjo Orovio, Puig-Samper, and García Morales, *La nación soñada*, deal with race: Jorge Ibarra, "Cultura e identidad nacional en el Caribe hispánico: el caso puertorriqueño y el cubano," and Lanny Thompson Womacks, "Estudiarlos, juzgarlos y gobernarlos: Conocimiento y poder en el archipelago imperial estadounidense." Some excellent recent work is reopening the race debate in Puerto Rico. See, for example, the issue of *Centro* 8, nos. 1 and 2 (spring 1996), the journal of the Center for Puerto Rican Studies, Hunter College, New York, given over to race and identity, which includes Miriam Jiménez Román, "Un hombre (negro) del pueblo: José Celso Barbosa and the Puerto Rican 'Race' Toward Whiteness," Juan A. Giusti Cordero, "AfroPuerto Rican Cultural Studies: Beyond *cultura negroide* and *antillanismo*," Roberto P. Rodríguez-Morazzani, "Beyond the Rainbow: Mapping the Discourse on Puerto Ricans and 'Race,'" and Juan José Baldrich et al., "Bibliography on Puerto Ricans and Race." See also Juan Angel

Giusti Cordero, "De Pandora a Elegguá: una lectura histórica de Rosario Ferré, The House on the Lagoon," *Historia y Sociedad,* Año 7 (1994). This compares with work on the Dominican Republic: Silvio Torres Saillant, "Hacia una identidad racial alternativa en al sociedad dominicana," *Op. Cit.* 9 (1997); Michiel Baud, "'Constitutionally White': The Forging of a National Identity in the Dominican Republic" in Oostindie (1996); Ernesto Sagás, "A Case of Mistaken Identity: Antihaitianismo in the Dominican Republic," *Latinamericanist* 29, no. 1 (1993). For Hispanic America, see the journals *América Negra* and *Palara.* For the French Antilles, see Michel Giraud, "Les identités antillaises entre négritude et créolité," *Cahiers des Amériques Latines* 17 (1994). There are some excellent recent single-country monographs: Richard and Sally Price, *Enigma Variations* (Cambridge, Mass.: Harvard University Press, 1995) and *Equatoria* (New York: Routledge, 1992); Michel-Rolphe Trouillot, *Culture, Color, and Politics in Haiti* (New Brunswick: Rutgers University Press, 1994); Peter Wade, *Blackness and Race Mixture: The Dynamics of Racial Identity in Colombia* (Baltimore: Johns Hopkins University Press, 1993); Nina S. de Friedemann, *La saga del negro: presencia africana en Colombia* (Bogota: Pontificia Universidad Javeriana, 1993); George Reid Andrews, *Blacks and Whites in São Paulo, Brazil, 1888–1988* (Madison: University of Wisconsin Press, 1991) and *The Afro-Argentines of Buenos Aires, 1800–1900* (Madison: University of Wisconsin Press, 1991); Winthrop R. Wright, *Café con Leche: Race, Class and National Image in Venezuela* (Austin: University of Texas Press, 1991); O. Nigel Bolland, *Colonialism and Resistance in Belize: Essays in Historical Sociology* (Benque Viejo del Carmen, Belize: Cubola Productions, 1988), chapter 9; Nina S. de Friedemann and Jaime Arocha, *De Sol a sol: génesis, transformación y presencia de los negros en Colombia* (Bogota: Planeta Editorial Colombiana, 1986). Excellent monographs on the racial dynamics of West Indian labor migration to the Central American isthmus are Aviva Chomsky, *West Indian Workers and the United Fruit Company in Costa Rica, 1870–1940* (Baton Rouge and London: Louisiana State University Press, 1996); Philippe I. Bourgois, *Ethnicity at Work: Divided Labor on a Central American Banana Plantation* (Baltimore: Johns Hopkins University Press, 1989); Michael L. Coniff, *Black Labor on a White Canal: Panama, 1904–1981* (Pittsburgh: University of Pittsburgh Press, 1985).

2. For recent works of reference, see Fernández Robaina (1969, 1971, 1986, 1988, 1991, 1996); Trelles y Govín (1927). For black political figures, see *Antonio Maceo* (1950); Gómez (1974, 1984); Serra (1907); Betancourt (1950, 1958, 1961). For the work of past black literary figures, see Plácido (1976, 1979); Manzano (1972); Zambrana (1873); Guillén (1972, 1987). A good bibliographical overview of race can be found in L. Pérez (1989).

3. Ortiz, a founding figure of *Archivos del Folklore Cubano* and *Estudios Afrocubanos,* has a voluminous list of publications, cited at length in the bibliography. See also the extensive work of Cabrera published in Miami. In Cuba, Bolívar Orostegui began to publish in similar directions (1990, 1996) and, in Miami, Castellanos and Castellanos (1988). For literature, three novelists are most cited:

Villaverde (1962 [1879]); Carpentier (1968 [1933], 1994); and Montejo and Barnet (1993 [1966]).

4. The latter is outlined in Sydney Mintz, *Caribbean Transformations* (Chicago: Aldine, 1994).

5. Howard Winant, "Rethinking Race in Brazil," *Journal of Latin American Studies* 24, no. 1 (February 1992: 173–92). Examples he gave were Abdias do Nascimento's project of Quilombismo, Benedita Souza da Silva as Partido Trabalhista federal deputy, an Assessoria para Assuntos Afro-Brasileiros set up in the Ministry of Culture, and the group Olodum. An excellent earlier overview is Jan Fiola, "Race Relations in Brazil: A Reassessment of the 'Racial Democracy' Thesis" (occasional papers series 24, Latin American Studies Program, University of Massachusetts at Amherst, 1990). See also Howard Winant, *Racial Conditions* (Minneapolis: University of Minnesota Press, 1994); Michael Omi and Howard Winant, *Racial Formation in the United States: From the 1960s to the 1980s* (New York: Routledge and Kegan Paul, 1986). The classics referred to are Gilberto Freyre, *The Masters and the Slaves* (New York: Knopf, 1946 [1933]) and *New World in the Tropics* (New York: Vintage, 1963 [1959]); Carl N. Degler, *Neither Black Nor White: Slavery and Race Relations in Brazil and the United States* (New York: Macmillan, 1971); Anani Dzidzienyo, *The Position of Blacks in Brazilian Society* (Minority Rights Group Report, 1971, 1979); Carlos A. Hasenblag and Nelson do Valle Silva, *Relações raciais no Brasil contemporâneo* (Rio de Janeiro: Rio Fundo Editora, 1992). See also Michael G. Hanchard, *Orpheus and Power: The Movimiento Negro of Rio de Janeiro and São Paulo, Brazil, 1945–1988* (Princeton: Princeton University Press, 1994).

6. Thomas E. Skidmore, "Bi-racial U.S.A. vs. Multi-racial Brazil: Is the Contrast Still Valid?," *Journal of Latin American Studies* 25 (May 1993): part 2, 373–86.

7. On the 1912 war, see also Fermoselle-López (1972a [1974]) and Orum (1975).

8. The other five particularities were the high level of black military participation in the nationalist wars, the high level of black organization and mobilization compared with other Latin American countries, the organization of the first black party in the hemisphere, the Partido Independiente de Color (Independent Colored Party), official antiblack violence, and a Cuban myth of racial equality in the nation based on racial fraternity in nationalist wars.

9. For the 1920s, see Schwartz (1977).

10. De la Fuente set out to provide substantive data and evidence on race in Cuba, given the more qualitative and at times speculative and highly polarized views that have been advanced. In this context see Duany (1988); C. Moore (1988a, 1988b); Cannon and Cole (1978); Booth (1976); Clytus (1970). A solid overview of the prerevolutionary twentieth century can be found in Jorge Ibarra, *Prologue to Revolution: Cuba, 1898–1959* (Boulder, Colo., and London: Lynne Rienner, 1998), chapter 8. Interesting comparative demographic analysis can be found, for the earlier period in Cuba, in Kiple (1976) and, for Brazil, in Peggy A. Lovell and Charles H. Wood, "Skin Color, Racial Identity, and Life Chances in Brazil," *Latin American Perspectives* 25, no. 3 (May 1998).

11. On black Caribbean migrant labor, see Carr (1998); García Domínguez (1988); Knight (1985b); Lundahl (1982); McCleod (1998); and Elizabeth Thomas-Hope, "The Establishment of a Migration Tradition: British West Indian Movements to the Hispanic Caribbean in the Century after Emancipation" in Colin G. Clarke, ed., *Caribbean Social Relations* (Liverpool: Center for Latin American Studies, 1978).

12. In effect, the life experiences of four generations were quite different. Those born in 1922–43 led the revolution and retained crucial positions of power. Those born in 1944–49 were too young to participate actively in the 1950s but were the first beneficiaries of revolution; those born in 1950–61 were too young to be active in the 1960s, and many were raised by older generations because of the intensive labor and political participation of their parents; and those born in 1962–76 represented the post-revolutionary baby boom and today's youth, with the most educational opportunities but without participation in transformative events, and with the greatest expectations but the least opportunities and least social and political involvement. At the same time, marriage patterns displayed high levels of racial endogamy, especially among whites: according to 1981 census statistics, 93.1 percent among whites, 70.1 percent among blacks, and 68.7 percent among those of mixed race.

13. Information on initiatives already under way can be found on the Web site http://www.afrocubaweb.com.

14. An Associated Press story on the UN Report contained clips from interviews with Cuban-American New Orleans-based middlemen involved in sending remittances, and with Miami-based economists who see the middlemen as amoral because they help maintain stability and hence the political status quo for the island regime. See Roxana Hegeman, "Lucrativo mercado negro de EU a Cuba," *Nuevo herald,* 28 November 1997.

15. This raises interesting issues for Cuba in the context of work being done on Caribbean transnational social networks, economic alliances, and political ideologies. See Linda Basch, Nina Glick Schiller, and Christina Szanton Blanc, *Nations Unbound: Transnational Projects, Postcolonial Predicaments, and Deterritorialized Nation-States* (Langhorne, Pa.: Gordon and Breach, 1994).

16. Fernando Coronil introduction, "Transculturation and the Politics of Theory: Countering the Center, Cuban Counterpoint" in Ortiz (1995). The parallel figure for Brazil is Gilberto Freyre: see Jeffrey Needell, "Identity, Race, Gender, and Modernity in the Origins of Gilberto Freyre's Oeuvre," *The American Historical Review* 100, no. 1 (February 1995). Comparisons have also been made between Ortiz and José Luis González, *Puerto Rico: The Four-Storeyed Country* (Princeton: Markus Wienner, 1993 [1980]). For Puerto Rico see Richard M. Morse, "Race, Culture and Identity in the New World: Five National Versions" in Oostindie (1996). Similarly, the work of Carbonell (1961) might be compared with that of Puerto Rican Isabelo Zenón Cruz, *Narciso descubre su trasero: el negro en la cultura puertorriqueña* (Narciso Discovers his Behind: The Black in Puerto Rican Culture) (Humacao: Editorial Furidi, 1974).

1. A Journalist's Story

1. Vedado was once an exclusive Havana neighborhood.

2. The Club Atenas (Athens Club) was an elite black club founded in Havana in 1918.

3. The 26 July movement was the underground urban backbone of the 1950s insurrection. It took its name from the attack on the Moncada Garrison in Santiago de Cuba on 26 July 1953.

2. The Only Black Family on the Block

1. Gerardo Machado ruled Cuba in 1925–33 and was toppled in the 1933 revolution.

2. 10 October was the outbreak of the 1868–78 Ten Years War, the first of Cuba's wars for independence from Spain; 20 May, Independence Day, marked the beginning of the Republic of Cuba, after four years of U.S. military occupation, 1898–1902; Noche Buena is the eve of 24 December, which is celebrated with a dinner in Catholic Hispanic tradition.

3. The Day of the Kings is on 6 January, Epiphany. In Catholic Hispanic tradition this is the day for giving children gifts.

4. Three Havana neighborhoods: Mantilla was working class, Lawton more middle class, and Diez de Octubre in between.

5. The date is used figuratively for the revolution. The U.S. embargo actually started later.

6. This was already changing at the time the interview was conducted. Now whole stretches of beach (at Varadero, for example) are for foreign tourists and out of bounds to Cubans, especially those who stand out as black.

7. In Spanish tradition, a girl is presented to society on her fifteenth birthday.

3. Issues of Black Health

1. Named after José Antonio Aponte, a free black who led the 1812 Aponte conspiracy.

2. Africa House was established in the 1980s in Havana, as a cultural center.

3. The Pioneer Organization comprises schoolchildren aged 5–13.

4. Unofficial exchange rates at the time were twenty-five to thirty Cuban pesos to the U.S. dollar.

4. Race Mixing in the Historical Novel

1. The 1870 Moret Law, implemented in 1880, was known as the law of the free belly (*vientre libre*) and established that the children born of slave women should henceforth be born free. Slavery was finally abolished in 1886.

2. Rojas explains that the term *pardo* refers only to mulattos with wealth and status.

3. The Casa de Beneficencia was the Havana orphanage that took in the elite's illegitimate offspring.

5. White Aesthetic/Black Ethic

1. Agustín Cárdenas for many years lived and sculpted in Paris.

2. Wifredo Lam also lived and painted outside Cuba, in Paris; he died recently. Manuel Mendive is the most famous of Cuban painters alive today, and lives and paints from his home in Santa María del Rosario, on the outskirts of Havana.

3. Jesús Menéndez and Aracelio Iglesias were black communist leaders of the sugar workers and dock workers, respectively. Both were assassinated in the late 1940s Cold War purge of strong, communist-led trade unions.

6. An All-Black Theater Project

1. "History Will Absolve Me" was Fidel Castro's defense plea at the trial for the 1953 attack on the Moncada Garrison. It subsequently became the blueprint for revolution.

2. Black communist Jesús Menéndez, general secretary of the sugar workers' union, was shot dead in 1948.

3. Sara Gómez was a black filmmaker who died young, in 1971, depriving the Cuban film industry of its only black female director. At the time of her death, she was completing a hard-hitting film on race and gender.

4. Black communist Lázaro Peña was the general secretary of the tobacco workers who was elected general secretary of the Cuban Trade Union Confederation. It was common in those days to secure a teaching post through a person of influence.

5. The term *negrometrajes,* a pun on the Spanish term for feature-length films, *largometrajes,* was popularly coined to refer to the trilogy of films of slavery made by black Cuban filmmaker Sergio Giral in the 1970s.

6. Juan Marinello was one of two communist members of the government in 1940.

7. *Memories of Underdevelopment,* directed by the late Tomes Gutiérrez Alea, is the 1960s classic of the Cuban film industry.

8. Carlos Rafael Rodríguez was the other communist member of the government in 1940.

7. Tackling Racism in Performing Arts

1. Alden Knight became particularly famous for reciting the poetry of Cuba's national poet, mulatto Nicolás Guillén. The poem "Tengo" (I Have) includes the line "Tengo lo que tenía que tener," which translates as "I have [under the revolution] what was my due."

2. Félix B. Caignet was a pioneer of the telenovela, or soap, on Cuban radio, and was famous throughout Latin America for the classic *El Derecho de Nacer* (Right to Be Born).

3. Eugenio Hernández was a black Cuban playwright who made his name in the 1960s with the play *María Antonia.*

4. The term *cara pálida* came into popular usage among blacks to refer to whites in the 1990s, around the time of dollar remittances and joint ventures creating osten-

sible racial differences between those who had and had not access to hard currency. It is, of course, taken from U.S. westerns in which Indians refer to whites as pale faces.

8. Poetry, Prostitution, and Gender Esteem

1. MAGIN was short-lived. The positions it espoused were not well taken by the FMC and it was closed down by the government.

2. The father of her children was the writer Manuel Granados, who died in Paris in 1998, after this interview. Ignacio, her son, is in Florida, after a preparatory period in Peru, studying for the monastery.

9. Africa . . . in Cuban Film

1. The black Virgen de Regla (Virgin of Regla), the brown Virgen de la Caridad del Cobre (Virgin of Our Lady of Charity of El Cobre), and Santa Barbara/Changó symbolize the fusion of Catholic and Afro-Cuban religions.

2. CARIMAC is the Caribbean Media Arts Center of the University of the West Indies (Mona), Jamaica.

3. Rupert Lewis is a historian at the University of the West Indies in Mona, Jamaica, who specializes in African Caribbean politics and history.

4. Barbadian writer George Lamming, Cuban writer Nicolás Guillén, and Jamaican dancer, choreographer, and writer Professor Rex Nettleford are all well known throughout the Caribbean.

5. Black Cuban filmmaker Sergio Giral now resides in Miami. For an interview with Giral shortly before he left Cuba, see Pedro Pérez Sarduy and Jean Stubbs, eds., *Afro-Cuba: An Anthology of Cuban Writing on Race, Politics and Culture* (Melbourne, Australia: Ocean Press; New York: Center for Cuban Studies; London: Latin American Bureau, 1993).

6. See Tomás González, "Sara, one way or another," in Pérez Sarduy and Stubbs, ibid., 1993.

10. Crafting the Sacred Batá Drum

1. Part of the initiation was to walk around the market square.

2. Evaristo Aparicio ("Picaro") was a famous drummer.

11. Grupo Antillano

1. Juan Formell is the band leader of Los Van Van.

2. Gastón Baquero recently died in Madrid.

12. A National Cultural Identity?

1. Domingo del Monte was famous in the early to mid-nineteenth century for his literary salon, encouraging literary criticism of Spain and slavery.

2. Evaristo Estenoz and Pedro Yvonet founded the Independent Colored Party of 1910 and were killed in the 1912 Race War.

3. Amadeo Roldán and Alejandro García Caturla were celebrated twentieth-cen-

tury Cuban composers who incorporated Afro-Cuban rhythm into classical music, to create a new school of Cuban music.

4. For an English-language translation of an extract from *Imaginary Dialogues*, see Rogelio Martínez Furé, "Imaginary dialogue on folklore" in Pedro Pérez Sarduy and Jean Stubbs, eds., *Afro-Cuba: An Anthology of Cuban Writing on Race, Politics and Culture* (Melbourne, Australia: Ocean Press; New York: Center for Cuban Studies; London: Latin American Bureau, 1993).

13. Diaspora and Nation

1. The integrationist ideas of the turn-of-the-century Afro-Cuban political leader Juan Gualberto Gómez are far less known than those of Hispano-Cuban José Martí, whom Gómez helped found the Cuban Revolutionary Party.

2. Morejón worked closely with and wrote extensively on Nicolás Guillén.

3. José Antonio Saco was an early-nineteenth-century advocate of Cuban economic development and free trade. He opposed the slave trade and slavery on economic and social grounds, not in defense of the slaves but because he espoused a highly exclusionary notion of *cubanidad*, one that celebrated *hispanidad* and advocated cleansing the island of its black African presence.

GLOSSARY OF AFRO-CUBAN TERMS AND NAMES

Abakuá male secret religious society founded in Havana in the nineteenth century by Africans of Calabar; known also as Ñañiguismo, one of the Afro-Cuban religions of today

añá the secret deposited in the sacred *batá* drums of Santería

ará blood brothers; tribe or community

Arará nation of ancient Dahomey, West Africa

Argayú *orisha* father of Changó

Babala wo/Babaloc ha high priest in Santería

Bantu nation of the Congo, West Africa

batá the three sacred drums of Santería: Okónkolo, Itótele, Iyá

bozalonzón the loose articulation of Spanish by African slaves

cabildo chapter of one of the black African organizations allowed in nineteenth-century Cuba

Carabalí nation from old Calabar, southern Nigeria, West Africa

Changó main *orisha* of fire, lightning, thunder, and war; syncretistic with the Catholic Santa Barbara

comparsa carnival dance group

Conga Afro-Cuban religion of Congo origin and from Angola, also known as Regla de Palo, Palo, Palo Monte, and Regla Conga, with its variants: Mayombe, Biriyumba, Quirimbaya

Congo nation of West Africa, comprising various groups: Muriaco, Loango, Real

conguero drummer in Carnival

danzón Afro-Cuban rhythm with French influence that emerged around the turn of the century

eggú spirit of the dead

Elegguá main *orisha*, opens the path for other *orishas*; syncretism with Catholic Saint Anthony

guaguancó Afro-Cuban rhythm
Ifá main *orisha* of fortune
Iroku/Irok o sacred silk-cotton tree
irú seed, race, class, genre, service
Itótele one of the three *batá* drums
Iyá one of the three *batá* drums
iyawó, pl. *iyawoses* initiate(s), who lower their heads on the Iyá
Lucumí nation of Yoruba origin, comprising various groups
mestizo/a of mixed race, born of one Indian and one white parent
mandinga nation of West Africa
mestizaje race mixing, or miscegenation
moreno/a old term for black
mulato/a mixed race, mulatto, born of one black and one white parent
Ñañigo practitioner of Ñañiguismo; see Abakuá
Ochún/Oshún main *orisha* of sexuality, rivers, and springs
Oggún principal *orisha* of iron and war; syncretistic with the Catholic Saint Peter and Saint John the Baptist
Okónk olo one of the three *batá* drums
Olofi supreme *orisha,* eternal father
Olú master *batá* drummer
orisha deity in Santería
Oyá *orisha* of cemeteries and lightning
palenque maroon settlement of runaway slaves
Palero practitioner of the Palo religion
Palo Afro-Cuban religion, also known as Regla de Palo and Palo Monte; of Bantu origin
pardo old term for mulatto
patakín stories or legends of Santería, in the oral tradition; handed down by the Yoruba people of Nigeria, West Africa
Santería Afro-Cuban religion of Yoruba origin, from Nigeria; syncretistic with Catholicism; also known as Ocha, Regla de Ocha, and Regla de Ifá
Santero/a priest/practitioner of Santería
Santo/a saint; initiate in Santería
son Afro-Cuban rhythm that emerged in nineteenth-century Cuba
tambor drum and drum ceremony
timbero drummer
Yemayá main *orisha* of the sea and motherhood

SELECTED BIBLIOGRAPHY

Though by no means exhaustive, this bibliography is intended to provide a comprehensive listing of titles dealing with race in Cuba. Invaluable periodicals for prerevolutionary Cuba are *Archivos del folklore* and *Estudios Afrocubanos*. Contemporary periodicals that might be consulted are *Anales del Caribe, Bohemia, Casa de las Américas, Del Caribe, Etnología y Folklore, Granma Weekly Review, Islas, Revolución y Cultura, Santiago,* and *Unión*. Some useful U.S. periodicals are *Afro-Hispanic Review, Calibán, Cimarrón, Cuba Update, Cuban Studies/Estudios Cubanos, The Black Scholar,* and *Palara*. See also *América Negra* (Colombia) and *Encuentro de la Cultura Cubana* (published by Cubans in Spain).

Agüero, Sixto Gastón. *Fundamentos de Ochún, Virgen de la Caridad.* Havana, 1963.
———. *El materialismo explica el espiritismo y la santería.* Havana, 1961.
Aguirre, Benigno. "Differential Migration of Cuban Social Races." *Conflict Studies* 24 (June 1972).
Aimes, Hubert H. S. *A History of Slavery in Cuba, 1511–1868.* New York, 1907.
Alarcón, Alexis. "¿Vodú en Cuba ó vodú cubano?" *Del Caribe 5,* no. 12 (1988).
Alén, Olavo. *La música de las sociedades de tumba francesa en Cuba.* Havana, 1986.
Alfonso, Domingo. *Poemas del hombre común.* Havana, 1964.
———. *Sueños en el papel.* Havana, 1959.
Alonso, Guillermo Andrew. *Los Ararás en Cuba: Florentina, la Princesa Dahomeyana.* Havana, 1992.
Alvarado Ramos, Juan Antonio. "Relaciones raciales en Cuba: Notas de investigación." *Temas 7* (1996).
Alvarez Mola, Martha Verónica, and Pedro Martínez Pérez. "Algo acerca del problema negro en Cuba hasta 1912." *Universidad de la Habana 179* (May–June 1966).
Amira, John, and Steven Cornelius. *The Music of Santería.* White Cliffs, Ind., 1992.
Amor, Rose Teresa. "Afro-Cuban Folk Tales as Incorporated into the Literary Tradition of Cuba." Ph.D. diss., Columbia University, 1969.
Antonio Maceo: Documentos para su vida. Havana, 1945.
Antonio Maceo: Ideología política, cartas y otros documentos. Havana, 1950.
Aparicio, Raúl. *Hombradía de Antonio Maceo.* Havana, 1967.
Appiah, Kwame Anthony, and Henry Louis Gates, Jr., eds. *Africana: The Encyclopedia of the African and African American Experience.* Civitas, 1999. CD-ROM, Microsoft Encarta Africana, 1998.

Arce, Angel C. *La raza cubana.* Havana, 1935.
Arenas, Reinaldo. *Graveyard of the Angels.* New York, 1987.
Arguelles, Aníbal, and Ileana Hodge. *Los llamados cultos sincréticos y el espiritismo.* Havana, 1991.
Arnes, David. "Negro Family Types in Cuban Solar." *Phylon* 2, no. 2 (1950).
Arredondo, Alberto. *El negro en Cuba.* Havana, 1939.
Bachiller y Morales, Antonio. *Los negros.* Barcelona, 1887.
Barcía, María del Carmen. *Burguesía esclavista y abolición.* Havana, 1987.
Barnet, Miguel. "The Untouchable Cimarrón." *New West Indian Guide/Nieuwe West-Indische Gids* 71, nos. 3 and 4 (1997).
———. *La vida real.* Havana, 1986.
———. *The African Presence in Cuban Culture.* University of Warwick, U.K., 1986.
———. *La fuente viva.* Havana, 1983.
———. *Akeké y la jutía.* Havana, 1978.
———. *La canción de Rachel.* Havana,1969.
———. *Isla de Guijes.* Havana, 1964.
———. *La piedrafina y el pavo real.* Havana, 1963.
Barredo, Pedro. *The Black Protagonist in the Cuban Novel.* Amherst, Mass., 1979.
Bascom, William R. "The African Heritage and Its Religious Manifestations." In *Background to Revolution: The Development of Modern Cuba,* edited by Robert Freeman Smith. New York, 1966.
———. "Yoruba Acculturation in Cuba." *Les Afro-Américains* no. 27 (1953).
———. "The Focus of Cuban Santería." *Southwestern Journal of Anthropology* 6, no. 1 (1950).
Bejarano, Margalit. "La inmigración a Cuba y la política migratoria de los Estados Unidos, 1902–1933." *Estudios Interdisciplinarios de América Latina y el Caribe* 4, no. 2 (July–December 1993).
Benítez-Rojo, Antonio. "La cuestión del negro en tres momentos del nacionalismo literario cubano." *Op. Cit.,* Universidad de Puerto Rico Centro de Investigaciones Históricas, no. 9 (1997).
———. *La isla que se repite: el Caribe y la perspectiva posmoderna.* Durham, N.C., and London, 1992.
Bergad, Laird W. *Cuban Rural Society in the Nineteenth Century.* Princeton, N.J., 1990.
———. "The Economic Viability of Sugar Production Based on Slave Labor in Cuba, 1859–1878." *Latin America Research Review* 24, no. 1 (1989).
Bergad, Laird, with Fe Iglesias García and María del Carmen Barcía. *The Cuban Slave Market, 1790–1880.* Cambridge, New York, and Melbourne, 1995.
Betancourt Bencomo, Juan René. "Castro and the Cuban Negro." *Crisis* 68 no. 5 (1961).
———. "Fidel Castro y la integración nacional." In "Recuento de la gran mentira comunista," *Bohemia* 51, no. 7 (1959).
———. *El negro: Ciudadano del futuro.* Havana, 1959.

————. *Doctrina negra: La única teoría certera contra la discriminación racial en Cuba.* Havana, 1958.

————. *Preludios de la libertad. La tragedia del negro y la táctica del partido comunista.* Havana, 1950.

Bettelheim, Judith, ed. *Cuban Festivals: An Anthology with Glossaries.* New York, 1993.

————. "Festivals in Cuba." In *Caribbean Festival Arts.* Washington, 1988.

"Blacks in Cuba." *Cuban Resource Center Newsletter* (special issue) 2, no. 6.

Blasier, Cole, and Carmelo Mesa-Lago. *Cuba in the World.* Pittsburgh, 1979.

Boggs, Vernon. *Salsiology: Afro-Cuban Music in the Evolution of Salsa in New York.* New York, 1992.

Bolívar Orostegui, Natalia. *Ifá: Su Historia en Cuba.* Havana, 1996.

————. *Los orishas en Cuba.* Havana, 1990.

Bolívar Orostegui, Natalia, and Carmen González. *Mitos y leyendas de la comida afrocubana.* Havana, 1993.

Booth, David. "Cuba, Color and the Revolution." *Science and Society* 40, no. 2 (1976).

Brandon, George Edward. *The Dead Sell Memories: An Anthropological Study of Santería in New York City.* Bloomington, Ind., 1993.

Brea, Rafael. "Presencia africana en los carnavales de Santiago de Cuba." *Del Caribe* 3, no. 10 (1987).

————. "Un día de San Juan en Los Hoyos." *Del Caribe* 2, no. 5 (July–September 1984).

Brock, Lisa, and Digna Castañeda Fuertes, eds. *Between Race and Empire: African Americans and Cubans before the Cuban Revolution.* Philadelphia, 1998.

Bueno, Salvador. *El negro en la novela hispanoamericana.* Havana, 1985.

Cabrera, Lydia. *Anagó: Vocabulario Lucumí (El Yoruba que se habla en Cuba).* Miami, 1986.

————. *Koeko Iyawó: aprende novicia.* Miami, 1980.

————. *Reglas de Congo: Palo Monte, Mayombe.* Miami, 1979.

————. *La Regla Kimbisi del Santo Cristo del Buen Viaje.* Miami, 1977.

————. *Anafarauna.* Madrid, 1975.

————. *Yemaya y Ochún. Kariochas, Iyalochas y Olorichas.* Madrid, 1974.

————. *La sociedad secreta Abakuá.* Havana, 1958.

————. *El monte.* Havana, 1954.

————. *Cuentos negros de Cuba.* Havana, 1940.

Calcagno, Francisco. *Aponte.* Barcelona, 1901.

————. *Poetas de color.* Havana, 1878.

Calvo Ospina, Hernando. *Salsa! Havana Heat, Bronx Beat.* London, 1995.

Canet, Carlos. *Lukumí: La religión de los Yorubas de Cuba.* Miami, 1984.

Cañizares, Raúl. *Walking the Night: The Afro-Cuban World of Santería.* Rochester, Vt., 1993.

Cannon, Terry, and Johnetta Cole. *Free and Equal. The End of Racial Discrimination in Cuba.* New York, 1978.

Cano Secade, María del Carmen. "Relaciones raciales, proceso de ajuste y política social." *Temas* no.7 (1996).

Carbonell, Walterio. *Crítica: ¿Cómo surgió la cultura nacional?* Havana, 1961.

———. "Africa y Cuba." *Lunes de revolución* 83, no. 15 (24 October 1960).

Carneado, José F. "La discriminación racial en Cuba no volverá jamás." *Cuba Socialista* 2, no. 5 (1962).

Carpentier, Alejo. *El reino de este mundo*. Río Piedras, Puerto Rico, 1994.

———. *Ecué-Yamba-O!: Historia afro-cubana*. Buenos Aires, 1968 [Madrid, 1933].

Carr, Barry. "Identity, Class and Nation: Black Immigrant Workers, Cuban Communism, and the Sugar Insurgency, 1925–1934." *Hispanic American Historical Review* 78, no. 1 (February 1998).

Casal, Lourdes. "Race Relations in Contemporary Cuba." *Minority Rights Group Reports* no. 7 (1979).

Casals, Jorge. *Plácido como poeta cubano: ensayo biográfico crítico*. Havana, 1944.

Castañeda, Digna. "The Female Slave in Cuba During the First Half of the Nineteenth Century." In *Engendering History: Caribbean Women in Historical Perspective*, edited by Verene Shepherd, Bridget Brereton, and Barbara Bailey. Kingston, Jamaica, and London, 1995.

Castellanos, Jorge. *La brujería y el ñañiguismo desde el punto de vista médico-legal*. Havana, 1916.

Castellanos, Jorge, and Isabel Castellanos. *Cultura afrocubana: El negro en Cuba 1492–1868*. Miami, 1988.

———. "The Geographic, Ethnologic, and Linguistic Roots of Cuban Blacks." *Cuban Studies/Estudios Cubanos* 17 (1987).

Castro, Fidel. *Cuba's Internationalist Foreign Policy: Fidel Castro Speeches*. New York, 1986.

Cepero Bonilla, Raúl. *Azúcar y abolición*. Havana, 1971.

Chrisman, Robert, ed. "Roundtable on the History of Racial Prejudice in Cuba." *The Black Scholar* (January–February 1985).

Clarke, Colin G., ed. *Caribbean Social Relations*. Liverpool, 1978.

Clytus, John. *Black Man in Red Cuba*. Coral Gables, Fla., 1970.

Cole, Johnetta B. "Race Toward Equality: The Impact of the Cuban Revolution on Racism." *The Black Scholar* 2, no. 8 (1980).

Comisión de Activistas de Historia. *Los palenques de los negros cimarrones*. Havana, 1973.

Corwin, Arthur F. *Spain and the Abolition of Slavery in Cuba, 1817–1866*. Austin, Tex., 1967.

Corzi Pi, Daniel. *Historia de Antonio Maceo: el Aníbal cubano*. Havana, 1943.

Cos Causse, Jesús. *Como una serenata*. Havana, 1988.

———. *Balada de un tambor y otros poemas*. Havana, 1988.

———. *Las islas y las luciérnagas*. Havana, 1981.

———. *Las canciones de los héroes*. Havana, 1974.

Costa, Octavio R. *Antonio Maceo, el héroe*. Havana, 1947.

Crimi, Bruno. "L'Afrique et la tentation cubaine." *Jeune Afrique,* 16 April 1976.

Cros, Mercedes. *La religión afrocubana.* Madrid, 1975.

Cruse, Harold. "Cuba y el negro norteamericano." *Casa* (August–September 1960).

Cuervo-Hewitt, Julia. *Aché, presencia africana: Tradiciones yoruba-lucumí en la narrativa cubana.* New York, 1988.

———. "Ifa: orácula Yoruba y Lucumí." *Cuban Studies/Estudios Cubanos* 13 (winter 1983).

Danger, Matilde, and Delfina Rodríguez. *Mariana Grajales.* Havana, 1975.

Daniel, Yvonne. *Rumba: Dance and Social Change in Contemporary Cuba.* Bloomington, Ind., 1995.

De Benoist, Joseph Roger. "Cuba-Afrique, Cubains avant tout." *Afrique* 29 (November 1979).

DeCosta-Willis, Miriam, ed. *Singular like a Bird: The Art of Nancy Morejón.* Washington, D.C., 1999.

De la Fuente García, Alejandro. "Recreating Racism: Race and Discrimination in Cuba's 'Special Period.'" Georgetown University, *Cuba Briefing Paper* 18 (July 1998a).

———. "Race, National Discourse, and Politics in Cuba: An Overview." *Latin American Perspectives* issue 100, 25, no.3 (May 1998b).

———. "Two Dangers, One Solution: Immigration, Race and Labor in Cuba, 1900–1930." *International Labor and Working-Class History* no. 51 (spring 1997).

———. "Negros y electores: Desigualdad y políticas raciales en Cuba, 1900–1930." In *La nación soñada: Cuba, Puerto Rico y Filipinas ante el 98,* edited by Consuelo Naranjo, Miguel A. Puig-Samper, and Luis Miguel García Mora. Madrid, 1996a.

———. "With All and For All": Race, Inequality, and Politics in Cuba, 1900–1930." Ph.D. diss., University of Pittsburgh, 1996b.

———. "Race and Inequality in Cuba, 1899–1981." *Journal of Contemporary History,* no. 30 (1995).

———. "Denominaciones étnicas de los esclavos introducidos en Cuba." *Anales del Caribe* 6 (1986).

De la Fuente García, Alejandro, and Laurence Glasco. "Are Blacks 'Getting out of Control'? Racial Attitudes, Revolution, and Political Transition in Cuba." In *Toward a New Cuba? Legacies of a Revolution,* edited by Miguel Angel Centeno and Mauricio Font. Boulder, Colo., and London, 1997.

Depestre, René. "On Culture, Politics, and Race in Cuba." *Socialism* 3, no. 5 (May 1986).

———. "Carta de Cuba sobre el imperialismo de la mala fe." In *Por la revolución, por la poesía.* Havana, 1969.

———. "Lettre de Cuba." *Présence Africaine* 4, no. 56 (1965).

———. "El que no tiene Congo." *Unión* (April–June 1965).

Deschamps-Chapeaux, Pedro. "Presencia religiosa en las sublevaciones de esclavos." *Del Caribe* 6, nos. 16 and 17 (1990).

———. *Rafael Serra y Montalvo: obrero incansable de nuestra independencia.* Havana, 1975.

———. *El negro en la economía habanera del siglo XIX*. Havana, 1971.

———. *El negro en el periodismo cubano en el siglo XIX*. Havana, 1963.

Deschamps-Chapeaux, Pedro, and Juan Pérez de la Riva. *Contribución a la historia de la gente sin historia*. Havana, 1974.

Deutschmann, David, ed. *Changing the History of Africa*. Melbourne, 1989.

Duany, Jorge. "After the Revolution: The Search for Roots in Afro-Cuban Culture." *Latin American Research Review* 23, no.1 (1988).

———. "Ethnicity in the Spanish Caribbean: Notes on the Consolidation of a Cuban Santero Ritual." *Ethnic Groups* 6 (1985).

———. "Stones, Trees, and Blood: An Examination of a Cuban Santero Ritual." *Cuban Studies/Estudios Cubanos* 12 (July 1982).

Duharte Jiménez, Rafael. "Tres mujeres hablan de prejuicios raciales." *América Negra* 12 (December 1996).

———. *Nacionalismo e historia*. Santiago de Cuba, 1989.

———. "El ascenso social del negro en la Cuba colonial." *Boletín americanista* 30, no. 38 (1988).

———. *El negro en la sociedad colonial*. Santiago de Cuba, 1988.

———. "La abolición de la esclavitud en Cuba: cronología comentada (1553–1886)." *Del Caribe* 4, no. 8 (1987).

———. "La huella de la emigración francesa en Santiago de Cuba." *Del Caribe* 3, no. 10 (1987).

———. *La rebeldía esclava en la región oriental de Cuba (1533–1868)*. Santiago de Cuba, 1986.

———. "Cimarrones urbanos en Santiago de Cuba." *Del Caribe* 2, no. 5 (July–September 1984).

———. *Seis ensayos de interpretación histórica*. Santiago de Cuba, 1983.

Duke, Cathy. "The Idea of Races: The Cultural Impact of American Intervention in Cuba, 1898–1912." In *Politics, Society, and Culture in the Caribbean. Selected Papers of the XIV Conference of Caribbean Historians*, edited by Blanca G. Silvestrini. San Juan, 1983.

Echanové, Carlos A. *La "Santería" cubana*. Havana, 1959.

Edreira de Caballero, Angelina. *Vida y obra de Juan Gualberto Gómez*. Madrid, 1984.

Entralgo, José Elías. "La mulatización cubana." *Casa* 36–37 (May–August 1966).

———. "Un forum sobre los prejuicios étnicos en Cuba." *Nuestro tiempo* (1959).

———. *La liberación étnica cubana*. Havana, 1953.

Epstein, Erwin H. "Social Structure, Race Relations, and Political Stability under U.S. Administration." *Revista/Review Interamericana* 8 (summer 1978).

Falk, Pamela. "Cuba in Africa." *Foreign Affairs* 65, no. 5 (summer 1987).

Fall, Babacar. "La crosade cubaine." *Afrique* 12 (1978).

Feijoó, Samuel. *El negro de la literatura folklórica cubana*. Havana, 1987.

———. *Mitología cubana*. Havana, 1986.

Fermoselle-López, Rafael. "Black Politics in Cuba: The Race War of 1912." The

American University, Washington, D.C., 1972. [*Política y color en Cuba: la guerrita de 1912*. Montevideo, 1974.]

———. "The Blacks in Cuba: A Bibliography." *Caribbean Studies* 12 (October 1972).

Fernández de Castro, José. "El aporte negro en las letras de Cuba en el siglo XIX." *Revista Bimestre Cubana* 38 (July–December 1936).

Fernández, Nadine T. "Race, Romance and Revolution: The Cultural Politics of Interracial Encounters in Cuba." Ph.D. diss., University of California, Berkeley, 1997.

———. "The color of love: Young interracial couples in Cuba." *Latin American Perspectives* 23, no. 1 (1996).

Fernández, Pablo Armando. *El vientre del pez*. Havana, 1989.

Fernández Retamar, Roberto. *Calibán y otros ensayos: nuestra América y el mundo*. Havana, 1979.

———. "Debunking the Black Legend: A Hard Look at the Historical Role of Spain in Latin America." *The UNESCO Courier* (August–September 1977).

Fernández Robaina, Tomás. "Los repertorios bibliográficos y los estudios de temas afrocubanos." *Temas* 7 (September 1996).

———. *Cultura afrocubana*. Havana, 1994.

———. *Bibliografía de temas afrocubanos: Suplemento*. Diskette. Havana, 1991.

———. *El negro en Cuba, 1902–1958: Apuntes para la historia de la lucha contra la discriminación racial*. Havana, 1990.

———. *Carlos M. Trelles y la "Bibliografía de autores de raza de color."* Havana, 1988.

———. *Bibliografía de temas afrocubanos*. Havana, 1986.

———. *Los santeros*. Havana, 1984.

———. *La prosa de Guillén en defensa del negro cubano*. Havana, 1982.

———. *Indice de revistas folklóricas*. Havana, 1971.

———. *Bibliografía de estudios afroamericanos*. Havana, 1969.

Fernández Sosa, Miriam. "Construyendo la nación: Proyectos e ideologias en Cuba, 1899–1909." In *La nación soñada: Cuba, Puerto Rico y Filipinas ante el 98*, edited by Consuelo Naranjo, Miguel A. Puig-Samper, and Luis Miguel García Mora. Madrid, 1996.

Ferrer, Ada. "Esclavitud, ciudadanía, y los límites de la nacionalidad cubana: La Guerra de los Diez Años, 1868–1878." *Historia Social* (1995a).

———. "To Make a Free Nation: Race and the Struggle for Independence in Cuba." Ph.D. diss., University of Michigan, 1995b.

———. "Social Aspects of Nationalism: Race, Slavery, and the Guerra Chiquita, 1879–1880." *Cuban Studies/Estudios Cubanos* 21 (1991).

Ferrer, Rodolfo M. "El problema negro en Cuba, su orígen, desarrollo y solución definitiva." *El militante comunista* (October 1986).

Fivel-Demoret, Sharon Romeo. "The Production and Consumption of Propaganda Literature: The Cuban Anti-Slavery Novel." *Bulletin of Hispanic Studies* 66 (January 1966).

Foner, Philip S. *Antonio Maceo: The "Bronze Titan" of Cuba's Struggle for Independence.* New York, 1977.

Fox, Geoffrey E. "Race and Class in Contemporary Cuba." In *Contemporary Communism,* 3d ed., edited by Irving Louis Horowitz. New Brunswick, N.J., 1977.

Franco, José Luciano. *Comercio clandestino de esclavos.* Havana, 1980a.

———. *Ensayos sobre el Caribe.* Havana, 1980b.

———. *Las conspiraciones de 1810–1812.* Havana, 1977.

———. *Contrabando y trata negrera en el Caribe.* Havana, 1976.

———. *Antonio Maceo: apuntes para una historia de su vida.* 3 vols. Havana, 1975.

———. *La diáspora africana en el Nuevo Mundo.* Havana, 1975.

———. *Ensayos históricos.* Havana, 1974.

———. *Los palenques de los negros cimarrones.* Havana, 1973.

———. *Historia de la revolución de Haití.* Havana, 1971.

———. "Presencia de Africa en América." *Tricontinental* 14 (1969).

———. *La vida heróica y ejemplar de Antonio Maceo.* Havana, 1963.

———. *La conspiración de Aponte.* Havana, 1963.

———. *Afroamérica.* Havana, 1961a.

———. *Ruta de Antonio Maceo en el Caribe.* Havana, 1961b.

———. *Folklore criollo y afrocubano.* Havana, 1959.

Friol, Roberto. *Suite para Juan Francisco Manzano.* Havana, 1977.

Frutos, Argelio. *Panteón Yoruba.* Holguín, 1992.

Fuentes, Jesús, and Grisel Gómez. *Cultos afrocubanos: un estudio etnolingüístico.* Havana, 1994.

Fulleda León, Gerardo. *Chago de Guisa.* Havana, 1989.

———. *Algunos dramas de la colonia.* Havana, 1984.

Galich, Manuel. "El indio y el negro, ahora y antes." *Casa* 36–37 (May–August 1966).

García Aguero, Salvador. "La discriminación, la ley y la trampa." *Fundamentos* 10, no. 95 (February 1950).

———. "Presencia africana en la música nacional." *Estudios Afrocubanos* (1937).

García Barrio, Constance S. "The Black in Post-Revolutionary Cuban Literature." *Revista/Review Interamericana* 8 (summer 1978).

García Cortés, Julio. *El santo o la Ocha.* Miami, 1983.

García Domínguez, Bernardo. "Festival e identidad." *Del Caribe* 6, nos. 16 and 17 (1990).

———. "Garvey and Cuba." In *Garvey: His Work and Impact,* edited by Rupert Lewis and Patrick Bryan. Jamaica, 1988.

———. "Baraguá: Independencia o abolición." *Del Caribe* 2, no. 5 (July–September 1984).

García González, Armando. "Ciencia y racismo en la enseñanza de la biología en Cuba." In *La nación soñada: Cuba, Puerto Rico y Filipinas ante el 98,* edited by Consuelo Naranjo, Miguel A. Puig-Samper, and Luis Miguel García Mora. Madrid, 1996.

Giral, Sergio. "Cuban Cinema and the Afro-Cuban Heritage." In *Cuba: Twenty-Five Years of Revolution*, edited by Sandor Halebsky and John Kirk. New York, 1985.

Gómez, Juan Gualberto. "Esclavitud y corrupción social." In *La cuestión de Cuba*. Madrid, 1984.

———. *Por Cuba libre*. Havana, 1974.

Gómez de Avellaneda, Gertrudis. *Sab*. Austin, Tex., 1993.

González, Reinaldo. *Contradanzas y latigazos*. Havana, 1983a.

———. *La fiesta de los tiburones*. Havana, 1983b.

González, Tomás. *Repertorio teatral*. Havana, 1991.

———. *Delirios y visiones de José Jacinto Milanés*. Havana, 1988.

González Bueno, Gladys. "La adivinación con el dilogún en la regla de la ocha." *Del Caribe* 6, no. 13 (1989).

———. "Una ceremonia de iniciación en regla de palo." *Del Caribe* 5, no. 12 (1988).

González Echevarría, Roberto. *Alejo Carpentier: The Pilgrim at Home*. Ithaca, N.Y., 1977.

González Wippler, Migene. *Santería: The Religion of Legacy of Faith, Rites, and Magic*. New York, 1989.

———. *Santería: African Magic in Latin America*. Garden City, N.Y., 1973.

Govín, Silvia. *Miscelánea de la santería*. Havana, 1990.

Graham, Richard (ed). *The Idea of Race in Latin America, 1870–1940*. Austin, Tex., 1990.

Granados, Manuel. *Expediente de hombre*. Havana, 1988.

———. *El viento en la casa-sol*. Havana, 1970.

———. *Adire y el tiempo roto*. Havana, 1967.

Greenbaum, Susan D. "Afro-Cubans in Exile: Tampa, Florida, 1866–1984." *Cuban Studies/Estudios Cubanos* 15 (winter 1985).

Griñán Peralta, L. *Maceo: Análisis caracterológico*. Havana, 1953.

Guanche Pérez, Jesús. "Etnicidad y racialidad de la Cuba actual." *Temas*, no. 7 (1996).

———. *Procesos etnoculturales de Cuba*. Havana, 1983.

Guevara, Ernesto. *Escritos discursos*. 4 vols. Havana, 1985.

Guillén, Nicolás. *Prosa de prisa*. Havana, 1987.

———. *Obra poética, 1920–1958*. 2 vols. Havana, 1972.

Guirao, Ramón, ed. *Cuentos y leyendas negras de Cuba*. Havana, 1942.

———. *Orbita de la poesía afrocubana 1928–1937*. Havana, 1938.

Guirao, Ramón. *Orbita de la poesía Afro-Cubana, 1926–37*. Havana, 1938.

Gutzmann, Rita. "La evolución de un tema: El negro en la obra de Alejo Carpentier." *Cuadernos americanos* 3 (1989).

Guzmán, Carlos. *Los secretos de la santería*. New York, 1984.

Hall, Gwendolyn Midlo. *Social Control in Slave Plantation Societies: A Comparison of St. Domingue and Cuba*. Baltimore, 1971.

Helg, Aline. *Our Rightful Share: The Afro-Cuban Struggle for Equality, 1886–1912*. Chapel Hill, N.C., and London, 1995.

———. "Afro-Cuban Protest: The Partido Independiente de Color, 1908–1912." *Cuban Studies/Estudios Cubanos* 21 (1991).

————. "Race in Argentina and Cuba, 1880–1930: Theory, Policies, and Popular Reaction." In *The Idea of Race in Latin America, 1870–1940*, edited by Richard Graham. Austin, Tex., 1990.

Hernández, Eugenio. *Teatro*. Havana, 1989.

Hernández, Eusebio. *Maceo: Dos conferencias históricas (1913 and 1930)*. Havana, 1968.

Hernández Artigas, J. "¡Negros no . . . ciudadanos!" *Revolución* 20 (February 1959).

Herrera, Georgina. *Granos de sol y luna*. Havana, 1978.

————. *Gentes y cosas*. Havana, 1974.

————. *G. H.* Havana, 1962.

Horrego Estuch, Leopoldo. *Maceo, héroe y carácter*. Havana, 1944.

Howard, Charles P., Sr. "The Afro-Cubans." *Freedomways* 4, no. 3 (1965).

Howard, Philip. *Changing History: Afro-Cuban Cabildos and Societies of Color in the Nineteenth Century*. Baton Rouge, La., 1998.

————. "The Spanish Colonial Government's Response to the Pan-Nationalist Agenda of the Afro-Cuban Mutual Aid Societies, 1868–1895." *Revista/Review Interamericana* 22, no. 1–1 (1992).

Ibarra, Jorge. "Cultura e identidad nacional en el Caribe hispánico: el caso puertorriqueño y el cubano." In *La nación soñada: Cuba, Puerto Rico y Filipinas ante el 98*, edited by Consuelo Naranjo, Miguel A. Puig-Samper, and Luis Miguel García Mora. Madrid, 1996.

————. "Regionalismo y esclavitud patriarcal en los departamentos Oriental y Central de Cuba." *Anales del Caribe* 6 (1986).

————. *Un análisis psicosocial del cubano 1898–1925*. Havana, 1985.

————. *Aproximaciones a Clio*. Havana, 1979.

————. *Nación y cultura nacional*. Havana, 1978.

————. *Ideología mambisa*. Havana, 1967.

Instituto de Ciencias Históricas. *La esclavitud en Cuba*. Havana, 1986.

Iznaga Beira, Diana. *Transculturación en Fernando Ortiz*. Havana, 1989.

————. *La burguesía esclavista cubana*. Havana, 1988.

————. "Fernando Ortiz y su hampa afrocubana." *Universidad de La Habana* 220 (May–August 1983).

James Figarola, Joel. "Aproximación al Carnaval de Santiago de Cuba." *Journal of Caribbean Studies* 7, nos. 2 and 3 (winter 1989/spring 1990).

————. *Sobre muertos y dioses*. Havana, 1989.

————. "Folklore y teatro en la cultura cubana." *Del Caribe* 1, no. 1 (July–September 1983).

Jones, Ronald E. "Cuba and the English-Speaking Caribbean." In *Cuba and the World*, edited by Cole Blasier and Carmelo Mesa-Lago. Pittsburgh, 1979.

King, Lloyd. "Mr. Black in Cuba." *African Studies Association of the West Indies* bulletin no. 5 (December 1972).

Kiple, Kenneth F. *Blacks in Colonial Cuba, 1774–1899*. Gainesville, Fla., 1976.

Klein, Herbert S. *Slavery in the Americas: A Comparative Study of Cuba and Virginia*. Chicago, 1967.

Knight, Franklin W. "Ethnicity and Social Structure in Contemporary Cuba." In *Ethnicity in the Caribbean,* edited by Gert Oostindie. Basingstoke and London, 1996.

———. "Cuba." In *Neither Slave Nor Free: The Freedom of African Descent in the Slave Societies of the New World,* edited by David Cohen and Jack P. Greene. Baltimore, 1985a.

———. "Jamaican Migrants and the Cuban Sugar Industry, 1900–1934." In *Between Slavery and Free Labor: The Spanish-Speaking Caribbean in the Nineteenth Century,* edited by Manuel Moreno Fraginals, Frank Moya Pons, and Stanley L. Engerman. Baltimore, 1985b.

———. "Slavery, Race, and Social Structure in Cuba During the Nineteenth Century." In *Slavery and Race in Latin America,* edited by Robert Brent Toplin. Westport, Conn., 1974.

———. *Slave Society in Cuba During the Nineteenth Century.* Madison, Wis., 1970.

Kutzinski, Vera. *Sugar's Secrets. Race and the Erotics of Cuban Nationalism.* Charlottesville, Va., 1993.

La Rosa Corzo, Gabino. *Los cimarrones en Cuba.* Havana, 1988.

Lachatañeré, Rómulo. *Oh, Mío Yemayá.* Havana, 1993 [1938].

———. *Obra completa.* Havana, 1993.

———. *Manual de santería.* Havana, 1942.

———. "El sistema religioso de los lucumíes y otras influencias africanas en Cuba." *Estudios afrocubanos* 3, nos. 1–4 (1939).

Lamore, Jean. "*Cecilia Valdés:* Realidad económica y comportamientos sociales en la Cuba esclavista de 1830." *Casa* 19, no. 110 (September–October 1978).

Lamounier, Lucia. "Between Slavery and Free Labour: Early Experiments with Free Labour and Patterns of Slave Emancipation in Brazil and Cuba." In *From Chattel Slaves to Wage Slaves: The Dynamics of Labour Bargaining in the Americas,* edited by Mary Turner. London, 1995.

———. "Cimarrones, apalencados y rancheadores en Puerto Príncipe." *Del Caribe* 4, no. 8 (1987).

Legré, Michel. "Les africains à Cuba." *Jeune Afrique* 18 (January 1978).

Leogrande, William. *Cuba's Policy in Africa 1959–1980.* Berkeley, Calif., 1980.

León, Argeliers. "Del sujeto al objeto de la creencia." *Del Caribe* 5, no. 12 (1988).

———. "Continuidad cultural africana en América." *Anales del Caribe* 6 (1986).

———. *Del canto y el tiempo.* Havana, 1984.

———. "El folklore: su estudio y recuperación." In *La cultura en Cuba Socialista.* Ministerio de la Cultura, Havana, 1982.

———. "Presencia del africano en la cultura cubana." *Islas,* no. 41 (January–April 1972).

———. *Música folklórica cubana.* Havana, 1964.

———. *Influencias africanas en la música cubana.* Havana, 1959.

León, Harvey. *Bibliografía del negro en Cuba.* Havana, 1966.

Lewis, Rupert, and Patrick Bryan, eds. *Garvey: His Work and Impact.* Jamaica, 1988.

López Lemus, Virgílio. "Regino Pedroso: Mi voz se elevará sobre la vida." *Del Caribe* 1, no. 2 (October–December 1983).

López Valdés, Rafael. "Las religiones de origen africano durante la república neocolonial en Cuba." *Del Caribe* 5, no. 12 (1988).

———. *Componentes africanos en el etnio cubano.* Havana, 1985.

———, and Pedro Deschamps Chapeaux. "La sociedad secreta 'Abakuá' en un grupo de obreros portuarios." *Etnología y folklore* 2 (July–December 1966).

Luis, William. *Literary Bondage: Slavery in Cuban Narrative.* Austin, Tex., 1990.

Lundahl, Mats. "A Note on Haitian Migration to Cuba, 1890–1934." *Cuban Studies/ Estudios Cubanos* 12 (July 1982).

Manuel, Peter. *Caribbean Currents: Caribbean Music from Rumba to Reggae.* Philadelphia, 1995.

Manzano, Juan Francisco. *Obras.* Havana, 1972.

———. *History of the Early Life of the Negro Poet.* London, 1840.

Márquez, Roberto. "Racism, Culture, and Revolution: Ideology and Politics in the Prose of Nicolás Guillén." *Latin American Research Review* 17 (1982).

———, ed. *¡Patria ó muerte! The Great Zoo and Other Poems by Nicolás Guillén.* Havana, 1973.

Martí, Jorge L. "La cuestión racial en la evolución constitucional cubana." *Política* 33 (April 1964).

Martí, José. "My Race." In *The America of José Martí.* New York, 1968 [1893].

———. *Obras completas.* Havana, 1963.

Martínez-Alier, Verena. *Marriage, Class, and Colour in Nineteenth-Century Cuba.* Oxford, 1974 [2d ed., Ann Arbor, 1989; *Racismo y sexualidad en la Cuba colonial,* edited by Verena Stolcke. Madrid, 1992].

Martínez-Fernández, Luis. *Fighting Slavery in the Caribbean: The Life and Times of a British Family in Nineteenth-Century Havana.* Armonk, N.Y. and London, 1998.

Martínez Furé, Rogelio. *Diwán africano: Poetas de expresión francesa.* Havana, 1988.

———. *Diálogos imaginarios.* Havana, 1979.

———. *Poesía anónima africana.* Havana, 1968.

———. *Poesía yoruba.* Havana, 1963.

Masferrer, Marianne, and Carmelo Mesa-Lago. "The Gradual Integration of the Black in Cuba: Under the Colony, the Republic, and the Revolution." In *Slavery and Race in Latin America,* edited by Robert Brent Toplin. Westport, Conn., 1974.

Mason, James. *Orin Orisa.* New York, 1992.

Matas, Julio. "Revolución, literatura y religión afro-cubana." *Cuban Studies/ Estudios Cubanos* 18 (winter 1983).

Matibag, Eugenio. *Afro-Cuban Religious Experience: Cultural Reflections in Narrative.* Gainesville, Fla., 1996.

Mauleón, Rebecca. *Salsa Guidebook for Piano and Ensemble.* Petaluma, Calif., 1993.

McCleod, Marc C. "Undesirable Aliens: Race, Ethnicity and Nationalism in the

Comparison of Haitian and British West Indian Immigrant Workers in Cuba, 1912–1939." *Journal of Social History* 31, no. 3 (1998).

McGarrity, Gayle. "Race, Culture, and Social Change in Contemporary Cuba." In *Cuba's Struggle for Development: Dilemmas and Strategies,* edited by Sandor Halebsky and John Kirk. Boulder, Colo., 1992.

McGarrity, Gayle, and Osvaldo Cárdenas. "Cuba." In *No Longer Invisible: Afro-Latin Americans Today,* edited by the Minority Rights Group. London, 1995.

Mendieta Costa, Raquel. *Cultura, lucha de clases y conflicto racial, 1878–1895.* Havana, 1989.

Menéndez, Lázara. "¡¿Un *cake* para Obatala?!" *Temas* 4 (October–December 1995).

———. *Estudios afrocubanos: selección de lecturas.* Havana, 1990.

Mesa Lago, Carmelo, and June Belkin, eds. *Cuba in Africa.* Pittsburgh, 1982.

Mestiri, Ezzédine. *Les Cubains en Afrique.* Paris, 1980.

Millet, José. "El espiritismo de cordón en el oriente de Cuba: un estudio de caso." *Del Caribe* 5, no. 12 (1988).

———. "Una ceremonia del culto radá: El loa blanche." *Del Caribe* 5, no. 11 (1988).

Millet, José, and Julio Corbea. "Presencia haitiana en el oriente de Cuba." *Del Caribe* 3, no. 10 (1987).

Minority Rights Group. *No Longer Invisible: Afro-Latin Americans Today.* London, 1995.

Moliner Castañeda, Israel. "Los Ñáñigos." *Del Caribe* 5, no. 12 (1988).

———. "Sublevaciones de esclavos en Cuba." *Del Caribe* 4, no. 8 (1987).

Montejo, Esteban, and Miguel Barnet. *Biography of a Runaway Slave.* London, 1993 [1966].

Montejo Arrechea, Carmen Victoria. *Sociedades de Instrucción y Recreo de pardos y morenos que existieron en Cuba colonial: período 1878–1898.* Veracruz, 1933.

Moore, Carlos. "Cuban Communism, Ethnicity and Perestroika: The Unmasking of the Castro Regime." *Caribbean Quarterly* 42, no. 1 (March 1996).

———. "Race Relations in Socialist Cuba." In *Cuba,* edited by Sergio G. Roca. Boulder, Colo., 1988a.

———. *Castro, the Blacks, and Africa.* Los Angeles, 1988b.

———. "Congo or Carabalí? Race Relations in Socialist Cuba." *Caribbean Review* 15, no. 2 (1986).

———. "Cuba: Ces noirs que partent." *Jeune Afrique* no. 1027 (September 1980).

———. "Le peuple noir a-t-il sa place dans la révolution cubaine?" *Présence Africaine* 24, no. 52 (1964).

Moore, Robin D. *Nationalizing Blackness: Afrocubanismo and Artistic Revolution in Havana, 1920–1940.* Pittsburgh, 1997.

———. "'Primitivist' Art and Afro-Cuban Music: Development Parallels in the Twentieth Century." *Journal of Caribbean Studies* 7, nos. 2 and 3 (winter 1989/spring 1990).

Morejón, Nancy. *Baladas para un sueño.* Havana, 1989.

———. *Piedra pulida.* Havana, 1986.

———. *Nación y mestizaje en Nicolás Guillén.* Havana, 1982.

———. *"Cecilia Valdés:* mito y realidad." In *Documentos de "Rompiendo Barreras."* *Encuentro de escritores del Caribe.* San Juan, 1979a.

———. *Parajes de una época.* Havana, 1979b.

———. *Octubre imprescindible.* Havana, 1978.

———. *Recopilación de textos sobre Nicolás Guillén.* Havana, 1974.

———. *Lengua de pájaro.* Havana, 1971.

———. *Richard trajo su flauta.* Havana, 1966.

———. *Amor, ciudad atribuída.* Havana, 1964.

———. *Mutismo.* Havana, 1962.

Moreno Fraginals, Manuel. "Particularidades de la esclavitud en Cuba." *Del Caribe* 4, no. 8 (1987).

———. *Africa in America.* Paris, 1984.

———. *La historia como arma y otros estudios sobre esclavos, ingenios y plantaciones.* Barcelona, 1983.

———. *El ingenio: el complejo económico-social del azúcar en Cuba.* Havana, 1978 [1964].

———, ed. *Africa in Latin America: Essays on History, Culture, and Socialization.* Mexico, 1977.

Morrison, Karen Y. "Race, Culture and Nation in the Works of Afro-Cuban Intellectuals from 1912 to 1940." Master's thesis, University of Florida, 1997.

Morse, Richard M. "Race, Culture and Identity in the New World: Five National Versions." In *Ethnicity in the Caribbean: Essays in Honor of Harry Hoetink,* edited by Gert Oostindie. Basingstoke and London, 1996.

Morúa Delgado, Martín. *Obras completas.* Havana, 1957.

Mosquera, Gerardo. *Exploraciones en la plástica cubana.* Havana, 1983.

Muguercia, Alberto, and Ezequiel Rodríguez. *Rita Montaner.* Havana, 1984.

Mullen, Edward J. *Afro-Cuban Literature: Critical Junctures.* Westport, Conn., 1998.

———. *"Los negros brujos:* A Reexamination of the Text." *Cuban Studies* 17 (spring 1987).

———, ed. *The Life and Times of a Cuban Slave: Juan Francisco Manzano, 1797–1854.* Hamden, Conn., 1981.

Murphy, Joseph M. *Santería: An African Religion in America.* Boston, 1988.

Murray, David. *Odious Commerce: Britain, Spain, and the Abolition of the Cuban Slave Trade.* London, 1980.

Naranjo Orovio, Consuelo. "En búsqueda de lo nacional: Migraciones y racismo en Cuba (1880–1910)." In *La nación soñada: Cuba, Puerto Rico y Filipinas ante el 98,* edited by Consuelo Naranjo, Miguel A. Puig-Samper, and Luis Miguel García Mora. Madrid, 1996.

Naranjo Orovio, Consuelo, and Armando García González. *Racismo e inmigración en Cuba en el siglo XIX.* Madrid, 1996.

Neimark, John Philip. *The Way of the Orisa.* San Francisco, 1992.

Nodal, Roberto. "The Black Man in Cuban Society: From Colonial Times to the Revolution." *Journal of Black Studies* 16, no. 3 (1986).

North, Joseph. "Negro and White in Cuba." *Political Affairs* (July 1963).

O'Kelly, James. *The Mambi-Land or Adventures of a Herald Correspondent in Cuba.* Philadelphia, 1874.

Olliz-Boyd, Antonio. "Race Relations in Cuba: A Literary Perspective." *Revista / Review Interamericana* 8 (summer 1978).

Oostindie, Gert, ed. *Ethnicity in the Caribbean: Essays in Honor of Harry Hoetink.* Basingstoke and London, 1996.

Orovio, Helio. *Diccionario de la música cubana biográfico y técnico.* Havana, 1992.

Ortiz, Fernando. *Cuban Counterpoint: Tobacco and Sugar.* Durham and London, 1995 [1947]. [*Contrapunteo cubano del tabaco y el azúcar.* Havana, 1940.]

———. "Martí y las razas." *Etnia y sociedad.* Havana, 1993.

———. *La fiesta afrocubana del 'Día de Reyes'.* Havana, 1992.

———. *Los bailes y la fiesta afrocubana del Día de Reyes.* Havana, 1992.

———. *La música afrocubana.* Madrid, 1975.

———. *Los negros curros.* Havana, 1973.

———. *Orbita de Fernando Ortiz.* Havana, 1973.

———. *Hampa afrocubana: los negros brujos.* 2d ed. Miami, 1973.

———. "La cocina afrocubana." *Casa* 36–37 (May–August 1966).

———. *La africanía de la música folklórica de Cuba.* Havana, 1965.

———. "Orígen geográfico de los afrocubanos." *Revista Bimestre Cubana* 71, no. 1 (1957).

———. "La sinrazón de los racismos." *Revista Bimestre Cubana* 70, no. 1 (1955).

———. *Los instrumentos de la música afrocubana.* Havana, 1955.

———. *La africanía de la música folklórica de Cuba.* Havana, 1950.

———. *El engaño de las razas.* Havana, 1945.

———. "La cubanidad y los negros." *Estudios afrocubanos* 3, nos. 1–4 (1939).

———. *Glosario de afronegrismos.* Havana, 1924.

———. *Los esclavos negros.* Havana, 1916.

Orum, Thomas T. "The Politics of Color: The Racial Dimension of Cuban Politics During the Early Republican Years, 1900–1912." Ph.D. diss., New York University, 1975.

Padrón Valdés, Abelardo. *El general José: apuntes biográficos.* Havana, 1973.

Palacios Estrada, Manuel. "El carnaval santiaguero durante la Guerra de los Diez Años." *Del Caribe* 3, no. 10 (1987).

Palmier, Stephan. "Against Syncretism: Africanising and Cubanising Discourses in North American Orisa-Worship." In *Counterworks: Managing Diverse Knowledge,* edited by Richard Fardon. London, 1998.

———. "Ethnogenetic Processes and Cultural Transfer in Caribbean Slave Populations." In *Slavery in the Americas,* edited by Wolfgang Binder. Wurburg, Germany, 1993.

———. "Afro-Cuban Religion in Exile: Santería in South Florida." *Journal of Caribbean Studies* 5, no. 3 (1986).

Paquette, Robert L. *Sugar is Made with Blood: The Conspiracy of La Escalera and the Conflict Between Empires over Slavery in Cuba.* Middletown, Conn., 1988.

Partido Comunista de Cuba. *África: Referencia* 3, no. 1 (1970).

Pedro, Alberto. "Cultura y plantación." *Del Caribe* 6, no. 16–17 (1990).

———. "Guanamaca: una comunidad haitiana." *Etnología y folklore* 1 (1976).

Peraza Sarausa, Fermín. *Infancia ejemplar en la vida heroíca de Antonio Maceo.* Havana, 1943.

Pereda Valdés, Idelfonso. *Lo negro y lo mulato en la poesía cubana.* Montevideo, 1970.

Pérez, Louis A., Jr. "Identidad y nacionalidad: Las raices del separatismo cubano, 1868–1898." *Op. Cit.,* Universidad de Puerto Rico Centro de Estudios Históricos, no. 9 (1997).

———. *Between Reform and Revolution.* New York and London, 1989.

———. "Politics, Peasants, and People of Color. The 1912 'Race' War in Cuba Reconsidered." *Hispanic American Historical Review* 56 (August 1986).

Pérez, Nancy, et al. *El Cabildo Carabalí Isuama.* Santiago de Cuba, 1982.

Pérez Alvarez, María Magdalena. "Los prejuicios raciales: sus mecanismos de reproducción." *Temas* no. 7 (1996).

Pérez de la Riva, Francisco. "Cuban Palenques." In *Maroon Societies: Rebel Slave Communities in the Americas,* edited by Richard Price. Baltimore, 1979.

———. *El monto de la inmigración forzada en el siglo XIX.* Havana, 1979.

———. "Una familia de color en Cuba: el pintor Vicente Escobar." *Trimestre* (1947).

Pérez de la Riva, Juan. *El barracón y otros ensayos.* Havana, 1975.

———. "La inmigración antillana en Cuba durante el primer tercio del siglo XX." *Revista de la Biblioteca Nacional "José Martí"* 17 (May–August 1975).

———. "La contradicción fundamental de la sociedad colonial cubana: trabajo esclavo contra trabajo libre." *Economía y Desarrollo* 2 (1970).

———. "Documentos para la historia de las gentes sin historia. Antiguos esclavos cubanos que regresan a Lagos." *Revista de la Biblioteca Nacional "José Martí"* 1 (1964).

———. Cuadro sinóptico de la esclavitud en Cuba y de la cultura occidental." *Actas del Folklore* 1, no. 5 (May 1961).

Pérez Sarduy, Pedro. "And Where Did the Blacks Go?" *Cuba Update* 17, nos. 4 and 5 (January–February and March–April 1998).

———. "Seven Dead Seasons." In *The Voice of the Turtle: An Anthology of Cuban Stories,* edited by Peter Bush. London: Quartet Books, 1997.

———. "¿Y qué tienen los negros en Cuba?" *Encuentro de la Cultura Cubana* no. 2 (fall 1996).

———. "Flash Back on Carnival: A Personal Memoir." In *Cuban Festivals: An Anthology with Glossaries,* edited by Judith Bettelheim. New York, 1993.

———. "Myth and History: Literary Reconstruction around the Life of a Maid in Prerevolutionary Cuba." *Notebook/Cuaderno, A Literary Journal* 6, no. 2 (1990).

———. "Open Letter to Carlos Moore." *Afro-Hispanic Review* 9, nos. 1 and 3 (January, May, and September 1990).

———. "The Ibelles and the Lost Paths." In *Under the Storyteller's Spell: Folk-Tales from the Caribbean*, edited by Charles Faustin. London, 1989.

———. *Cumbite and Other Poems*. New York, 1990. [*Cumbite y otros poemas*. Havana, 1988.]

———. *Surrealidad*. Havana, 1967.

Pérez Sarduy, Pedro, and Jean Stubbs. Latin America and Cuba sections in *Afropaedia*. Cambridge, 1999.

———. Introduction to *No Longer Invisible: Afro-Latin Americans Today*, edited by the Minority Rights Group. London, 1995.

———. *Afro-Cuba: An Anthology of Cuban Writing on Race, Politics and Culture*. Melbourne, New York, and London, 1993. [*AfroCuba: una antología de escritos cubanos sobre raza, política y cultura*. San Juan, 1998.]

Petras, Elizabeth McLean. *Jamaican Labor Migration: White Capital and Black Labor, 1850–1930*. Boulder, Colo., 1988.

Plácido. *Poesías*. Havana, 1979.

———. *Los poemas más representativos de Plácido*. Chapel Hill, N.C., 1976.

Portilla, Juan. *Jesús Menéndez y su tiempo*. Havana, 1987.

Portuondo, José Antonio. *El pensamiento vivo de Maceo*. Havana, 1962.

Portuondo Linares, Serafín. *Los independientes de color: historia del Partido Independiente de Color*. Havana, 1950.

Quiñones, Tato. *Ecorie Abakuá*. Havana, 1994.

———. *A pie de obra*. Havana, 1987.

———. *Al final del terraplén el sol*. Havana, 1971.

Ramos, José Antonio. "Cubanidad y mestizaje." *Estudios Afrocubanos* 1, no. 1 (1937).

"Report from Cuba." *The Black Scholar* 8, nos. 8–10 (summer 1977).

Ring, Harry. *How Cuba Uprooted Race Discrimination*. New York, 1961.

Ríos, Soleida. *Entre mundo y juguete*. Havana, 1987.

———. *De pronto abril*. Havana, 1979.

Risquet, Juan F. *Rectificaciones: la cuestión político-social en la isla de Cuba*. Havana, 1900.

Rivas Muñoz, Mercedes. *The Cuban Antislavery Novel (1838–1882)*. Ph.D. diss., University of Seville, 1989.

Robert, Karen. "Slavery and Freedom in the Ten Years War, Cuba, 1868–1878." *Slavery and Abolition* 13 (December 1992).

Rodríguez, Ileana. "Cecilia Valdés de Villaverde: raza, clase y estructura familiar." *Areíto* 5, no. 18 (1979).

Rodríguez Morejón, Gerardo. *Maceo: héroe y caudillo*. Havana, 1943.

Rodríguez Sarabia, Aida. *Mariana Grajales: madre de Cuba*. Havana, 1957.

Roig de Leuchsenring, Emilio. *Ideario cubano III. Antonio Maceo*. Havana, 1946.

———. *Revolución y república en Maceo*. Havana, 1945.

———. *La vida heroica de Antonio Maceo*. Havana, 1945.

Rojas, Marta. *Santa lujuria*. Havana, 1999.

————. *El columpio de Rey Spencer.* Santiago de Chile, 1994.

————. *La cueva del muerto.* Havana, 1983.

————. *El aula verde.* Havana, 1982.

————. *El que debe vivir.* Havana, 1978.

————. *Tania la guerrillera inolvidable.* Havana, 1971.

————. *Escenas del Vietnam.* Havana, 1969.

————. *La generación del centenario en el juicio del Moncada.* Havana, 1965.

Rushing, Fannie T. "Afro-Cuban Participation in Slave Emancipation and Cuban Independence, 1865–1895." Ph.D. diss., University of Chicago, 1992.

Saldaña, Excilia. *Poemas de la noche.* Havana, 1989.

————. *Kele, Kele.* Havana, 1987.

————. *Enlloró.* Havana, 1967.

Sánchez, Julio. *La religión de los orichas: Creencias y ceremonias de un culto afrocaribeño.* San Juan, 1978.

Sandoval, Mercedes C. *La religión afrocubana.* Madrid, 1975.

Santovenia, Emeterio S. *Raíz y altura de Antonio Maceo.* Havana, 1943.

Sarabia, Nydia. *Historia de una familia Mambisa: Mariana Grajales.* Santiago de Cuba, 1975.

Sardinha, Dennis. *The Poetry of Nicolás Guillén.* London, 1976.

Sarracino, Rodolfo. *Los que volvieron a África.* Havana, 1988.

————. *La injerencia británica en las rebeliones abolicionistas cubanas.* Havana, 1986.

————. *La guerra chiquita: Una experiencia necesaria.* Havana, 1982.

Schwartz, Rosalie. "The Displaced and the Disappointed: Cultural Nationalists and Black Activists in Cuba in the 1920s." Ph.D. diss., University of California, San Diego, 1977.

Scott, Rebecca J. "Raza, clase y acción colectiva en Cuba, 1895–1902: la formación de alianzas interraciales en el mundo de la caña." *Op. Cit.,* Universidad de Puerto Rico Centro de Investigaciones Históricas, no. 9 (1997).

————. "'The Lower Class of Whites' and 'the Negro Element': Race, Social Identity, and Politics in Central Cuba, 1899–1909." In *La nación soñada: Cuba, Puerto Rico y Filipinas ante el 98,* edited by Consuelo Naranjo, Miguel A. Puig-Samper, and Luis Miguel García Mora. Madrid, 1996a.

————. "The Boundaries of Freedom: Postemancipation Society in Cuba, Louisiana and Brazil." In *Inside Slavery: Process and Legacy in the Caribbean Experience,* edited by Hilary McD. Beckles. Kingston, Jamaica, 1996b.

————. "Cuba: Questions sociales, raciales et politiques d'une transition à l'autre." *Problèmes d'Amérique Latine* 17 (1995).

————. "Defining the Boundaries of Freedom in the World of Cane: Cuba, Brazil and Louisiana after Emancipation." *American Historical Review* 99 (February 1994).

————. *Slave Emancipation in Cuba: The Transition to Free Labor, 1860–1899.* Princeton, N.J., 1985.

Serra, Rafael. *Para blancos y negros: ensayos políticos, sociales y económicos.* Havana, 1907.

Serviat, Pedro. *El problema negro en Cuba y su solución definitiva.* Havana, 1986.

————. "La discriminación racial en Cuba, su orígen, desarrollo y terminación definitiva." *Islas* 66 (May–August 1980).

Smallwood, Lawrence. "African Cultural Dimensions in Cuba." *Journal of Black Studies* 6 (December 1975).

Smart, Ian. *Nicolás Guillén, Popular Poet of the Caribbean.* Columbia, Mo., 1990.

Sosa Rodríguez, Enrique. *El carabalí.* Havana, 1984.

————. *Los Ñáñigos.* Havana, 1982.

Stubbs, Jean. "Social and Political Motherhood of Cuba: Mariana Grajales Cuello." In *Engendering History: Caribbean Women in Historical Perspective,* edited by Verene Shepherd, Bridget Brereton, and Barbara Bailey. Kingston, Jamaica, and London, 1995.

————. "Fernando Ortiz' Afro-Cuban Festival 'Day of the Kings'." In *Cuban Festivals: An Anthology with Glossaries,* edited by Judith Bettelheim. New York, 1993.

Suárez y Romero, Anselmo. *Francisco: el ingenio o las delicias del campo.* Havana, 1967 [1839].

Taylor, Frank F. "Revolution, Race, and Some Aspects of Foreign Relations in Cuba Since 1959." *Cuban Studies/Estudios Cubanos* 18 (1988).

"Thirtieth Anniversary of the Cuban Revolution." *The Black Scholar* 20, nos. 5 and 6 (1972).

Thomas-Hope, Elizabeth. "The Establishment of a Migration Tradition: British West Indian Movements to the Hispanic Caribbean in the Century after Emancipation." In *Caribbean Social Relations,* edited by Colin G. Clarke. Liverpool, 1978.

Thompson, Robert Farris. *Flash of the Spirit: African and Afroamerican Art and Philosophy.* New York, 1984.

Thompson Womacks, Lanny. "Estudiarlos, juzgarlos y gobernarlos: Conocimiento y poder en el archipélago imperial estadounidense." In *La nación soñada: Cuba, Puerto Rico y Filipinas ante el 98,* edited by Consuelo Naranjo, Miguel A. Puig-Samper, and Luis Miguel García Mora. Madrid, 1996.

Toledo, Armando. *Presencia y vigencia de Brindis de Salas.* Havana, 1981.

Torres Cuevas, Eduardo, and Eusebio Reyes. *Esclavitud y sociedad. Notas y documentos para la historia de la esclavitud negra en Cuba.* Havana, 1986.

Trelles y Govín, Carlos M. "Bibliografía de autores de la raza de color en Cuba." *Cuba contemporánea* 43 (January 1927).

UNESCO. *Introducción a la cultura africana en América Latina.* París, 1970.

————. "Homenaje a Cirilo Villaverde." *Cuba en la UNESCO* (March 1964).

Urban, C. Stanley. "The Africanization of Cuba Scare, 1853–1855." *Hispanic American Historical Review* 37 (February 1957).

Urfé, Odilio. "Music and Dance in Cuba." In *Africa in Latin America,* edited by Manuel Moreno Fraginals. New York, 1977.

Urrútia, Gustavo E. "El prejuicio en Cuba." In *Negro Anthology,* edited by Nancy Canard. London, 1934.

Valdés, Nelson P. "Revolutionary Solidarity in Angola." In *Cuba in the World,* edited by Cole Blasier and Carmelo Mesa-Lago. Pittsburgh, 1979.

Valdés, Sergio. "Las lenguas africanas y el español cololoquia de Cuba." *Santiago* 31 (September 1978).

Valdés-Cruz, Rosa. "The Black Man's Contribution to Cuban Culture." *The Americas* 34 (October 1977).

Veguer, Pascual B. Marcos. *El negro en Cuba.* Havana, 1955.

Velasco, Carlos de. "El problema negro." *Cuba contemporánea* 1 (February 1913).

Villaverde, Cirilo. *La peineta calada.* Havana, 1979.

———. "Diario del rancheador." *Revista de la Biblioteca Nacional "José Martí"* 67, no. 1 (January–April 1973).

———. *Cecilia Valdes.* New York, 1962 [1879].

Weis, Judith A. "Traditional Popular Culture and the Cuban 'New Theater': Teatro Escambray and the Cabildo de Santiago." *Theatre Research International* 14 (summer 1989).

Williams, Lorna Valerie. *The Representation of Slavery in Cuban Fiction.* Columbia, Mo., 1994.

Wilson, Leslie N. *La poesía afroantillana.* Miami, 1979.

Wolf, Donna M. "The Cuban 'Gente de Color' and the Independence Movement, 1879–1895." *Revista/Review Interamericana* 5 (fall 1975).

Zambrana, Antonio. *El negro Francisco.* Havana, 1873.

Zarragoitia, Ledesma L. *Maceo.* Havana, 1945.

Zeuske, Michael. "The Cimarrón in the Archives: A Re-Reading of Miguel Barnet's Biography of Esteban Montejo." *New West Indian Guide/Nieuwe West-Indische Gids* 71, nos. 3 and 4 (1997).